CUBA 1933

Prologue to Revolution

IN THE NORTON LIBRARY

Cuba 1933: Prologue to Revolution
by Luis E. Aguilar N712

Cuba: The Making of a Revolution
by Ramon Eduardo Ruiz N513

CUBA 1933

Prologue to Revolution

Luis E. Aguilar

The Norton Library

W·W·NORTON & COMPANY·INC·

NEW YORK

First published in the Norton Library 1974
by arrangement with Cornell University Press

Published simultaneously in Canada
by George J. McLeod Limited, Toronto

Books That Live
The Norton imprint on a book means that in the publisher's estimation it is a book not for a single season but for the years.
W. W. Norton & Company, Inc.

Library of Congress Cataloging in Publication Data
Aguilar, Luis E.
Cuba 1933; prologue to revolution.
(The Norton library)
Reprint of the ed. published by Cornell University Press, Ithaca, N.Y.
Includes bibliographical references.
1. Cuba—History—Revolution, 1933. 2. Cuba—History—1895- I. Title.
[F1787.5.A66 1974] 972.91'06 73-18214
ISBN 0-393-00712-X

Printed in the United States of America
1 2 3 4 5 6 7 8 9 0

To my parents in Cuba, with gratitude.

To my children, Louis, George, and Elizabeth Anne, with love and hope.

"Todo noble tesón al cabo alcanza
a fijar las justas leyes del destino."
[Noble tenacity finally results in
restoring the justice of the laws of fate.]

ENRIQUE HERNÁNDEZ MIYARES
Cuba, 1915

Contents

Preface

Historians writing about Cuba today commonly make a great mistake. They dismiss what happened in Cuba before Castro and ignore the earlier struggles, triumphs, and defeats of the Cuban people. Sometimes this tendency arises from ignorance; occasionally it is the result of political partiality; usually it is born of a desire for oversimplification. Some recent studies have even attempted to discover parallels between the Mexico of 1910, the Bolivia of 1952, and the Cuba of 1959. One common factor—a more or less successful revolution—has caused some historians to overlook the historical past of these three nations, and important racial, economic, and cultural differences.

This book is a modest attempt to correct the historical perspectives on Cuba. In 1959, Cuba was not the somnolent Mexico of Porfirio Díaz or the remote Bolivia of the tin barons. By the mid-1920's Cuba had already entered a revolutionary period from which she emerged deeply and radically transformed: a popular revolutionary party had been formed; a constitution emphasizing social legislation had been adopted; a new sense of nationalism prevailed; and the necessary forces for an economic revival were present. Some of the programs and ideas which seemed radical and new to those who ignore Cuban history evolved to a great extent from the ideals and frustrations of the revolution of 1933. These historical links are significant and interesting. They illumine present-day Cuban history.

Of the many persons, some still in Cuba, to whom I am indebted for making this book possible, there are a few who deserve special mention: the former President of Cuba, Dr. Carlos Prío Socarrás, who graciously tolerated long hours of questioning; the late José Emilio Obregón (Machado's son-in-law), who not only talked candidly about Machado's personality, but also gave me old newspaper clippings and pamphlets of the period; Joaquín Martínez Saenz, founder of the secret revolutionary society ABC and former President of the Cuban National Bank, who wrote me two long letters explaining ABC's historical position; Juan Antonio Rubio Padilla, a former member of the Student Directory of 1930, whose remarkable memory provided me with many insights; and last but not least, a group of the "generation of 1933," whose presence in and around Washington, D.C., forced them to suffer my continuous demands for details and explanations —Felipe Pazos, Carlos Martínez, and Jústo Carrillo. For them, and for Isa and Gerardo Canet, Fernando and Joanna Leyva, and Jorge and Diana Beruff, I would like to recall an old Hispanic tradition of the era when writers had time to be polite to their readers, and say:

> "Lo que esta obra valga, por ellos va logrado;
> Yo sólo puse el esfuerzo y lo menguado."
> [What is good in this book is because of them;
> I only add the effort and the limitations.]

Translations from the Spanish have been made by the author unless otherwise noted.

L. E. A.

Georgetown University
Washington, D.C.

CUBA 1933 ✦✦✦✦✦✦

Prologue to Revolution

I Creation of the Republic

Struggle for Independence

From 1808 to 1825, while most of the Spanish colonies in Latin America succeeded in transforming the initial crisis caused by the French invasion of Spain into a vast movement for independence, the "ever faithful" island of Cuba remained relatively quiet and peaceful. The very few Cubans who at that time began to consider the possibility of independence relied more on any outside help they could obtain from Simón Bolívar or from Mexico or the United States than on the support of the people of the island.[1]

Many factors conditioned the apparent passivity of the Cubans—geographical and political isolation, underpopulation,[2] lack of a national conscience—but a growing economy was probably the most influential. The Cuban economy developed differently from the economies of the continental colonies. There, at the beginning of the nineteenth century, a creole elite had already achieved enough economic power to

[1] For a history of the first Cuban conspiracies and rebellious movements against Spain, *Inicidiadores y primeros mártires de la revolución cubana*, by Vidal Morales y Morales (3 vols.; Havana: Consejo Nacional de Cultura, 1963), is essential.

[2] The census of 1817 reported the total population of the island as 553,033; this figure represented an increase of 103 per cent since 1792 (Hubert H. S. Aimes, *A History of Slavery in Cuba, 1511–1868* [New York: Putnam's, 1907], p. 89).

chafe under Spanish commercial and political control.[3] In Cuba the period 1790–1830 marks the first stage of real economic growth, the rapid transformation of a rather stagnant market into one of the wealthiest colonies of the world.

This accelerated process, this "leap forward," was in response to a series of well-known events, of which the two most important were the independence of the United States in 1783, which opened a new and expanding market for Cuban products, and the decline of Haiti as a sugar and coffee producer after the slave revolt of 1791. It was Cuba's good fortune to have an alert minority, creoles headed by Francisco de Arango y Parreño (1765–1837), who realized the vast possibilities of the moment and proposed sound economic programs. Also lending support and cooperation to many of the creoles' initiatives was the rule by a series of sympathetic colonial officers, who even went so far as to oppose some Spanish regulations whose application would have hindered economic growth.[4] As a result, as an analyst of the period puts it: "In the half century from 1790 to 1839, the expansion of trade in Cuba seems almost miraculous. In that period real income multiplied more than fifty times." In the same period of time the number of sugar haciendas on the island jumped from about 400 to more than 800.[5]

[3] A good example of this attitude was the increasing demand for free trade and mercantile reforms in Santiago de Chile, Buenos Aires, and Montevideo, from 1793 to 1808. See Ricardo Levene, *Ensayo histórico sobre la Revolución de Mayo y Mariano Moreno* (Buenos Aires: Libreria El Ateneo, 1949), vol. I, ch. xiii, and Hernán Ramirez Necochea, "The Economic Origins of Independence," in R. A. Humphreys and John Lynch, *The Origins of Latin American Revolutions, 1808–1826* (New York: Knopf, 1965), pp. 169–183.

[4] For example, in November 1799 a royal decree abolished the provisional right to trade with nations not involved in the Spanish War; Captain-General Someruelos suspended its application.

[5] Roland T. Ely, *La economía cubana entre las dos Isabeles, 1492–1832* (Bogotá: Aedita Editores, 1962), pp. 87, 111. Using different

Under these favorable conditions it was natural that the creoles could not yet regard Spain as an obstacle to their progress and that they were, in general, very reluctant to adopt any political position that could endanger their recently acquired prosperity. Furthermore, sugar expansion required the importation of an increasing number of African slaves. This continuous growth of the black population was a matter of concern to many on the island. For years Spanish authorities used the menace of a slave insurrection to paralyze all Cuban initiative for reform or rebellion. As late as 1874, D. Mariano Cancio-Villa Amil, Spanish Intendant in Cuba, warned Cuban rebels that independence could only result in Negro dominance or Anglo-Saxon control of the island.[6] The tragic example of Haiti, so close to Cuban shores, helped to temper any political extremism. Finally, the Spanish defeat on the continent forced many Spanish families to seek refuge in Cuba, the last stronghold of the Spanish empire. These families helped to counterbalance the Negro immigration, as well as aiding the island's expanding economy; but they also brought with them an ultra-Hispanism, an intransigent "loyalism" which reinforced Spanish control. Eventually, though, their arrogance and their disdain for the creoles became a source of friction with the Cubans.

With prosperity and economic growth also came leisure and an intellectual awakening, the *crise de conscience* of the

---

figures, another writer points out the powerful expansion of the sugar industry in the same period: in 1775 the number of sugar mills was around 600, in 1846 there were 1,442 (Jacobo de la Pezuela, *Diccionario geográfico, estadístico, histórico de la isla de Cuba* [Madrid: Imprenta del Establecimiento del Mellado, 1863], I, 56–61).

[6] See his *Situación económica de Cuba* (Madrid, 1876), p. 18. According to Manuel de la Cruz (*Obras completas* [Havana and Madrid, 1926], VII, 25–28), the common efforts of whites and blacks during the first war for independence (1868–1878) dispelled once and for all those fears among white Cubans.

creole population of Cuba. In 1795, at the Seminar San Carlos, Father José Agustín Caballero (1762–1835) initiated an offensive against the outdated "scholasticism" that reigned in education. He was followed by Father Felix Varela (1787–1853), a young philosopher eager to open Cuba to modern ideological currents. Almost simultaneously, the first truly important poet, José María de Heredia (1803–1839), made the name of Cuba prominent on the continent. With them and after them, educators and philosophers like José de la Luz y Caballero (1800–1862), historians and essayists like José Antonio Saco (1797–1879), writers and literary mentors like Domingo del Monte (1804–1853), and many others promoted an effervescent cultural atmosphere. With energy and enthusiasm this expanding group studied and rediscovered the past, the economic resources, and the culture of Cuba. Their activity and their influence were felt in every sector of the population. In 1831 a highly regarded cultural magazine, the *Revista bimestre de Cuba*, appeared; in 1833 the Cuban Academy of Literature was founded. Technical studies were inaugurated; education was reorganized and improved. In 1831 a proud Saco was writing: "We must be extremely satisfied to notice the complete revolution experienced in all branches of our primary education, and in many of the secondary branches also. . . . From now on our families will not be compelled to send their children abroad in order to obtain a proper education." [7]

It was soon evident, however, that the intellectual effort was turning into a search for a national conscience. José de la Luz y Caballero summed up the common aspirations of this brilliant generation when he wrote to a friend in Paris: "Everybody here is full of enthusiasm. I have donated all my

[7] Quoted in Antonio Bachiller y Morales, *Apuntes para la historia de las letras en Cuba* (Havana: Imprenta de P. Massana, 1859), I, 29.

books to the Ateneo [a cultural society] . . . so return quickly, my friend, and bring with you books, paintings, rocks and every possible thing for our Ateneo. This is our motto: Let us join our efforts, let us improve our culture, let us build a Fatherland, let us build a Fatherland!" [8] But to build a Fatherland implied a break with the colonial spirit of the "ever faithful island" of previous times. Inevitably, the *crise de conscience* ushered in a period of political and armed struggle against Spain.

On the other hand, while writers and intellectuals were awakening a national spirit among Cubans, the political and economic policy of Spain was changing from a friendly or neutral attitude to one of suspicion and increasing control. Already in 1825, when the first Cuban conspiracies against Spain were discovered, a royal decree gave the Captain-General of the island authority to rule the colony as "a city under siege." In 1833, General Miguel Tacón was appointed Captain-General. One of the soldiers defeated by the patriots on the continent, Tacón brought with him suspicion and hate of everything creole, and a firm belief that only stern authority could prevent Cuban independence. It was he who forced Saco into exile and tried to stifle the emerging Cuban cultural energies. His government marked a turning point on the island. While material progress continued for a time, political and intellectual efforts suffered under an increasing official severity. As a Cuban historian writes: "No longer was the island a true part of Spanish territory, no longer did the children of this land have the same rights as those born in Spain. All Spanish law was modified when applied to Cuba." [9]

[8] José de la Luz y Caballero, *De la vida íntima: Epistolario y diarios* (Havana: Editorial de la Universidad, 1945), p. 194.

[9] Juan M. Leiseca, *Historia de Cuba* (Havana: Libreria Cervantes, 1925), p. 169.

Creole reaction to this policy was predictable: after 1835 conspiracies against Spanish rule multiplied. But the atmosphere was not yet ripe for an open revolt against the colonial government. The majority of those who wanted to change the political conditions of Cuba were divided into two basic groups: annexationists and reformists. The former believed, with Gaspar Betancourt Cisneros (1803–1866), that the only way to expel Spain from Cuba, and avoid a long and dangerous war, was to annex the island to the United States. The latter thought that Cuba was rich and powerful enough to force Spain to make political and economic concessions. Annexationism was basically supported by slave owners who looked to the South of the United States for protection and support. Reformism was defended by liberals who, like José Antonio Saco, preferred evolution to revolution and feared the absorption of Cuba's new nationalism and culture by the voracious vitality of the United States.

Annexationism reached its peak with the two expeditions of Narciso López, former officer of the Spanish army, who with American backing landed briefly at the port of Cárdenas in 1850 but was forced to retreat for lack of popular support, and again in the province of Pinar del Río in 1851, under the false impression that a rebellion had started on the island. Captured by the Spanish forces, López and a great number of his officers (many of whom were Americans) were immediately executed. The failure of these expeditions, the cogent arguments of Saco, and the growing crisis between North and South in the United States eroded the support for the annexationist cause.[10]

[10] In 1852, even Betancourt Cisneros, increasingly alarmed by certain American attitudes, had changed his position to a revolutionary stand: "Without revolution," he proclaimed, "there will be no rights, no virtue, no honor for the Cubans . . . without revolution Cuba will not be for the Cubans" (quoted in Max Henriquez Ureña,

At the same time, the reformists gathered support, and finally their opportunity came. In November 1865 a royal decree convened a Junta de Información, whose members were to be partially elected by Cuban city councils, which would report and advise the Spanish government about the reforms that were necessary on the island. In the elections of March 1866, the reformists showed their strength: of the sixteen members elected twelve belonged to their cause.[11] With great hope and a detailed program calling for free trade, tax reforms, and progressive abolition of slavery, the delegates departed for Spain. The result of their efforts was a mortal blow for the reformist cause. In April 1867 the Spanish government abruptly dissolved the Junta, and contrary to its suggestion imposed a 10 per cent increase on the general taxes of the island.

During 1866–1867, Cuba was feeling the impact of an international economic crisis. This new financial burden, plus the humiliation of the Junta, provoked discontent and resentment. For many Cubans it seemed that only independence would free the island from arbitrary rule, corruption, and abuse, and that only through armed rebellion could independence be gained. In 1868, the most progressive elements among the creoles, those for whom the Spanish policy hurt both patriotism and financial interests, were ready to give everything, to risk their lives and their wealth in a war with Spain. On October 10, 1868, in the small town of Yara in Oriente Province, Carlos Manuel de Céspedes with a group of other *hacendados* (plantation owners) and patriots rose up in arms against Spain, abolished slavery, and proclaimed the indepen-

---

Panorama histórico de la literatura cubana [New York: Las Americas, 1963], I, 241).

[11] Ramiro Guerra y Sánchez, *Manual de historia de Cuba* (Havana: Consejo Nacional de Cultura, 1962), p. 483.

dence of Cuba. Reformism was dead; the struggle for independence began.

For ten long and arduous years, alone and with no aid, the Cuban people fought for their independence, forcing Spain to pour into the island ten times more troops than she had sent to fight in the entire continent. "It was a general belief among us that the character of this people was not apt for war," reported Spanish General Martínez Campos, "but in the fight whites and Negroes alike had shown us quite the contrary. . . . If they don't have among them great generals, they have something much more necessary: remarkable guerrilla fighters." [12] But, in spite of all these efforts, the Ten Years' War ended in defeat. In 1878, with a firm guarantee from Spain of a better deal for Cuba, the last rebels put down their weapons.

A few consequences of this long struggle contributed decisively to the Cuban experience. Not only had the blood and sacrifices of so many Cubans transformed independence into a national cause, but, at the very moment when a landed aristocracy was establishing firm political and economic control over most parts of Latin America, that class was defeated and decimated in Cuba. While the Argentine gaucho was being wiped out by the cattle owners, while the Mexican rurales were beginning to secure Mexico for the owners of great estates (latifundistas), the most enlightened representatives of the Cuban land owners had plunged with their class into disaster. For even those creoles who had remained loyal to Spain felt the effects of colonial hatred. Writes an investigator of the period:

At this time there were decisive changes in the economic structure. This was the first moment in which the control of the sugar

[12] Luis Estévez y Romero, *Desde el Zanjón hasta Baire* (Havana: Tipografía la Propaganda Literaria, 1899), p. 5.

industry passed from the creole's hands to other hands, mainly those of the "loyal" Spaniards. Many partisans of the revolution, or even those only suspected of being sympathizers, lost their properties. . . . Even small properties were affected, and consequently their essential role as a source of agricultural diversification was weakened.[13]

The seeds of a powerful native oligarchy controlling land and wealth were not allowed to grow in the island, and this kind of an elite, at least in the typical and traditional Latin American form, will never rise in Cuba.

Second, until the economic crisis provoked by the war, there had been little American capital invested in Cuba. Now, profiting from the bankruptcy of many Spanish and Cuban capitalists, and taking advantage of a general fear for the future of the island, American money moved in and began to acquire land, sugar, and mining interests. In 1896, Richard Olney, then Secretary of State, estimated the American investment in Cuba at about $50,000,000. Great as this growth—and its collateral political influence—was, it is well to remember that, as Leland Jenks put it: "In 1898 the Yankees were not the owners of Cuba. Except for certain valuable mining concessions, they did not own any important part of Cuban territory. The railroads were British. Many other enterprises were Spanish. There were no American banks in Cuba. . . . The United States controlled only the sugar market." [14]

[13] H. E. Friedlander, *Historia económica de Cuba* (Havana: Jesús Montero, 1944), pp. 422–423.

[14] Leland H. Jenks, *Nuestra colonia de Cuba* (Buenos Aires: Editorial Palestra, 1960), p. 63. This argument of Jenks' refutes the often repeated assertion (usually based on Jenks' figures) that "by the beginning of the year 1895, Cuba had definitely been converted into an economic colony of the United States." For this side of the argument, see Philip S. Foner, *A History of Cuba and Its Relations with the United States* (New York: International Publishers, 1963), II, ch. 23, and Emilio Roig de Leuchsenring, *Conclusiones fundamentales sobre*

After the Ten Years' War, the politically active sector of Cuban society was again divided into two groups: those who had faith in the Spanish promises for autonomy, and those who still nurtured the hope of independence. The first group, by far the most important in the decade after the war, organized a party popularly called "Autonomista"; the second group, lacking direction and a definite program, either disbanded and went into exile or waited in silence on the island.

But Spain did not change. In spite of promises and programs, in spite of minor concessions, it became more and more evident to many Cubans in the early 1890's that Spain was incapable of making any real effort to change the conditions in Cuba. Through their meetings and publicity the Autonomists had stirred new hopes and spread the desire for reform, but had repeatedly failed to obtain it. In 1892, voicing their frustration and their growing concern with the Cuban political dilemma, the party issued a manifesto to the nation. If the Spanish government continued its policy of ignorance, repression, and persecution, they warned, then the moment would arrive when, after having "dissolved our party, the nation must make radical decisions. The responsibility of that future will fall on those who prefer the use of force to the exercise of justice." [15]

So the cause of separatism, nurtured by disillusion and desperation and guided now by the genius of José Martí (1853–1895), began to gain the upper hand. As a further symptom of the change in attitude, in 1893 Rafael Merchan, one of the most important spokesmen of the party, and a select group of Autonomists openly backed the road of revolution.[16]

---

la guerra libertadora cubana de 1895 (Mexico City: El Colegio de México, 1945).

[15] Estévez y Romero, p. 474.

[16] See Rafael Merchan, *Cuba, justificación de sus guerras de independencia* (Havana: Dirección de Cultura, 1961).

It was the task and the enormous contribution of Martí to build the fighting instrument, the medium by which all the diverse attitudes and convictions would be organized into a common effort for the independence of Cuba. In January 1892, after years of patient work, El Partido Revolucionario Cubano (the Cuban Revolutionary party) was born. The reasons, justifications, and political ideas of the new movement were published in a document written by Martí. A few months later Máximo Gómez, Antonio Maceo, and the best veterans of the Ten Years' War joined Martí in preparing for the coming war.

A detailed explication of the political ideas and the social objectives of Martí is a tempting subject, especially since today they are a sort of battlefield between Marxists and anti-Marxists.[17] But to understand certain Cuban reactions after independence it is enough to say that Martí had three objectives: (1) He envisaged a brief war, which would avoid vast destruction on the island and would not provoke the rise of militarism and the intervention of the United States—a possibility Martí feared the most. (2) He hoped to establish a republic with justice for everyone, a government capable of abolishing social and racial inequalities. (3) And he conceived

[17] As with every prolific creative writer, Martí can be quoted in justification of opposing ideas. The Marxists tend to stress his anti-imperialist stand; see, for example, Emilio Roig de Leuchsenring, *Martí anti-imperialista* (Havana: Dirección de Cultura, 1961). Non-Marxists point to his clear rejection of Marx and of social violence; for example, Jorge Mañach, *El pensamiento político y social de Martí* (Havana: Edición Oficial del Senado, 1941), esp. pp. 21–22. It is worth mentioning that before Castro's government, Cuban Communist writers easily conceded the non-Marxist, and almost antisocialist, position of Martí. Two good examples are: Julio Antonio Mella's judgment of Martí (1929) in *La lucha revolucionaria y el imperialismo* (Havana: Editora Popular de Cuba y del Caribe, 1960), p. 95; and Carlos Rafael Rodríguez, *José Martí and Cuban Liberation* (New York: International Publishers, 1953), principally pp. 13–15.

of a republic with agricultural diversification and free of economic dependence. Martí constantly warned against depending on one crop and one buyer as a situation that would inevitably end in political domination.[18]

Grasping at every cent that could be acquired, calming the impatient, encouraging the doubtful, Martí, by the end of 1894, had gathered a well-equipped expedition that was to strike the initial and decisive blow at the unsuspecting Spanish forces. But three days before the scheduled departure from the Florida coast, the government of the United States detained the three ships at Fernandina, and confiscated the war material. In spite of this disaster, it was too late to turn back. The leaders of the revolution continued with their plans, and on February 24, 1895, the fight for independence started once more. Three months later Martí, who had landed in the eastern part of Cuba with General Máximo Gómez, was killed in a skirmish with the Spanish forces.

And so, for reasons beyond his control, the dreams and aspirations of Martí were unfulfilled. Far from a short and glorious war, the struggle for independence dragged on for more than three years, with the utter destruction of Cuban economic wealth used as one of the principal weapons of the rebel forces. As early as June 1896, General Maceo instructed Brigadier José M. Aguirre to "destroy every building which could offer shelter and defense to the enemy, and to destroy all tobacco and corn which could be found gathered in that territory." [19] The basic idea was to avoid the mistake of the Ten Years' War, when Spain used the profits of Cuban trade to pay for the war, and, by destroying all sources of wealth in

[18] The "Resolutions of the Cuban Revolutionary Party" and the so-called "Manifesto de Montecristi" best express the political thought of Martí; see *Obras completas* (Havana: Editorial Lex, 1946), I, 298–353, and II, 240–247.

[19] Unpublished order of Maceo, No. 284 (the original in the personal records of the author).

Cuba, to force Spain to carry the economic burden of the long campaign. The tactic was successful; after two years of conflict Spain was at the limit of her financial possibilities, but the cost to the Cubans was appalling. The first census taken after the war estimated that the population of the island had decreased by 12 per cent and that two-thirds of its wealth had been destroyed. In the provinces of Matanzas and Santa Clara more than nine-tenths of the horned cattle had disappeared, and of well over a million animals, less than one hundred thousand remained.[20]

In addition, the event that Martí feared most eventually occurred—American intervention.

American Intervention and the Platt Amendment

On April 11, 1898, President McKinley submitted his famous message to Congress declaring that "in the name of humanity, in the name of civilization, *in behalf of endangered American interests* . . . the war in Cuba must stop." Those endangered interests had been growing in Cuba throughout the nineteenth century, for the rich island had received the attention of the United States throughout almost every period of that nation's history. Preceding McKinley, Grover Cleveland had stated in his annual message to Congress on December 7, 1896, that the nation's concern for Cuba was "by no means of a wholly sentimental or philanthropic character. . . . Our actual pecuniary interest in it is second only to that of the people and government of Spain." [21]

The reply of Congress to McKinley's message was the

[20] *Informe sobre el censo de Cuba* (Washington, D.C.: Department of War, 1900), p. 44; David F. Healy, *The United States and Cuba, 1898–1902* (Madison: University of Wisconsin Press, 1963), p. 63. In 1902 the sugar crop reached only 795,000 tons, with a total price of $29,981,000. See Ramiro Guerra, "Saldo de la república," *Revista trimestre* (Havana), Oct.–Dec. 1948, pp. 8–10.

[21] Healy, p. 11 (italics mine).

Joint Resolution of April 20, empowering the President to use the army and navy to end Spanish rule in Cuba. This resolution, following the traditional policy of the American government, did not recognize the existence, or independence, of the Cuban Republic or the Cuban army, which had been fighting since 1895. Nevertheless, the famous Teller Resolution stated that the United States had no disposition or intention to exercise sovereignty, jurisdiction, or control over the island.

By December 1898, the "splendid, little war" was over. The ideology of expansionism defended by such Americans as Fiske, Strong, Burgess, and Mahan [22] had received the best of blessings, that of an easy victory, and American businessmen, who had accepted reluctantly the necessity of war, were hailing the incalculable opportunities for trade and exploitation opened up by the conquest of Puerto Rico and the Philippines. To this new appetite, which many Cubans began to recognize with growing apprehension, the Teller Resolution, which had pledged the United States to an independent Cuba, was an antidote. But some Americans regarded it as an obstacle that was to be overcome or at least, as the *Journal of Commerce* suggested, a declaration that "must be interpreted in a sense somewhat different from that which its author intended it to bear." The American flag, then, was to float over Cuba until "law" and "order" were assured.[23]

It is worth mentioning for a balanced picture of the situation that there were numerous groups in the United States that opposed this attitude and combated the emergence of "American imperialism." While American Catholicism expressed its mild opposition through the voice of Cardinal Gibbons, Arch-

[22] See Julius W. Pratt, "The Ideology of American Expansion," *Essays in Honor of William E. Dodd* (Chicago: University of Chicago Press, 1935).

[23] Quoted in Julius W. Pratt, "American Business and the Spanish American War," *Hispanic-American Review*, XIV (May 1934), 200.

bishop of Baltimore, whom President McKinley consulted on the matter of retaining the Philippines,[24] many labor leaders, who had previously acknowledged the necessity of helping the Cubans in their fight for freedom, were now outspoken in their criticism of the U.S. government. In November 1898, a disillusioned Samuel Gompers wrote: "Where has flown this great outburst of our sympathy for the self-sacrificing and liberty loving Cubans? Is it not strange that now, for the first time, we hear that the Cubans are unfit for self-government . . . ?"[25]

For many Cubans, American intervention, received with initial enthusiasm, quickly became a source of concern and anxiety. After three years of war and sacrifice victory had come, but it had not been cleanly gained by the Cuban machete; rather, the impressive cannons of a foreign army had taken full command of the island, and this force was unwilling even to recognize the Cubans as valuable allies. With their soldiers excluded from the cities by the American army, with no clear official policy on the part of the United States government, the Cubans were suspended in a political limbo. Spain had assuredly been defeated, but independence was still obscured on a distant horizon. Cubans had even been deprived,

[24] See John Bilshi, "The Catholic and American Imperialism," *Historical Records and Studies*, XLVII (1959), 140–195.

[25] Samuel Gompers, "Imperialism, Its Dangers and Wrongs," *American Federationist*, V (Nov. 1898), 182. Almost simultaneously the British press, which had extended a sort of caustic welcome to the U.S. for its entry into what it called "cosmic society," recorded the changing mood of the Americans. In the spring, they wrote, the theme was a divine call to help the noble Cubans. "In July it was known that the call was not at all divine; that the Cubans ('ambitious only for plunder and revenge') needed regulation by a strong hand; that to allow independence to Cuba would be a crime against humanity" ("The U.S. War of Awakening," *Blackwood's Edinburgh Magazine*, Sept. 1898, pp. 436–437).

as Manuel Sanguily, a fiery defender of Cuba's sovereignty, expressed it, "their healthy minute of historical revenge." Protected by the Americans, the most reactionary and anti-Cuban Spanish elements were allowed to stay on the island and keep their fortunes and possessions. As usual, no one expressed the collective apprehension better than a poet. On returning from the United States and seeing the American flag on Morro Castle, Bonifacio Byrne wrote bitterly:

> Al volver de distante ribera,
> con el alma enlutada y sombría,
> afanoso busqué mi bandera
> y otra he visto en lugar de la mía. . . .
>
> [On returning from a distant place,
> with a soul veiled and sombre,
> anxious I look for my banner
> and another meets my gaze. . . .]

Meanwhile Cuba was under American control. The first American military occupation of the island lasted from January 1, 1899, to May 20, 1902. As we have seen, the economic and social conditions of the island were terrible. General John R. Brooke, the first military governor, and his successor, General Leonard Wood, undertook with great energy the work of reconstruction: roads were built, hospitals and schools erected, yellow fever was stamped out, and cities received proper sanitary attention.

The Americans also had to face innumerable problems in dealing with the people, trying to calm the natural anxieties of many Cubans who waited for a clear definition of the political future of their nation. As no government or representative of the Cuban nation had been officially recognized, relations with the leaders of the so-called National Assembly [26] and

[26] The National Assembly (Asamblea del Cerro) was formed, without national elections, in 1899.

with the officers of the Cuban army were far from easy. After several conflicts and bitter disputes between American authorities and Cuban representatives, and even among Cubans themselves, primarily in regard to the payment of $3,000,000 to the Cuban soldiers who had fought in the war, the Assembly and the army disbanded, and the task of governing Cuba eased.

But the cloud over the future persisted. After a visit of Military Governor Wood to Washington in July 1900, President McKinley decided that it was time to initiate the process of establishing an independent Cuba. As a first step, a convention would be summoned to prepare a Cuban constitution. Naturally, the drafting of such a constitution would not commit the United States to withdrawal by any particular date, but it would be an easy way to soften the Democratic party's charges of imperialism "which were being hurled at the administration with renewed vigor in that election year." [27] At the end of July, Wood issued a call for the election of delegates in September. On November 5 the Constitutional Convention met in Havana. It would be the duty of the delegates, Wood told them in the opening speech, first to frame a constitution for Cuba, and only "when that has been done," to decide on future relations with the United States.[28] Working slowly, but without any interference from the American authorities, the delegates, many of whom had been members of the National Assembly, finished the body of the constitution in early February 1901, and then began to study the touchy problem of relations with the United States. On that subject the American officials were not so tolerant. While the American Congress studied the problem, Wood began speak-

[27] Russell H. Fitzgibbon, *Cuba and the United States, 1900–1935* (Menasha, Wis., 1935), p. 71.

[28] Rafael Martínez Ortiz, *Cuba, los primeros años de independencia* (Paris: Imprimerie Lux, 1921), I, 173.

ing to the Cuban delegates about the necessity of concrete concessions to the American government.[29] On February 25, 1901, Senator Orville H. Platt introduced in Congress the famous amendment that bears his name, as a rider to the army appropriation bill. The Platt Amendment stipulated conditions under which the United States government would intervene in Cuban affairs. It also proposed establishment of an American naval base in Cuba. On March 2, after congressional debate and signing by the president, the bill became law. The relations between Cuba and the United States had been clearly defined by the Congress of the United States. It remained only for the Cubans to accept the *fait accompli.*

In spite of the assurances of the then Secretary of War of the United States, Elihu Root, that "the United States Government does not wish and is not attempting to intervene in the Cuban Government," [30] there was strong opposition in Cuba to the terms of the Platt Amendment and especially to Point III, which gave the United States the right to intervene in Cuba under very broad conditions. In a speech on March 26, at the Cuban Convention, Enrique Villuendas, one of the members of a commission appointed to consider the amendment, presented an adverse report. He objected to the entire amendment, for, he said, its acceptance was beyond the powers of the Convention, and specifically because "it reserves to the United States the faculty of deciding when independence is threatened, and when, therefore, they ought to intervene." [31] Other members of the Convention were less explicit, but many sectors of Cuban public opinion—the press,

[29] Domingo Mendez Capote, *Trabajos* (Havana: Molina y Compañía, 1929), p. 39.

[30] *Ibid.*, p. 41.

[31] *Memoria de los trabajos realizados por le Convención Constituyente* (Havana: P. Ruiz, 1905), p. 425.

patriotic clubs, and political groups—expressed vehement opposition to it.

But the situation was in fact unalterable. Even Manuel Sanguily finally conceded: "Independence with some restrictions is better than a military regime." [32] After visiting Washington and receiving further reassurance from Mr. Root regarding the self-determination and sovereignty of Cuba, the Cuban commission considering the Platt Amendment returned to Cuba and presented its report. On June 12, by a majority of one, the Constitutional Convention adopted the Platt Amendment as an annex to the Cuban Constitution.

From this time on, the amendment—its imposition upon Cuba, the bitter denunciation of it by a number of Cubans, the analysis of its pernicious influence on the development of a true and responsible Cuban government—would remain an ever present subject in Cuba, a leitmotif for all those who wanted to inflame anti-American feelings.[33]

Juan Gualberto Gómez, one of the most distinguished leaders of the war against Spain, considered the Platt Amendment a political imposition which "reduced the independence and sovereignty of the Cuban republic to a myth," and other Cubans reacted sternly, but the fact that its approval guaranteed the withdrawal of the American army was accepted by many as fair compensation, as a necessary compromise to open the way for political independence. As Enrique José Varona never tired of insisting, the important thing for the Cubans now was to gather all their energies, to rally all their efforts for the common cause of the republic

to resist the enormous pressure of foreign interests which are

[32] Quoted in Martínez Ortiz, I, 257.

[33] A recent and excellent review of opinion and bibliography on the subject is James H. Hitchman, "The Platt Amendment Revisited: A Bibliography," *The Americas*, XXIII (1967), 343–370.

surrounding us. We are a people broken by a long period of internal struggles, subjected to the expansionist force of a very powerful nation. What form will this expansion take? Is it going to be reduced only to an economic and civilizing influence, or would it take the form of political dominance? That will depend on our capacity to resist, that is, on our social cohesion.[34]

"The Americans are going to leave," General Máximo Gómez supposedly said; "it is our primary duty to avoid any stumbling which could bring them back."

But after some initial firm steps that encouraged a general sense of optimism, the Republic stumbled and brought the Americans back.

First Steps of the Republic, 1902–1906

The Constitution of 1901 provided for a presidential system of government similar to that of the United States and incorporated a lengthy Bill of Rights with particular emphasis on the separation of Church and State. The president could be re-elected for a second term and universal manhood suffrage was established in modification of the electoral law of the military government which had given the franchise only to adult males who were literate, owned a small amount of property, or had served in the Revolutionary Army.

As provided by the Constitution, presidential elections were held in December 1901. On May 20, 1902, with great enthusiasm, Tomás Estrada Palma, who had succeeded Martí as the head of the Revolutionary party, took command of the government of the island from Governor-General Leonard Wood. The President was not, unfortunately, a true representative of the nationalistic Cuban forces. A quiet, honest, hardworking man, Estrada Palma had lived almost his entire life outside of Cuba and deeply admired the United States. He preferred a politically dependent, but free and stable,

[34] Editorial from his newspaper *Patria*, April 1, 1899.

Cuba to a sovereign and independent republic that might follow the turbulent pattern of Latin America[35]—a conviction that eventually would result in disaster for Cuba.

Apart from the initial and deep disillusion caused by the Platt Amendment, the future of the island seemed bright at the moment. Many of the tremendous social and political problems which for decades had disturbed Latin America were not present in Cuba or appeared much less important: Cuba had no powerful and traditional oligarchy trying to control political channels and paralyzing all progress. The nucleus of this potential oligarchy had dispersed in 1878, and their successors, or those who would have been their successors, were hard hit by the years of revolution and destruction from 1895–1898. In more than one way, Cuba was a fresh society, a nation where class divisions were not acute or stratified. In 1898, after a vain attempt to stir up socialist ideas, the founders of the ephemeral Cuban Socialist party (which survived only four months) disbanded and joined another political party.[36] But, for almost the same reasons—the absence of native capitalists and of a landed aristocracy—Cuba was also, as will be seen, a land open and defenseless before the invasion of foreign capital.

There was no religious conflict in Cuba. The Church was not the all-powerful institution of Mexico or Colombia, and the Catholic feeling of the population lacked the fanaticism and intense concern that existed in Spain and in other countries of Latin America. The laxness of this religious feeling, which had been criticized by certain ecclesiastical

[35] Jenks, p. 107.

[36] The founder was a Cuban poet, Diego Vicente Tejera. For a history of the party and a survey of Tejera's ideas, see José Rivero Muñiz, *El primer partido socialista cubano* (Las Villas: Universidad Central, 1962), and Luis E. Aguilar, ed., *Marxism in Latin America* (New York: Knopf, 1968), pp. 70–74.

voices,[37] was clearly shown by the ease with which Church and State were separated in the Constitution, and in the absence of religious slogans or ideas in the first political parties organized in the republic. The attitude for or against religious ideas was not strong enough to justify a political banner.[38]

Finally, the racial situation was also quite different from the rest of Latin America, especially from those regions where Indians formed a large segment of the population. In Cuba the relationship between white and Negro (the original Indian population disappeared early) had been, in comparison with other places where slavery reigned, rather relaxed. As far back as 1826, Baron Humboldt had noticed the ease with which slaves could obtain freedom under Spanish laws, and the familiarity with which slaves and *libertos* (freed slaves) were treated by Cuban families.[39] The proverbial laxness of the Spaniards in sexual relations, nowhere more evident than in the Caribbean, furnished another bridge between the races. These intertwined themes of desire, love, and conflict between white and Negro, plus the fascination with Cuba's most beautiful product, the mulatta, form an entire literary current. Beginning with *Petrona and Rosalia*, written in 1838 by Felix Tanco y Bosmeniel, and *Francisco*, written in 1839 by Anselmo Suárez y Romero, heightened in 1882 with the publication of *Cecilia Valdés* by Cirilo Villaverde, this cur-

[37] See, for instance, *Oradores cubanos coloniales* (Madrid: Serafin Hdez, 1879), pp. 46–48.

[38] Martínez Ortiz, I, 88.

[39] For the racial situation during colonial times see "An Integrated Community: Cuba," in the excellent book by Herbert S. Klein, *Slavery in the Americas* (Chicago: University of Chicago Press, 1967), pp. 194–227; Alexander Humboldt, *Ensayo político sobre la isla de Cuba* (Havana: Archivo Nacional de Cuba, 1960), p. 179. Visiting Havana a few years later (1839), Fanny Calderón de la Barca noticed that even among the "social elite," to have Negro ancestors or Negro traits was not considered, "as in the U.S., any disgrace" (*Life in Mexico* [New York: Doubleday, 1970], p. 31).

rent has continued uninterrupted down to the novels, poetry, and folklore of the present day.

In the field of music, furthermore, breaking through the assumed disdain of the upper classes, African tunes and Negro rhythms combined with Spanish forms to create the soul of Cuban music. Since the arrival of the earliest slaves, African influence was felt in popular dances and songs. Not only were free Negroes organizing societies for their own entertainment (one of the first on which there is information can be dated in 1598), but even Spanish authorities permitted and encouraged dances among the slaves.[40] "Some time later those African or Cuban musicians, already initiated in the art of composition, formed those famous dancing orchestras which the refined society enjoyed so much; for then (the nineteenth century) as now dancing was the dominant passion in Cuba, and no one could give *sandunga* (flair) to rhythm and music as the Negroes." [41]

The black population contributed not only to Cuban musical development; they also founded schools and towns. By 1899, in spite of the high percentage of illiteracy (72 per cent among Negroes), they had established twenty-five newspapers which, run entirely by Negroes, spread throughout the island their aspirations and desires.[42]

In 1868, the first act of the Cuban patriots was to proclaim the abolition of slavery and to free the slaves. From then on the black man of Cuba fought side by side with the white in the effort for independence; many blacks rose to the rank of general, such as Guillermón Moncada, Flor Crombet,

[40] Alejo Carpentier, *La música en Cuba* (Mexico City: Fondo de Cultura Económica, 1946), pp. 222, 223.

[41] Gaspar Aguero y Barreras, "El aporte africano a la música popular cubana," in *Estudios Afro-Cubanos* (Havana: Separata, 1940–1946), V, 121.

[42] Pedro Deschamps Chapeaux, *El Negro en el periodismo cubano en el siglo XIX* (Havana: Ediciones Revolución, 1963), p. 11.

Quintín Banderas, and last but certainly not least, the supreme hero of the War of Independence, Antonio Maceo. It was significant that in 1899, during the first military occupation, certain American newspapers accused the U.S. army of introducing Southern race prejudice into Cuba, where racial relations had previously been smooth.[43]

Free from such social, religious, and racial impediments, the young republic experienced also a quick economic recovery. But in this field the basic weakness of Cuba showed immediately. The Platt Amendment was followed in 1903 by a commercial Treaty of Reciprocity which embodied terms diametrically opposed to Martí's objectives. This treaty assured Cuba of a 20 per cent tariff preference on her sugar entering the United States. The market was thus wide open, meaning that Cuba could supply all the sugar the United States wanted to buy. In return, Cuba granted tariff preferences to certain American products.

The effect of such an apparently advantageous position, along with the absence of powerful native capital that could have checked the invasion of foreign capital, was to make Cuba almost totally dependent upon the American market and the price of sugar. The trend that had appeared in 1878 was now a dominant force; Cuba began to be engulfed by the American economy.

Sugar production rose steadily from 300,073 long tons in 1900 to 1,163,258 long tons in 1905. At the same time, American investments in Cuba jumped from $50 million in 1896 to $205 million by 1911. In 1905 an estimated 13,000 American colonists had bought land in Cuba for about $50 million.[44]

[43] Healy, p. 61. This is not to imply that there was no racial prejudice in Cuba, but it was not bitter or general, it had complex economic causes, and it was limited to a few sectors of social life.

[44] José R. Alvarez Díaz *et al.* (for the Cuban Economic Research Project), *A Study on Cuba* (Miami: University of Miami Press, 1963),

President Estrada Palma was an honest man whose main concern was to build more schools than barracks and to keep a watchful eye on the manipulation of public funds. In 1905 the government could show a very positive balance for its activity. In 1902 the reserve in the Treasury of the Republic was $539,994.99; in 1904 it had increased to $7,099,584.86. In addition to the tremendous sugar expansion, other branches of agriculture were also growing rapidly. Cattle, for example, which numbered 125,229 in 1901, had jumped to 1,703,069 in 1904. Another good sign was the growing number of immigrants, principally Spaniards, who were coming to the island: in 1902 there were 6,316; in 1905 the number was 38,628.[45]

Unfortunately, as Máximo Gómez had foreseen, political mistakes were soon to plunge the new republic, with its still shaky institutions, into civil strife and, consequently, a second military occupation. At the beginning of 1904, the different regional political groups had gathered into several regional parties of which the two most important were El Partido Republicano Conservador (Republican Conservative party) and El Partido Liberal Nacional (National Liberal party). While both were preparing themselves for the presidential contest of 1905, Estrada Palma, extremely satisfied with the results of his government, yielded to those who were pressuring him to seek re-election. Immediately a new party was organized, El Partido Moderado (Moderate party), and to the consternation of all other political sectors the powerful machinery of the government was used to build the electoral

---

p. 233; *Investment in Cuba* (Washington, D.C.: U.S. Department of Commerce, 1956), p. 9; Julio Le Riverand, *Historia económica de Cuba* (Havana: Escuela de Comercio, 1963), p. 214.

[45] R. Iznaga, *Tres años de república* (Havana: Rambla, Bouza, 1905), pp. 28–29, 32.

strength of that party. Forced by this pressure, the other two parties united to present a common ballot opposed to Estrada Palma. And, while tension mounted in Cuba, Máximo Gómez, the old hero of independence, perhaps the only man who could have averted the tragedy, died.

On September 23, 1905, the elections were held. Because of governmental control over the electoral machinery, the opposition refused to participate, and Estrada Palma, probably in ignorance of the extent of the fraud, was elected for a second term. The fraud of the elections and the continuation of a policy of harassment of the opposition provoked an insurrection. In August 1906 rebellion was general and the government seemed incapable of controlling it. Facing the reluctance of the American government to intervene on his behalf, Estrada Palma decided to resign, creating a political vacuum which would force the Americans to intervene.[46] On September 28, 1906, he presented to the Cuban Congress his own and his cabinet's resignations. That same day he asked U.S. Commissioners Taft and Bacon to relieve his administration of custody of the Treasury. Taft immediately ordered the landing of a small body of marines to protect the Treasury. The following day Taft, with President Roosevelt's approval, issued the proclamation of intervention by the United States under the Platt Amendment. The Cuban Republic had failed.

[46] President Roosevelt had sent Secretary of War Taft and Assistant Secretary Bacon as commissioners to find a solution. Their report was critical of the Cuban government and hurt Estrada Palma. See Fitzgibbon, pp. 118–119. Estrada Palma was apparently following the suggestion of the American Consul who advised him to ask for American intervention. See *Census of the Republic of Cuba, 1919* (Havana: Maza, Arroyo y Caso, 1929), p. 148. For a good study of these and the following events from the American point of view see Allan Reed Millet, *The Politics of Intervention: The Military Occupation of Cuba, 1906–1909* (Columbus: Ohio State University Press, 1968).

2 Failure of the Republic, 1906-1925

Second American Intervention and Its Consequences

The second intervention in Cuba (1906–1908) was quite different from the first. Thrust upon an American government that did not want or need it, devoid of patriotic fanfare or military glory, it was a quick expedient to cope with an embarrassing Cuban political problem. And to handle it, the provisional governor, Charles E. Magoon, relied on political solutions. Bureaucratic positions were widely distributed to calm factional disputes; public works contracts were liberally granted; flexibility reigned. Personally honest, the Governor took several positive initiatives and helped reorganize Cuban political life toward returning the government to the Cuban people. Unfortunately his system encouraged political corruption. But for an understanding of the history of Cuba it is less essential to defend or accuse Magoon (certainly the *bête noir* of Cuban historians) than to evaluate the impact on Cuba of this second American intervention.[1] On this point

[1] For a study and evaluation of Magoon's role in Cuba, see David Lockmiller, *Magoon in Cuba 1906–1909* (Chapel Hill: University of North Carolina, 1958); also, Hugh Thomas, *Cuba, the Pursuit of Freedom* (New York: Harper & Row, 1971), pp. 480–495. The herculean work of Thomas, which covers the history of Cuba from

the testimony is overwhelming. Psychologically or, perhaps, sociologically speaking, the second intervention proved disastrous for Cuba.

The presence of American troops on the island, the evident failure of the first government, and the fact that the Cubans themselves had invited foreign rule provoked a wave of pessimism and disillusionment throughout every level of Cuban society. It was no longer possible to maintain even a pretense of faith in self-government or the shadow of an illusion about independence. The corps of Cuban writers and politicians, who had fought for independence and who, in spite of the Platt Amendment, had remained optimistic about the future of the island, now expressed dismay. In 1906, Gonzalo de Quesada, close friend of Martí, wrote in this somber mood to Ambassador Márquez Sterling: "Do you remember my previous deep pessimism? . . . Do you remember how you then accused me of seeing everything through a dark glass? . . . Alas, later you yourself turned pessimistic and the fears of us both were realized." [2] At about the same time Francisco Figueras, in the prologue to a study of Cuba, expressed this bitter conclusion: "When I finished my reading I was both defeated and convinced. Defeated in my old ideals and convinced that Cuba lacked the capacity to be an independent nation." [3]

With this weakening of the forces that represented the best hopes and dreams for a healthy, honest, and vigorous republic, all the latent elements of irresponsibility and immorality were

---

1762 to 1966, was published when this book was ready for the printer. That is why only a few references to that important contribution will be found in it.

[2] Gonzalo de Quesada, *Documentos históricos* (Havana: Editorial de la Universidad, 1965), p. 311

[3] *Cuba y su evolución colonial* (Havana: Imprenta Avisador Comercial, 1907), p. 5.

unleashed. Profiting from the still vast ignorance of the population, encouraged by a large Spanish population who, harboring resentment for the recent defeat, voiced their contempt for and mockery of every Cuban effort,[4] and supported by the increasing political and economic control of the United States over the island, the worst political elements emerged as the driving forces of the nation. The period of 1909–1925 is one of continuous decline of the moral and political standards of the island. In the background, the mass of the population took refuge in an attitude of irreverence toward everything that had any national or spiritual value. This popular reaction, a mixture of disillusion and drollery, of bitterness and biting humor, called *choteo criollo,* became a national characteristic, a psychological escape from unpleasant social realities.[5]

The best minds of Cuba clearly realized the causes for this rapid deterioration. Deprived of the responsibility of deciding her own destinies, the republic had become a political instrument for the protection of many foreign economic interests, and some national ones which had allied themselves with the conquerors. With a few exceptions, to rule in Cuba really meant to obey—to harken to the demands of the socioeconomic complex which actually controlled the republic. Thus exempted from governing the nation, political hands were free to "administer" public funds. Toleration for dishonesty was the reward for political compliance, and there was no strong nationalistic force that could break this vicious circle. The enlightened patriciate had been decimated in the fight for independence, and the opportunists, newcomers, and specu-

[4] The negative influence of certain sectors of the Spanish population in Cuba has been studied by Alberto Lamar Schweyer in *La crisis del patriotismo* (Havana: Editorial Martí, 1929).

[5] See Jorge Mañach, *Indagación del Choteo* (Havana: Editorial Lex, 1936).

lators who replaced them, without any trace of patriotism, had taken advantage of American penetration and become interested defenders of the status quo. These were pragmatic men who derided idealism and considered nationalism only an empty slogan for electoral campaigns. They formed a powerful group of lawyers, politicians, *hacendados*, and merchants who believed that the Americans held in their hands the key to a golden future, and that nothing should be done to imperil the "privileged" position of Cuba.

In 1902, alarmed by news that the American government was hesitant to sign the Commercial Reciprocity Treaty with Cuba, some of the most influential representatives of the Cuban economy—lawyers, politicians, businessmen—met at the Tacón Theater in Havana. They urgently demanded the signing of the Treaty "not because of a particular class interest, but because of the interest of the entire country," as one of the speakers said: "With this treaty we would save national production, and with national production our entire existence; for once Cuba is under American hegemony; having solved the economic problem, all her other problems are secondary." Accord No. 4 of the meeting declared that "the salvation of the Cuban wealth depends entirely on the government of the United States." [6] Thus were economic and political dependence accepted by these groups who, considering themselves spokesmen for the entire nation, proclaimed that "alliance" with the Americans was the only way to prosperity.

This atmosphere explains the agonized cry of Enrique José

[6] *Discursos pronunciados en el Teatro Tacón* (Havana, 1902), pp. 5, 7, 44. The relevance of the meeting can be measured by the prominence of the speakers. Among them were Alfredo Záyas, future president of the Republic; Rafael Montoro, brilliant orator, future senator and vice presidential candidate; Antonio Sánchez de Bustamante, distinguished lawyer and internationalist, later president of the Supreme Court of the League of Nations.

Varona, "We are back in the colony!" and the poetic lament of Felipe Pichardo Moya:

> y para oponer a la invasión de tantos males,
> no tenemos mas
> que las débiles lanzas de los cañaverales . . ."
>
> [and to oppose the invasion of so many evils
> we only have
> the fragile lances of our sugar canes . . .]

and the harsh words of Jesús Castellanos in 1911, when he denounced the materialism then engulfing the island:

> Among us a practical man is a machine to make money, without benefit to society; he is the physician who ignores biology and knows only how to dispatch prescriptions; he is the uncultivated lawyer who does not even know the history of his nation; he is, in one word, the merchant to whom the grave problems of the fatherland should always be sacrificed to the results of the next *zafra* [sugar crop] . . . a contemptible leading class which, perhaps, some day in the future will be forced to render an account for the destruction of the country. . . . We must react while there is still time against this ferocious mercantilism which is blinding us to a realization of our true destiny.[7]

But the ferocious mercantilism could not be stopped by criticism or by appeals to patriotism. In 1917, yielding temporarily to pessimism, Varona paused in his preaching of civic duties to make this acid summary of Cuban politics: "Has our political life been one of progress? . . . Yes, a progressive muddle." In 1924 Carlos M. Trelles wrote an essay on "The

[7] Jesús Castellanos, *Los optimistas* (Havana: Academia Nacional de Artes y Letras, 1915), pp. 124–125. It is fair to remember that this mercantilistic aspect of Cuban society was not new. Back in 1824 Felix Varela bitterly remarked: "In Cuba there is no political opinion, there is only mercantile opinion" (*El habanero* [Havana: Editorial de la Universidad, 1945], p. 17).

Progress and Retrogression of Cuba." And in the same year—only twenty-two years after independence—Fernando Ortiz analyzed "the decadence of Cuba."[8]

Unless one understands this negative atmosphere that debilitated the Cuban national conscience, it is difficult to grasp the extraordinary significance of the events of the twenties. Aided by a crisis that shattered the economic structure of the island, the generation of the twenties rebelled against the environment of corruption and decadence, renewed the old dreams of sovereignty and independence, and aroused the dormant nationalism of the Cuban people.

To appreciate this explosive situation, it is essential to examine the most important political and economic developments of the period (1909–1925) that formed its fuse.

Political Developments, 1909–1925

During the second intervention, two political alliances were organized in Cuba: the Conservative party, which was born mainly from the dissolution of the ill-fated Moderate party of Estrada Palma; and the Liberal party, which, defending a platform of "Cubanism" and reform, was the more popular of the two. Before abandoning Cuba, the Americans supervised another election. On November 14, 1908, the Liberal candidate, General José Miguel Gómez, was elected president. In 1912 the Conservative candidate, General Mario Menocal, won the election and was re-elected in 1916 amid outcries

[8] Enrique José Varona, *Con el eslabón* (Manzanillo, 1927), p. 11; Carlos M. Trelles, "El progreso y el retroceso de Cuba," *Revista bimestre cubana*, July–Aug. 1924; Fernando Ortiz Fernández, *La decadencia cubana* (Havana: La Universal, 1924). The short stories and novels of Luis Felipe Rodríguez (e.g., *La conjura de la ciénaga*, 1924) and Carlos Loveira y Chirino (*Generales y doctores*, 1922; *Juan Criollo*, 1928) provide a realistic and bitter picture of the conditions of Cuban society in this period.

from the Liberals of fraud and coercion. In 1920 Alfredo Zayas, a former Liberal now at the head of the small Partido Popular and supported by the Conservatives, was elected and remained in power until 1925, when Gerardo Machado y Morales was sworn in as President of the republic.

But the names of the candidates or the parties do not mean very much. The real essence of politics, the interplay of programs and ideas, did not exist. Conservatives changed positions with Liberals and vice versa; the political struggle was limited to differing slogans and the personal appeal of individuals. The real objective was to gain power in order to distribute positions and privileges among followers. Speaking in the Chamber of Representatives, José Antonio González Lanuza, a professor at the University of Havana and an honest man, acutely defined the political mechanism in Cuba: "Our political parties are merely cooperatives organized for bureaucratic consumption."

Of course, the causes for this situation went beyond a question of collective morals. The reasons for the abnormal growth of bureaucracy, for the transformation of politics into a struggle for survival, were rooted in the social and economic conditions of the island. With a large part of the land and sugar industry in American hands, and with the Spaniards still controlling most of the centers of trade in the cities, politics was one of the few fields open to Cubans in their own land. It was no accident that until the 1930's a bureaucratic position in Cuba was called *un destino*, "a destiny," a salvation, and that electoral campaigns were celebrated as the "second *zafra*" of the island.

Accordingly, a position in the bureaucracy became a dreamed-of booty and government an instrument to supply the necessities—or the luxuries—of many. Public funds were wasted or used for the personal benefits of those who had access to them. Illegal contracts for public works were awarded at impressive rates, helping to create heavy financial burdens on the government. Honesty was a luxury that no politician could afford in this struggle for the survival of the unfit. Several times—in 1908, in 1917, in 1919, and in 1921—opposition groups revolted or threatened to revolt, claiming, not without reason, that elections had been fraudulent. But the revolts, or the gestures of rebellion, usually led to more shady transactions and became an accepted play in the political game. When occasionally things became too serious, American intervention or the simple threat of American intervention was restraint enough.

The decisive factor was American influence. After 1906 almost every major political aspirant looked to the U.S. State Department for approval, and American influence supported many national and antinational causes. So powerful was the American economic-political complex that, for example, in 1920 the Liberals proposed as candidate for the vice-presidency one of the American directors of the sugar trust "Cuban Cane." "They thought," wrote Márquez Sterling, "that by associating sugar magnates with the candidacy of the party, the [Platt] Amendment would watch over the honesty of the elections." [9]

On the other hand, after the second intervention, American foreign policy had become tougher on Cuba. The protection of the growing American interests on the island demanded stronger measures than Root's cautious interpretation of the Platt Amendment. The result was the famous "preventive policy" and "dollar diplomacy" of William Howard Taft and Philander Chase Knox, a diplomatic formula that diminished the necessity of another intervention by augmenting American political control. Consequently, the Department of

[9] Manuel Márquez Sterling, *Las conferencias del Shoreham* (Mexico City: Ediciones Botas, 1933), p. 35.

State adopted "an attitude of constant and critical watchfulness in order that representation might be made to avoid, if possible, the development of any situation in Cuba which might call for intervention."[10] In January 1911, for example, a bill authorizing the improvement of several Cuban ports was approved by Congress. Because of recent debates concerning the interpretation of the law, the new American Minister, John B. Jackson, requested a clarification of the policy. Knox's reply was very enlightening:

> Because of its special treaty relations with Cuba . . . the Department considers that besides the direct protection of American interests you are to endeavour, by friendly representation and advice, *to deter the Cuban government from enacting legislation which appears to you of an undesirable or improvident character.*[11]

On other occasions, the "friendly advice" took more concrete forms. On January 17, 1912, Secretary of State Knox sent a note to the Cuban government in regard to the increasing unrest created by a movement of veterans of the War of Independence, who were demanding the ouster of pro-Spanish elements from political positions. His note expressed "grave concern" and recommended that Cuba forestall any development which might force the United States to decide "what measures it must take." The hint was more than enough: the veteran movement renounced its violent tactics and proclaimed its desire to work "for the benefit of all Cubans."[12]

In May of that same year the marines landed in Cuba,

[10] Russell H. Fitzgibbon, *Cuba and the United States, 1900–1935* (Menasha, Wis., 1935), p. 145.

[11] Dana G. Munro, *Intervention and Dollar Diplomacy in the Caribbean, 1900–1921* (Princeton: Princeton University Press, 1964), p. 472 (italics mine).

[12] *El País* (Havana), Feb. 4, 1912, p. 1; Fitzgibbon, p. 149. This "Movimiento de los Veteranos," formed by General Emilio Núñez (1861–1919), represented another aspect of the Cuban struggle against the still powerful Spanish elements in the island.

against the express wishes of President Gómez, to protect American interests from the supposed disorders that might result from a minor racial uprising. This episode, the only one of its kind in Cuba, deserves some clarification. In 1908, with the island still under Magoon's rule, a group of black people who felt they were excluded from all political opportunities founded the Agrupación Independiente de Color (Independent Colored Association). The leader of the movement was a former soldier of the Army of Independence, a bricklayer in Havana, Evaristo Estenoz. This organization soon became a political party that appealed to colored people exclusively; however, it failed to win a single position in the elections of 1908 (which ended the provisional American government).

After that failure, the Colored Independents intensified their racial propaganda in the pages of the newspaper *Previsión*. Several distinguished colored politicians, among them the president of the Senate, Martín Morúa Delgado, considered this tactic erroneous and presented to the Cuban Congress a projected law—quickly approved—by which all parties composed exclusively of persons of one race were outlawed. To force the abolition of that law, and following the example of other Cuban groups which, as noted earlier, threatened to revolt in order to force the government to accede to their wishes, the Colored Independents took the road of armed insurrection in 1912. Only minor groups, principally in Oriente Province, joined the improvised revolt, which proved to be a tragic mistake. The possibility of negotiating with the Cuban government faded rapidly under American pressure. Alarmed by exaggerated reports of the rebellion, the American government landed marines in Guantánamo, Havana, and Manzanillo, while several warships were ostentatiously sent toward Cuba.[13] Fearing another occupation of the island,

[13] Munro, pp. 478–479.

President Gómez protested this unrequested so-called help, guaranteed that the Cuban government could quell the rebellion, and, indeed, moved quickly to restore order. Under the circumstances, the Cuban government felt a show of force was necessary. The repression was unusually harsh, and the rebellion was easily put down. Estenoz, Ivonet, and all the minor leaders of the movement were killed, and hundreds of others who had joined the rebellion or were even remotely connected with it were summarily executed. The Independent Colored party ceased to exist.

It must be pointed out that the two most prominent leaders of the revolt (Estenoz and Ivonet) were not Cubans (they came from the Dominican Republic and Haiti), that the majority of the black people of Cuba did not join the movement, and that the principal colored figures of the island, Morúa Delgado and Juan Gualberto Gómez among them, condemned the action of Estenoz as a deviation from the common ideal of the Cuban people. In 1951 the Marxist review *Fundamentos* criticized the movement, concluding: "The ideology of the Independent Colored Party was typically petit-bourgeois. In their declarations and attitudes is often visible the influence of anarchism, its inflammatory terminology, its appeal to individual violence, its faith in the effect of threats." Sergio Aguirre, another Cuban Marxist, concludes: "It was an erroneous movement." [14]

[14] From *Fundamentos*, No. 110 (May 1951); quoted in Sergio Aguirre, *El cincuentenario de un gran crimen* (Havana: Departamento de Instrucción Revolucionaria, n.d.), pp. 29, 30. For a pre-Castro history of the movement, see Serafín Portuondo Linares, *Los independientes de color* (Havana: Minerva, 1937). Using basically non-Cuban sources, Hugh Thomas gives excessive importance to this episode (pp. 515–524). Perhaps that is why he concludes: "The movement fell away, almost as mysteriously as it had begun" (p. 523). There is no mystery if one considers the small number of those involved.

In February 1917 the Liberal party took up arms over the fraudulent elections held by President Menocal. So popular was their cause, so evident the abuse, that in the first two days the rebels controlled Santiago de Cuba, a great part of Oriente Province, and almost all of Camaguey Province. The revolt spread like fire throughout the island; "it seemed as if the government could not stop it."[15] Then William Elliot González, the American Minister in Cuba, received instructions to issue notices to the press that the United States would not support a government that came into power by unconstitutional means.[16] Shortly afterward, the "powerful" revolution dissolved into the air. In spite of its failure, the marines occupied Santiago, Guantánamo, Manzanillo, and several other cities. The "notices" of Mr. González became a landmark in the history of Cuba.

In 1919 both political Liberal and Conservative parties agreed to a revision of the electoral code and decided to invite the American General, Enoch H. Crowder, who had kept in touch with recent Cuban affairs, to help them in rewriting the code. In spite of President Menocal's opposition, Crowder was sent to Cuba as a personal representative of the President of the United States to supervise the settlement of political disputes and to offer his advice on the implementation of financial reforms. Symbolically, he arrived on a battleship, the "Minnesota," aboard which he held his first conferences. He remained an advisor until January 1923, when he was appointed the first Ambassador to Cuba, an office he held until 1927.

The struggle between President Zayas and General Crowder was long and, at times, bitter. To at least one historian, in a

[15] Juan M. Leiseca, *Historia de Cuba* (Havana: Libreria Cervantes, 1925), p. 513

[16] Fitzgibbon, p. 157.

rather superficial simplification, it was a struggle between Evil and Good.[17] Crowder, "the personification of that aggressive altruism which has given the world its great proconsuls," [18] did try to impose certain fiscal and political reforms on Cuba: a reduction in the budget, a revision of the bank system, modification of the electoral law. He had in his favor the poor economic condition of the island, the need for loans, and the usual threat of intervention. He was also the representative of powerful American business interests and had the backing of several Cuban financial groups. Until about 1923, Crowder's influence was paramount in Cuba. That year President Zayas, with a loan of $50,000,000 already received from the Morgan firm, decided to strike back, attacking the famous "Honest Cabinet" which had been "suggested" by Crowder in 1922. Some of its members considered themselves permanent because they had American backing. For this confrontation Zayas had in his favor a growing resurgence of nationalism in Cuba, and another change of attitude in the American State Department. In June the entire Cabinet was reorganized. While Crowder asked for a more "aggressive attitude by the United States," Secretary of State Hughes assured the Cuban Ambassador that the United States had no intention of intervening in Cuba as long as the Cuban government proved stable and sound.[19]

[17] Charles E. Chapman, *A History of the Cuban Republic* (New York: Macmillan, 1927), p. 413. Years later Crowder told Ambassador Guggenheim: "When I returned from Cuba to Chicago and witnessed the corruption of municipal politics in that city, I felt a sense of shame in recalling that memorandum I sent to President Zayas" (Harry F. Guggenheim, *The United States and Cuba* [New York: Macmillan, 1934], p. 157).

[18] Leland H. Jenks, *Nuestra colonia de Cuba* (Buenos Aires: Editorial Palestra, 1960), p. 224.

[19] Robert F. Smith, *The United States and Cuba* (New Haven: Yale University Press, 1961), p. 97.

The era of direct interference was ending. With mounting criticism of the United States in Latin America, and realizing that order and stability could be better kept if they allowed their national allies to have greater political freedom, the State Department reverted to a policy of restraint toward interference in Latin American internal affairs. It was characteristic of the period that a corrupt Cuban president had helped nationalism to triumph in Cuba.

Economic and Social Developments, 1909–1925

Economically, two important developments occurred during the years 1909–1925: (*a*) expanding sugar cultivation along with growth of great estates (latifundios) and (*b*) growing penetration and dominance of American capital. These phenomena represent the acceleration of earlier trends, and their impact and influence were deeply felt in Cuban society during this period.

The conditions with which Cuba started its independent life —under the Platt Amendment and the Treaty of Reciprocity of 1903—encouraged both phenomena. The Reciprocity Treaty reduced the duty paid on Cuban sugar marketed in the United States by 20 per cent, and thus other potential markets were disregarded for a long time. It is true that by 1902 sugar had become the main source of the island's national income, leaving far behind the other resources: cattle, tobacco, and coffee.[20] But the new incentives accelerated this process and turned sugar into the all-powerful king of the Cuban economy. Between 1903 and 1914, Cuban sugar production and sugar exports to the United States more than doubled. In

[20] In 1902, sugar represented 47.9 per cent of the total production of the island (*Resúmenes estadísticos seleccionados* [Havana: Ministerio de Hacienda, 1959], p. 26).

1900 the Cuban share of world sugar production was 2.7 per cent; in 1915 it had increased to 15.4 per cent.[21]

The First World War added tremendous momentum to this expansion. In July 1914 the average price of sugar sold in Havana was 1.93 cents per pound. The following month, when the war started, the price jumped to 3.36 cents per pound. Until 1920 this upward trend remained almost constant, creating a wave of investment, speculation, and expansion. During the period 1900–1913, in spite of favorable conditions, only seventeen new mills were constructed in Cuba, while in the five years from 1914–1918 twenty-five new mills were built. During this period, the raising of cattle and the cultivation of other foodstuffs—even coffee—suffered. In 1919 the census reported: "The great increase in sugar manufacturing during the last year has affected the coffee plantations by taking their workingmen and land. Several coffee plantations have been converted into sugar plantations." [22] Forest areas again began to disappear in Cuba, as they had in the final decades of the eighteenth century, when 500 *caballerías* of forest were sacrificed annually to sugar. (One *caballería* is equal to 32 acres.) By 1830 the figure had climbed to 2,000, when the most precious trees and wood of Cuba—ebony, mahogany, and the like—were cut and burned.[23]

The expansion of latifundios for sugar production soon affected not only the peasants and those who cultivated other minor agricultural products, but also a very imporant economic group in Cuba: the *colonos*—those who cultivated the

[21] *Anuario azucarero* (Havana: Ministerio del Comercio Exterior, 1961), XXV, 27, and 33; José R. Alvarez Díaz *et al.*, *A Study on Cuba* (Miami: University of Miami Press, 1965), p. 233.

[22] *Census of the Republic of Cuba, 1919* (Havana: Maza, Arroyo y Caso, 1929), p. 950.

[23] Manuel Moreno Fraginals, *El ingenio* (Havana: Comisión Nacional Cubana de la UNESCO, 1964), pp. 74–75.

cane and, unable to grind it themselves, sold it to the mills. This group, who had remained independent and rather powerful until the second intervention, began to lose ground rapidly when the mill owners initiated a vast program of land acquisition in order to guarantee their own supply of cane and reduce their production costs. In 1927, for example, the Cuban American Sugar Company owned six sugar mills and 14,867 *caballerías* of land.[24] As the majority of these great companies were owned by American firms, the *colonos* increasingly began to press for some protection from their government and, consequently, joined those who were beginning to defend nationalistic programs as a matter of collective survival.

The agricultural workers also felt the impact of this sugar expansion. To keep the cost of production low and, at the same time, to meet the demand for more and more *macheteros* (cane-cutters), the sugar mills pressured the government to authorize the immigration of Haitians and Jamaicans, who were willing to work for less than the Cuban workers. In 1912, reversing a policy that had been traditional in Cuba since the time of Félix Varela, President Gómez gave the United Fruit Company permission to import 1,400 Haitians.[25] From then on, legally and illegally, thousands of poorly paid workers from the lowest social level, most of whom could not speak Spanish, poured into the island, keeping salaries down and

[24] Lowry Nelson, *Rural Cuba* (Minneapolis: University of Minnesota Press, 1950), p. 96.

[25] Ramiro Guerra y Sánchez, *La industria azucarera de Cuba* (Havana: Cultural, 1940), p. 179. For a protest against this policy, see Carlos de Velasco, *Aspectos nacionales* (Havana: Jesús Montero, 1915), pp. 57–68. As late as 1932, Juan Marinello was accusing imperialist interests of bringing Haitians and Jamaicans to Cuba "to weaken and divide the Cuban proletariat." See his "El Negro en los Estados Unidos," *Repertorio americano* (Costa Rica), Dec. 10, 1932, pp. 340–341.

halting, at least in some provinces like Oriente, the homogenization process of the nation.

The year 1920 marked the peak and, to a certain extent, the turning point of this period. An unexpected demand for sugar in the international market and the removal of war price controls in the United States sent the sugar prices sky high. From 7.28 cents per pound in November 1919, the price of sugar climbed in March 1920 to 13.54 cents, in April to 19.56, and in May to 22.51. The sugar crop of 1919–1920 was sold at $1,022,000,000 and brought the island more money than had all the crops from 1900 to 1914. A golden era seemed about to open up for Cuba. The suddenness of this opportunity made everyone dizzy with dreams and greed. Everything was sacrificed for the smiling golden idol of sugar; everybody borrowed money to plant more sugar and the banks were more than generous in lending it. With no fiscal policy and no governmental control a wave of speculation, economic irresponsibility, and inflation swept the island. A Cuban poet said: "Hasta las cañas se volvieron doradas" ("Even sugar cane became golden"). Then disaster struck. In June 1920 the price of sugar dropped to 20.31 cents per pound, in July it was 18.56, in September 10.78, in October 9.00, and in December 5.51. At the beginning of 1921 the dream was over, and Cuba was faced with a devastating economic crisis which affected every segment of the population. Peasants, *macheteros*, *colonos*, and *hacendados* suffered enormously.

The domestic banking system almost totally collapsed. In 1920 foreign banks held only 20 per cent of the total deposits in Cuba; in 1923, more than 76 per cent of the total deposits were in foreign banks.[26] In 1919 American interests controlled

[26] Henry C. Wallich, *Monetary Problems of an Export Economy: The Cuban Experience, 1914–1917* (Cambridge: Harvard University Press, 1950), pp. 65–69.

68 sugar mills and 51 per cent of the total production.[27] During and after the crisis, with neither credit nor reserves to continue production, many *colonos* and *hacendados* lost their property or were forced to sell it at extremely low prices. In 1921, Cubans could find credit facilities only by yielding to conditions imposed by American banks.[28]

But the crisis had its salutary effects. American economic penetration, the "ferocious mercantilism" attacked by Castellanos, had shown its ruinous potential. One is tempted to use Marxist terminology and say that the crisis of 1921 made evident the basic contradiction resulting when a national bourgeoisie allies itself with an imperialist foreign power. But this explanation oversimplifies a complex problem, for precisely because of previous economic conditions, a Cuban bourgeoisie did not exist at that time. The power of American economic interests had made impossible the normal development of a Cuban bourgeoisie; in its place arose a potential middle class—inarticulate *colonos, hacendados,* merchants, and professionals—under the overriding influence of American economic penetration. In 1927, when many Cuban economic groups were already aware of the possibly disastrous results of their dependence on the Americans, the economist Raúl Maestri still concluded: "In our land there are Cuban capitalists, bourgeois, and proletarians. There is not a Cuban capitalism, a Cuban bourgeoisie, or a Cuban proletariat." In the same year, Emilio Roig de Leuchsenring observed: "Weak and divided, our middle class is, in some respects, in worse condition than our proletariat. Our middle class must awake and unite." [29]

[27] Alvarez Díaz *et al.*, p. 238. In 1919, Spanish interests dominated 17.3 per cent of the sugar production. Cuban participation was reduced to 22.8 per cent.

[28] Jenks, p. 228.

[29] Raúl Maestri, *El latifundio en la economía cubana* (Havana: Ediciones Revista Avance, 1929), p. 17; Roig de Leuchsenring, *Los problemas sociales en Cuba* (Havana: Imprenta El Ideal, 1927), p. 32.

But after 1921, with their solid economic ground suddenly transformed into quicksand, the disjointed members of various Cuban economic groups rapidly discovered their common plight, and that nationalism could be their trench and the state could be their shield. Only under the impact of disaster did these various groups realize how right Manuel Sanguily had been when, at the beginning of the Republic's history, he vainly tried to limit the foreign purchase of Cuban land.[30] How much more convenient it would have been to have followed Varona's call for an honest and efficient government which could protect them in time of need. Some Cubans now also realized how practical those idealistic men had been, and how improvident their own pragmatism.

The immediate result of this collective awakening was a profound change of attitude among the most important Cuban economic groups. Resentment against American penetration came hand in hand with the beginning of an economic nationalism which demanded protective legislation for Cuban interests, honesty in government, and a re-evaluation of Cuban-American relations. In 1921 a prominent young Cuban lawyer, Luis Machado, initiated the attack against the generally accepted interpretation of the Platt Amendment, arguing that it was not supposed to give the United States the right to intervene in Cuba "at will," and suggesting that Cuban-American differences be settled by arbitration under the aegis of the League of Nations.[31] Voicing this growing attitude, the Cuban Senate in 1922 adopted a set of resolutions protesting American interventions in the affairs of the Cuban government. In 1923 "nationalism" was the battle cry beginning to rally such diverse characters as President Zayas,

[30] For the text of this projected law and Sanguily's speech, see Manuel Sanguily, *Defensa de Cuba* (Havana: Municipio de la Habana, 1948), pp. 109–111.

[31] Luis Machado, *La Enmienda Platt* (Havana, 1922), pp. 79–118.

hacendado José Tarafa, young students like Julio A. Mella, General García Vélez, and intellectual Fernando Ortiz. Economist and historian Ramiro Guerra gave the most eloquent expression of this collective feeling. Indicting sugar latifundios as the root of all Cuban evils, Guerra concluded: "But latifundism is so strong and powerful in our country that it is impossible to fight it without appealing to the State to intervene in defense of the nation. . . . The Republic must come with all its resources to save and assist the people who created it. . . . Absolutely defenseless, the Cuban people turn their eyes toward the Republic. It is the duty of the Republic to come to the rescue." [32]

It is important to note that this emerging nationalism was not offensive, but defensive. It was not basically anti-American; it was essentially pro-Cuban: "We must fight against latifundio not to destroy, but to create," wrote Ramiro Guerra. The economic disaster of 1921 had opened many eyes to the necessity of protecting vital national interests and of curbing with legal measures, not violent methods, unrestricted American influence.[33] In 1922 a law regulating the

[32] Ramiro Guerra y Sánchez, *Azúcar y población en las Antillas* (3d ed.; Havana: Cultural, 1944), p. 156. The first edition was published in 1927.

[33] Some authors (Smith, p. 103, and Herbert L. Matthews, *Fidel Castro* [New York: Simon and Schuster, 1969], p. 46) have tried to overemphasize the anti-Americanism of the period. To prove their point, they quote the *New York Times*' quotation (June 22, 1922) of a headline in *La Nación:* "Hatred of North Americans will be the religion of Cubans." A careful reading of the most important Cuban publications of those years does not support that interpretation. On the other hand, *La Nación*, a newspaper which lasted about four years (1921–1925), was founded and directed by Manuel Márquez Sterling, who later became Cuban Ambassador in Washington and who certainly never displayed violent anti-American feelings. A single headline of an ephemeral newspaper is not enough to infer a national mood.

contracts for government loans in the sugar industry, devised for the protection of the Cuban *colonos*, was the first important step toward state intervention in the national economy. In that same year a prominent liberal politician attracted national attention by writing a series of articles demanding a restrictive interpretation of the Platt Amendment in order to free Cuban energies and allow economic growth. In 1923 a Cuban Junta for National Reform was formed to study the urgent economic and social reforms needed in Cuba.

Side by side with this "moderate" economic nationalism—a nationalism without radicalism, aimed basically at the creation of a just balance between American and Cuban interests—another, more violent and radical, nationalism was growing in Cuba. Rooted in passion more than in statistics, expressed in anger more than in legal arguments, this second nationalism was voiced by students, intellectuals and leftist elements who, as shall be seen later, were responding to a broad anti-Yankee feeling which was sweeping Latin America at the time.

Occasionally both currents used the same terminology and seemed identical—the slogan "All for Cuba and Cuba for all" was on every tongue—but slowly, certain differences became noticeable. Moderate nationalism was espoused by practical men who knew, or thought they knew, how much nationalism should be mixed with economic development to avoid an explosive combination. Those who supported the second kind, which was much more vague and undefined, were precisely attracted by the explosive possibilities of this newfound nationalism. The one group spoke of modifying the terms of the Platt Amendment, and of a more efficient political structure in Cuba; the other demanded the abrogation of the Amendment and a total renovation of the political and the social structure of the nation.

Initially the economic nationalism of the more important

groups, the "moderate" nationalism, was the most decisive. Already powerful in 1923, its adherents looked for a political champion for their cause. Thus the national elections of 1924 acquired new importance for many elements in Cuba. One of the candidates in those elections was the man who had written of the necessity to limit the interpretation of the Platt Amendment, and in favor of a national economic policy. He was to become the symbol and the hope of many aspirations or, as he was later called, "the instrument of destiny." This was Gerardo Machado y Morales.

3 *The Elections of 1924*

In 1924 the corruption of the Zayas government and the long association of the Conservative party with that government produced a powerful revival of Liberalism. Divided between Zayistas, who wanted the President to seek a second term, and Menocalistas, who followed former President Menocal in his new bid for power, the Conservative party was suffering internal deterioration and weakness. It was clear to the majority of observers that the candidate the Liberal party would select in 1924 was going to be the next president of Cuba. Thus the attention of the nation was focused on the internal struggle of the Liberal party.

After the death of José Miguel Gómez in 1921, two figures appeared as the potential leaders of the Liberal party: Colonel Carlos Mendieta and General Gerardo Machado. Mendieta was by far the more popular of the two. A veteran of the War of Independence, he had always been a steadfast supporter of the Liberals and had shown, in a country noted for its turncoat politicians, a remarkable loyalty to his party's principles. Famous for his courage, he was still more respected and admired for his reputation of honesty. In a nation with newly emerging political forces, which after the economic disaster of 1920 was crying for change, the figure of Mendieta was surrounded by an aura of popularity. For many Cubans he seemed to be the instrument of national regeneration. But

Mendieta's ability did not match this historical task. A well-read man of few words, inclined toward passive patriotism, Mendieta was more prone to follow decisions than to make them. Still worse, he seems to have never quite understood the complexities of any political situation.

Machado was quite the opposite. Outspoken and friendly, he made a point of being attentive to everyone, to win support from all circles. He did not have an impressive record in either war or peace, although he had been Secretary of Government under Gómez, where he displayed a tough policy toward labor. Furthermore, he was very ambitious and understood the mysterious dialectic of political transactions, and his cautious economic nationalism, acceptable by then to many American interests, had gained him powerful allies. It is an accepted fact of Cuban history that Machado had the backing of Henry W. Catlin, President of the Electric Bond and Share Company, and of powerful Spanish interests.

The two rivals operated on different levels. Mendieta had the sympathy and the support of the masses of the party. Wherever he went spontaneous popular demonstrations greeted him. Machado worked quietly for the control of the assemblies of the party, visited the leaders of different factions, made promises, and negotiated deals. Mendieta was a popular man but not a politician; Machado was above all a politician. "The triumph of Machado," said one of his most distinguished followers later, "is basically due to his being the most perfect and complete of all Cuban politicians." [1] Which, considering the species, was very dubious praise.

In June 1924 the General Assembly of the Liberal party elected Gerardo Machado as the official candidate. The disappointment of the masses of the party was so deep, the opposition to this decision so general, that a word from Mendieta

[1] Clemente Vázquez Bello in *Revista parlamentaria de Cuba*, VI (Sept. and Oct. 1926), 250.

could have provoked its complete rejection, causing the dissolution of the Assembly and the convocation of a new one. Many of Mendieta's sympathizers urged him to appeal to the Liberals to overturn the decision of the Assembly.[2] But, as always, Mendieta hesitated and finally decided to retire to private life: he wrote, "I don't want my popularity to be used against the high levels of my party." [3] With this patriotic, but perhaps not very wise, decision the road was open and clear for Machado.

The following month Machado published his political platform for the upcoming elections. In this platform he cleverly incorporated all the elements which were already in the political atmosphere of Cuba. He called it "the Platform of Regeneration." Its ten points may be summarized as follows: (1) strict limitation on the powers of the state, (2) opposition to the growth of bureaucracy in all public services, (3) constitutional reforms to assure honesty in elections, (4) revision of the permanent treaty to "free our Constitution from the Appendix [4] [so that] Cuban sovereignty shines with complete national independence," (5) construction of roads and improvement in communications, (6) more schools, (7) better sanitary services, (8) promotion of "good immigration," (9) professionalization of the army and the avoidance of any military interference in political or civil affairs, and (10) payment of public debts and the avoidance of new national loans.[5]

This platform was condensed, for political purposes, into

[2] See, for example, "Ahora o nunca Coronel!" *Diario de Cuba,* June 28, 1924, p. 1.

[3] Mendieta to José Beruff, July 1, 1924 (from the private collection of Dr. Jorge Beruff, grandson of Mendieta).

[4] The Platt Amendment was generally referred to as "the Appendix" in Cuba because of its adoption as an annex to the Cuban Constitution in 1901.

[5] *Revista parlamentaria de Cuba,* III (July 1924), 316–319.

one slogan which captured the imagination of the Cubans: "Water, roads, and schools." And when the Conservatives, with Menocal as their candidate, published a photograph of the General on horseback, the Liberals answered with a photograph of Machado among the masses and the slogan *Con el pueblo y a pie* ("With the people and on foot").

In November 1924, after a political campaign in which violence was not totally absent,[6] the elections were held. Machado carried five of the six provinces. The following day the newspaper *El País* proclaimed, "An era of regeneration has begun in Cuba."

It was highly symptomatic of the new atmosphere that the word "regeneration" was on all tongues, even before Machado adopted it for his campaign. It was likewise symptomatic that the triumphant political party expounded the necessity of revising relations with the United States. A general desire for reform and a revival of nationalism were the key sentiments of the period.

Actually, Machado represented a middle road, a meeting point for the rising moderate economic nationalism of several Cuban groups with the powerful American interests, who had by then realized that a certain degree of nationalism in Cuba was not only tolerable but advantageous. They recognized, as Leland Jenks expressed it, "that their right to intervene in Cuba to avoid anarchy, despotism or irresponsibility, had created precisely the conditions it wanted to avoid." Thus the similarity of words and programs. "It is necessary," wrote businessman José Tarafa in Havana in 1924, "for the Americans to understand that sovereignty means prosperity, and that a prosperous Cuba is the best guarantee for their investments." United States diplomat Dwight Morrow echoed

[6] *El País,* for example, reported on October 19 a shooting attack on the train carrying Menocal to Oriente Province. One person was killed.

this same tone: "American businessmen who have differences with the Cuban people should first seek remedies for their alleged wrongs through the ordinary channels in Cuba. They should not look to Washington." [7] In Machado's case, the alliance was more than theoretical. Until 1924 he had been vice-president of the Electric Bond and Share Company, and in 1925, the new President's son-in-law, José Emilio Obregón, was made notarial attorney for the Chase Bank in Havana.[8]

If Machado's nationalism was tempered by his own convictions and by the influence of powerful "friends," his program of "regeneration" also had certain initial weaknesses, for he had obtained the nomination of the Liberal party through trickery and shady deals, and a less than honorable pact with President Zayas had assured the benevolent neutrality of the government during the elections.[9] He had proclaimed the necessity of avoiding military intervention in political affairs, but even before his election he had convinced General Monteagudo of his sympathy and support for the army, and offered certain privileges for the officers if he were elected.[10]

After the elections and before taking office as President,

[7] Jenks, *Nuestra Colonia de Cuba* (Buenos Aires: Editorial Palestra, 1960), p. 275; "Entrevistas," *La Acción* (Havana), Jan. 15, 1924, p. 4; Robert F. Smith, *The United States and Cuba* (New Haven, Conn.: Yale University Press, 1961), p. 114.

[8] For Machado's relations with American business interests see Raymond Leslie Buell, "The Caribbean Situation: Cuba and Haiti," *Foreign Policy Reports*, IX, No. 8 (June 21, 1933), p. 84, n. 9.

[9] José Emilio Obregón, stated in an interview in New York, Oct. 24, 1965, that as the Assembly of the Liberal party was to be held in Nueva Paz, a town near Havana and connected with the capital by a single railroad, Machado bribed the conductors of the only train, so only half of the Mendietistas were able to reach the town in time to vote. Zayas allegedly received the right to control half of the total *colecturías* (places where Lottery tickets are sold) of the republic. This allegation is supported by numerous sources.

[10] Interview with José Emilio Obregón, who was present when this arrangement was made.

Machado paid a visit to the United States, where he met President Coolidge and was received and entertained by several American business groups. He assured everyone that he was a champion of better commercial and political relations between the United States and Cuba, and that social unrest was not going to be tolerated in his country. Then, in the words of one historian, "he returned to Cuba and the Presidency in May 1925, with the praises of American businessmen ringing in his ears." [11]

In all fairness it should be acknowledged that Machado's political sins—his links with American interests, his dubious pacts with politicians and military officers—were less than venial. In a nation where submission to American pressure had been the rule, and corruption was the essence of politics, Machado's stand for nationalism and his promises of honest government were a firm step forward for the republic, an evident sign for many that times were changing for the better.

And so, on May 20, 1925, amid unusual cheering and enthusiasm, Gerardo Machado y Morales was inaugurated as the fifth President of Cuba. His term was supposed to last until 1929.

[11] Smith, p. 114. For Machado's speeches, and those in his honor during that trip, see his *The Visit of the President-Elect of Cuba* (Washington, D.C., 1925).

4 *Machado as President, 1925-1927*

Cuba seemed finally to have entered an era of stability, progress, and true nationalism. The elections of 1924 were basically honest, and the new President had emphatically stated that his "true glory would be to hold elections as honest as those held in November and never to seek re-election."[1] In his first informal message to the Congress of the Republic, Machado made a realistic analysis of the economic difficulties of Cuba and promised "a government sober, honest, and constructive."[2] His cabinet was made up of well-known and respected men, and one of them, José María Barraqué, Secretary of Justice, announced that the basic task of this new government was "to put Cuba in contact again with her high destinies."

Almost immediately after taking office, the President presented to Congress a public works bill which initiated the most ambitious projects that the republic had known. Salient features in the final law were: (*a*) the construction of a much needed central highway which would connect Santiago de Cuba in the extreme eastern province, Oriente, to Pinar del Río, the most western of all Cuban provinces, with a road 1,179 kilometers long; (*b*) the erection of a national capitol for the Congress of the Republic; and (*c*) the initiation of

[1] *Revista parlamentaria de Cuba*, III (Dec. 1924), 516.

[2] *Ibid.*, p. 157.

such projects as expansion of the famous Malecón (an esplanade), for the embellishment of Havana.[3]

For the first time, the Cuban government began to try to control sugar production in order to avoid the hitherto almost absolute freedom of the *hacendados*. On May 3, 1926, the so-called Verdeja Act became law. Considering the decline in prices experienced in 1925 and the ever present risk of overproduction (the 1925 crop was 5,190,000 tons), the law limited the sugar crop of 1926 to 10 per cent less than the previous year. Supplementary decrees prohibited the cutting of virgin forest for the purpose of planting more cane and stipulated that work in the sugar mills (the start of which could vary from early December to late February) would begin on January 1, 1927. The sugar crop could not exceed four and one-half million tons, and a quota system (which provided that sugar mills were to buy cane from all the *colonos* in proportion to their production) was established for the protection of the *colonos*.[4] This restriction on Cuban production, even if beneficial in the short run, had encouraged other nations to expand their sugar industry; as a result, in October 1927 the government created a Sugar Defense Commission and a Sugar Export Company which would control the production and export of sugar.

Machado had also announced plans for diversifying agriculture and protecting the development of Cuban industry. In 1926, in words which sounded refreshingly new and patriotic, the President proclaimed: "Let us assure our political independence through economic independence."[5] In 1927, tariffs

[3] Milo A. Borges, *Compilación ordenada y completa de la legislación cubana* (Havana: Editorial Lex, 1952), I, 584.

[4] *Ibid.*, p. 627.

[5] Gerardo Machado, *Por la patria libre* (Havana: Imprenta de F. Verdugo, 1926), p. 9.

were raised by the Custom-Tariff Law to protect certain agricultural products and nascent small industries. As a result, affected sectors of the Cuban economy began to improve: fruits, rice, and cacao, for example, increased production rapidly after 1927. In July 1929, another law created a commission "for the defense and publicity of tobacco." Industries such as textiles and fishing also received encouragement for growth.[6]

In addition to assuming the firm direction of economic matters, the government proclaimed its intention to carry out a program of "regeneration." A law for the protection of public employees was proposed in June 1925, which stated that "merit and honesty and not political considerations will be the only roads to promotion in every branch of the State."[7] A series of laws issued in April 1927 created technical schools and schools of commerce and manual work. A much publicized, if not very effective, program for the regeneration of the prostitutes of Havana was announced in December 1926, as well as the creation of special schools for their rehabilitation. In a speech at the Lyceum, Secretary Barraqué reiterated that the government of Machado was making a supreme effort "to clean all the rooms of our Cuban house."

Considering the immediate past of Cuba and the spectacular programs and actions of the new government, it was no wonder that Gerardo Machado became, after a few months in power, the most popular president the island ever had. In September 1926 the University of Havana conferred on him

[6] "Undoubtedly, the Custom Tariff of 1927 was the most important legislation of an economic nature enacted during the first three decades of the twentieth century, and may be called the first economic effort made by the Cuban government directed toward augmenting the national production" (José R. Alvarez Díaz *et al.*, *A Study on Cuba* [Miami: University of Miami Press, 1965], p. 222).

[7] "Los Nuevos Proyectos," *Excelsior*, June 26, 1925, p. 1.

an honorary doctorate; in November a popular collection provided funds to erect a monument to his mother in Santa Clara; he was proclaimed *hijo predilecto* (favorite son) of twenty-five towns in the first two years of his government; politicians and journalists tried to outdo each other by referring to him with such titles as "El Titán," "El Egregio," "El Supremo." A story spread throughout the island that Machado had once asked the mayor of a town he was visiting, "What time is it?" and the mayor, with a smile that would have been the envy of the most obsequious courtier of Versailles, answered, "The time you wish, my General."

Far more dangerous than this fawning was the attitude of the political parties. Already in December 1925, Wifredo Fernández, a brilliant writer and a leader of the Conservative party, proclaimed that Machado's programs were so "full of patriotism and devotion for Cuba that true opposition was unpatriotic." [8] Instead, Mr. Fernández proposed *la oposición cooperativa* (cooperative opposition). The suggestion was immediately adopted by all parties, and in 1926 Liberals, Conservatives, and the small Popular party were working together supporting Machado in a movement that was popularly known as *cooperativismo*. In 1926, for all practical purposes, Machado had no political opposition. In a manifesto to the people, published in October 1926, the President declared his profound satisfaction at the spectacle of "all Cubans working for a common ideal. Today in Cuba all is harmony." [9]

Under this façade were some grumbling and resistance, barely visible at first. From the beginning, Machado had shown that he was not a soft politician who hesitated to take drastic measures whenever someone crossed his path. In August 1925

[8] Wifredo Fernández, "Los nuevos horizontes," *Heraldo de Cuba*, Dec. 9, 1925, p. 2.

[9] *Revista parlamentaria de Cuba*, VI (Sept. and Oct. 1926), 217.

the newspaper, *El Día*, whose editor was Commandant Armando André, published a series of cartoons criticizing several political figures. One of these cartoons was directed, with extremely poor taste, toward a personal affair of Machado. On August 20, André was assassinated at the door of his home. The affair served as a warning to everyone that the new President had a very somber sense of humor indeed. André was only the first in a steadily growing list.

The submissive attitude of the Congress and the danger of yielding to Machado's increasing demands for extraordinary powers were early denounced by some courageous legislators. On December 26, 1926, speaking in the Chamber of Representatives, Conservative Carlos Manuel de la Cruz accused his colleagues of violating the Constitution by giving the executive "faculties that are only granted in time of war or national emergency." [10] But the Chamber approved the President's request for power by an overwhelming majority.

Considering Machado's political convictions, his record as Secretary of Government during the Gómez administration (1908–1912), and his authoritarian character, it was natural that labor would suffer at times from his actions. As candidate and later as President, Machado had stated his conviction that foreign and native capital should receive full guarantee for development and his vow that no strike would last more than twenty-four hours under his regime. He intended to keep his word. Prone to solve all problems *manu militari*, he had a natural distrust for every form of social agitation, which he considered to be provoked by "professional and foreign agents." The avant-garde of a proletariat, then in the process of expansion and organization, found in him a natural and sometimes harsh opponent. In the first years of his term, as we

[10] Carlos Manuel de la Cruz, *Proceso histórico del machadato* (Havana: Imprenta La Milagrosa, 1935), p. 24.

shall see later, several labor leaders paid with their lives for their efforts to organize unions.

The assassination of André and the death of some labor leaders, the unrelenting attitude of the government toward labor unions, and the signs of a repressive policy against any vocal opposition did not, at first, affect Machado's popularity. Nor did the fact that the President had forgotten the tenth point of his platform and in 1926 was negotiating two loans, one from the J. P. Morgan firm for $9 million and the second from the Chase National Bank for $40 million [11]—clear proof that American interests considered Machado a profitable nationalist. After all, the central highway was under construction, giving employment to thousands of workers, and everybody could see the new improvements in Havana and other cities of the republic. The economic situation had improved, and for the first time in years no public scandal had shaken a government. The honesty of the administration seemed above reproach. Moderate nationalism was beginning to pay off. The year 1926 ended in a general atmosphere of optimism.

But very soon, additional motives encouraged various groups to take a firm stand against the government. A new and disturbing factor, unforeseen by those who had only sought a champion for economic nationalism, appeared on the horizon —Machado's increasingly evident desire to remain in power.

[11] Alvarez Díaz *et al.*, p. 217.

5 Extension of Powers and Re-election, 1927-1928

The impact of Machado's personality, the lack of true leadership in the political parties, and the noxious tendency to follow dogmatic individuals were felt in Cuban politics from the very beginning of the republic. As early as July 1925, two months after Machado took office, the leaders of the Liberal party visited him to propose his re-election.[1] In 1926, when *cooperativismo* was working smoothly and the three political parties were competing for the favor of the President, the idea of re-election gained force. But an obstacle remained—Machado's repeated declaration that "re-electionism is the source of all evils" and his promise not to seek re-election. At the same time, with increasing impudence, Machado began to show his appetite for power. On November 11, 1926, he addressed the provincial delegations of the Liberal party:

My government hopes to go on receiving, as up to now, the decided cooperation of the Congress, but if it should not have it, for the benefit of the Fatherland, under the banner of the Constitution, I, myself, alone, am capable of avoiding two years of lost effort.

And then he added:

I know that some of those who are hearing me will brand these declarations as anti-constitutional and will think that I am a dis-

[1] *Revista parlamentaria de Cuba*, IV (May–June 1925), 206.

guised partisan of dictatorship: *but if dictatorship were necessary to keep alive the memory of those who fell on the field of heroism, I, myself, alone*, with the help of those of you who are willing to follow me, am more than capable of carrying out this purpose. So now you know where I stand. The press can reproduce my words. Perhaps those who disagree will not be against me, but I will be against them! [2]

After these words there could be no doubt that Machado was willing to move toward dictatorship if necessary to carry out what he considered his ideals of government. It was imperative then for Machado to find a formula which would avoid re-election and yet keep him in power. Wifredo Fernández, whose fertile political imagination created *cooperativismo*,[3] is credited with having found the answer: to alter the Constitution in order to extend for two more years the term of office of the President and the Senators.[4] The pretext for this modification was supposed to be precisely eliminating from the Constitution the right of re-election. So, under the aegis of suppressing once and for all the root of all evils, "re-electionism," Machado's term was to be extended until 1930.

Politically speaking, the idea of prolonging the term while avoiding the hated re-election was a brilliant one. For in Cuba and in Latin America, generally, re-election is considered the

[2] *Ibid.*, VI (Nov.–Dec. 1926), 268–269 (translation and italics mine). It was highly symptomatic of the situation that after the speech the magazine reproduced an AP cable which stated that Machado's words "had created surprise in Washington, but the feeling in the capital is that there would be no objection to support a dictatorship in Cuba" (p. 270).

[3] It is fair to mention that several times Machado proclaimed that he himself was the initiator and responsible for the "cooperativist" movement.

[4] This step had been considered during Menocal's second term in office (Manuel Márquez Sterling, *Las conferencias del Shoreham* [Mexico City: Ediciones Botas, 1933], p. 31).

first step toward dictatorship. But apparently neither Machado nor Wifredo Fernández took into consideration the effect of this move on the political ambitions of others. With the bait of a general extension of power, politicians all jumped into the project with such wholehearted support that the proposed extension exceeded the initial plan. The Chamber of Representatives (Cámara de Representantes) debated the proposal in April 1927, and agreed to present it to the future Constituent Assembly with a modification which would extend the term of the President, Senators, and Representatives to May 1933—not two, but five more years. With little opposition to this proposal (in the Chamber of Representatives it was approved by a vote of 94 to 8; the best speech in opposition was made by Ramón Zaydin[5]), the Congress finally approved a plan for the modification of the Constitution which contained these basic points: (1) include the Isle of Pines as territory of Cuba, (2) extend to women the right to vote, (3) acknowledge the right of minority parties to be represented in the Senate, (4) stiffen rules for future modification of the Constitution, (5) augment the number of Senators from four to six for each province, elected for a term of nine years, (6) eliminate the vice-presidency, (7) elect the President for a six-year term without the right of re-election, (8) prolong the term of the present President for two years, and (9) hold an election for a Constituent Assembly to consider the revision of the Constitution.[6]

Immediately the President proclaimed his satisfaction at being spared "the necessity of re-election,"[7] and his displea-

[5] See his *Discurso contra la prórroga de poderes* (Havana: Imprenta Bouza, 1928).

[6] See *Texto del proyecto de reforma de la constitución* (Havana: Congreso de la República, 1927).

[7] *Heraldo de Cuba*, April 16, 1927, p. 1.

sure with those who had opposed the formula. Machado's desire to extend his term of office forced him to retreat from his nationalistic position in favor of what he considered his American allies. A man raised under the shadow of American omnipotence in Cuba, Machado always believed, almost to the end of his career, that while he could handle his Cuban opponents, he could not survive a break with the Americans. When he visited the United States in 1925, he proclaimed that "the payment of interest for the public debt should be considered as a sacred and primary obligation. Never, for any reason, should we fail to comply." [8] He never abandoned that policy. As a consequence of this conviction, as soon as he began to move toward a confrontation with several Cuban groups who opposed his political ambition, he tried immediately to secure the favor of the Americans through economic concessions. He still took the trouble to make a gesture toward Cuban nationalism by legalizing the sovereignty of Cuba over the Isle of Pines,[9] but almost simultaneously he made more than a cursory bow to American interests on the island. A law was proposed in Congress that would: (*a*) authorize the companies controlling electricity and transportation (all of them American) to expropriate land, property, or rights pertaining to the Cuban State or to private citizens, if so needed for expanding their services; and (*b*) reduce substantially the taxes to be paid by those companies.

[8] *Discurso pronunciado por el general Gerardo Machado en el banquete del Hotel Astor* (Washington, D.C.: Pan American Union, 1925), p. 4.

[9] The Isle of Pines was always part of the Cuban territory. In 1902 and 1904, the United States accepted Cuban sovereignty over the island, but the presence and pressure of numerous American farmers on the island delayed the ratification of the treaty until 1925. At this time, hence, the declaration of the Congress was more a gesture than a nationalistic victory.

Protesting against the law, Representative Carlos Manuel de la Cruz remarked angrily in the Chamber of Representatives: "In Havana the bleeding that these companies have imposed on the Cuban people has been accepted since 1902. . . . This Chamber should know that in Cuba the production cost of an electric kilowatt is one cent and a half, and for that same kilowatt our people pay seventeen cents. . . . This law creates a privilege, establishes a monopoly, and forbids competition." [10] Nevertheless, the law was approved.

The opposition to the formula for modifying the Constitution and extending the term of the President came basically, as shall be seen later, from a recently founded political group called La Unión Nacionalista, from some members of Congress, and from the students of the University. But it is doubtful that, if passed with the terms the Congress had approved, the project for reforming the Constitution would have provoked general opposition. After all, the extension was for only two years and it represented the disappearance of the dreaded right of re-election. Juan Clemente Zamora, Professor of Constitutional Law at Havana University, wrote a series of articles defending the project and maintaining that the two extra years were necessary "to guarantee the transformation from one system to the other," [11] from allowing re-election to forbidding it.

As planned by the government, on April 14, 1928, the members of the newly elected Constituent Assembly met for the first session. According to Article 115 of the 1901 Constitution, then in effect, the Constituent Assembly had to limit it-

[10] Carlos Manuel de la Cruz, *Proceso histórico del machadato* (Havana: Imprenta La Milagrosa, 1935), pp. 55–57. The text of the proposed law appears at the beginning of the speech by Dr. de la Cruz.

[11] Juan Clemente Zamora, *Estudios sobre el proyecto de reforma constitucional* (Havana: Rambla, Bouza, 1927), p. 55.

self to approval or rejection of the reform project already approved by Congress. But the electoral laws had been modified so that the delegates were all *Machadistas;* they all came from the ranks of the parties which had defended *cooperativismo;* and they were all eager to show their loyalty to the President. And so the Assembly violated Constitutional rule, modified the Congressional reform project, and declared on its own authority that the principle of no re-election could not be retroactive. Breaking all protocol, the Assembly unanimously declared in the session of May 10:

> The Constitutional Convention does not hesitate to reaffirm that General Gerardo Machado y Morales, because of his commitments and his antecedents as founder of the Republic, is faced with the inevitable obligation of accepting a new presidential term.[12]

Machado could run for a new six-year term in 1928; his presidential administration would end on May 20, 1935. After that date, the reform would become law and no president could aspire to a second term. Humbly but cheerfully Machado proclaimed that "the enthusiastic and visible consent of almost all the people, leaves me no other alternative than to accept a new presidential term." [13]

When the text of the new law was made public, the evident illegality of its provisions, the abject attitude of the Assembly, and the applause throughout the government dispelled the last doubts: the long shadow of dictatorship had been extended over Cuba. It was then that many Cubans decided to oppose Machado openly.

Since 1927, when the first articles and statements defending

[12] *Diario de sesiones de la Asamblea Constituyente* (Havana, 1928), 12th session, p. 5.

[13] De la Cruz, p. 67.

the reform of the Constitution appeared, Colonel Carlos Mendieta had come out of retirement and organized La Unión Nacionalista as a political party to combat Machado's policy. In February of that year the protest of the students against the extension of Machado's term was so violent that the University was closed "indefinitely." [14]

Deriding this opposition, Wifredo Fernández used his peculiar dialectic: "The proper thing to do for anyone who accuses a government of being tyrannical and murderous is to try to overthrow it by revolutionary methods. . . . But in Cuba a revolution is not proper for it brings in a foreign power." [15] Privately, he assured the President that there was no reason for concern. He is supposed to have said: "We have the support of the Americans, and the most important political forces are with us. Who cares about the shouting of some groups of *muchachos* [kids]." [16] They should have cared. Eventually, those shouting *muchachos* ruined all their political plans, sent Machado into exile, and coerced Wifredo Fernández to commit suicide in prison. They represented the forces of a new Cuba. It is now time to draw a profile of these emerging forces.

[14] *Revista parlamentaria de Cuba*, VII (Mar.–Apr. 1927), 80.
[15] *Ibid.* (Sept.–Oct. 1927), 201.
[16] Interview with José Emilio Obregón, New York, Oct. 24, 1965.

6 Winds of Change

In Latin America, the "Roaring Twenties" signified a period of unrest and transformation. From every direction revolutionary winds blew their portents. Echoes of the Mexican Revolution and the Constitution of 1917 awakened the political consciences of many young groups. The effect of the university reform in Córdoba, Argentina, in 1918 spread rapidly throughout Latin America. The postwar economic crisis shook the political structure of many Latin American nations. The vibrating thunder of the Russian Revolution, although remote and obscure, attracted the attention of the workers. Communist parties and radical groups appeared in several countries. The voices of rebellion and anti-Americanism became a chorus: from the Uruguayan writer José E. Rodó to the Argentine sociologist José Ingenieros; from the Colombian novelist José Vargas Vila to the Peruvian José Carlos Mariátegui (a Marxist writer) and political leader Víctor Raúl Haya de la Torre; from the Mexican philosopher José Vasconcelos to the Chilean labor leader Luis E. Recabarren; a new creed of Latinism, Indianism, nationalism—essentially anti-Yankeeism—resounded throughout Latin America. Even Rubén Darío, the poet of castles and princesses, cautioned with his famous somber query: "Es que tántos millones de hombres hablaremos inglés?" (Will so many million men speak English?) At the end of the decade the name of Augusto

César Sandino, who was fighting Yankee troops in Nicaragua, became briefly a symbol and a continental cause.

Prompted by all these currents as well as by the course of national events that culminated in the economic crisis of 1920, the first signs of a new attitude appeared in Cuba. Protesting intellectuals, rebellious students, struggling labor organizations, and leftist political groups—in a sort of spontaneous combustion—began to express a collective urgency for radical change. Machado's determination to remain in power and to quell every protest was a direct challenge to these forces. Confrontation was inevitable.

The Intellectuals

As already mentioned, another type of nationalism, more radical and fiery than the economic brand, began to appear at the same time. This second current had its source in intellectual circles. Born of a deep sense of national frustration and nourished by the ideological trends reaching Cuba from other countries, voices of rebellion multiplied. In 1921 a young mulatto poet from Oriente Province, José M. Poveda, passionately proclaimed: "We are not a new literary school. . . . We want to be the New Fatherland!" [1] In Havana a group of young writers with the avowed objective of reforming Cuban intellectual life pooled their efforts and formed the Grupo Minorista (Minority Group) in 1923. Their concerns were essentially artistic and literary, but, as one of the members wrote, they were "a group of young leftist intellectuals . . . interested also in the social and political problems of Cuba, America, and the world, willing to face those problems in a radical and progressive way." [2] The group considered itself a

[1] Cintio Vitier, *Lo cubano en la poesía* (Las Villas: Universidad Central, 1958), p. 292.

[2] Carlos Ripoll, *La generación del 23 en Cuba* (New York: Las Americas, 1968), p. 50.

"minority" only in its artistic opinions for, as Rubén Martínez Villena explained later, "as spokesmen of the people, as expression of the masses, we were indeed a majority." [3] Following such aspirations, they soon became involved in political affairs. On March 18, 1923, at a meeting of the Academy of Science, Erasmo Reguiferos Boudet, Secretary of Justice in President Zayas' cabinet, was invited to sit at the head table. Immediately Rubén Martínez Villena (who, as a leader of the Communist party, was to play an important role in the anti-Machado struggle), voiced his displeasure at the invitation and repudiated, on behalf of all Cuban intellectuals, the corruption of the government represented there by the Secretary of Justice. He then walked out of the Academy, followed by a group of thirteen. The following day they published a document, "The Protest of the Thirteen," which attracted national attention; in it they energetically condemned all "those corrupted politicians who degrade the fatherland," and announced their intention to repeat the protest in any similar situation in the future.[4] This defiant attitude was a symptom of changing times. "With this group," wrote Juan Marinello later, "a new and different attitude appeared among Cuban intellectuals who until then had never expressed directly and militantly, with personal risk, their nonconformity with government corruption." [5] All were tried by the government, but the legal process died out with no consequences. The names of most of those who signed the Protest later became famous in Cuba.[6]

After the Protest of the Thirteen, the Cuban intellectual

[3] See "Declaración del grupo minorista," in *Orbita de Rubén* (Havana: Ed. Union, Colección Orbita, 1965), p. 224.

[4] *Ibid.*, p. 112. [5] Ripoll, p. 49.

[6] Among the better known were Jorge Mañach, Juan Marinello, Francisco Ichaso, José Z. Tallet, Calixto Masó, Alberto Lamar Schweyer, and Felix Lizaso.

atmosphere was charged with a different electricity. The isolated cries of despair were transformed into exalted patriotism, serious research on national problems, or a chorus of social protest. In their search for leaders this generation turned to José Martí, the poet, who became a revered idol, and Enrique José Varona, the old philosopher whose lonely voice had long decried the social ills of Cuba. Rebellious nationalism was the keynote of the new spirit. In 1926 the poem "Las Carretas" (The Carts) of Agustín Acosta beautifully expressed the general attitude. Describing the slow march of carts across Cuban fields, loaded with sugar cane, "carrying Cuba's future on their shoulders," the poem ended with these lines repeated by hundreds of Cubans:

Van hacia el coloso de hiérro cercano,
van hacia el ingenio norteamericano,
y como quejándose, cuando a él se avecinan
¡con cuantas cubanas razones, las viejas carretas rechínan!

[They go toward the near colossus of iron,
they go toward the North American sugar mill,
and when they approach it, as if complaining,
with how many Cuban reasons the old carts creak, creak!]

At the same time and in the same tone Felipe Pichardo Moya wrote his "Poema de los cañaverales" (Poem of the Cane Plantation), expressing the agony of Cuban land, defenseless under a foreign economic yoke. The following year one of the first poems with social content appeared in Cuba, "Salutación al taller mecánico" (Salutation to the Mechanical Workshop) by Regino Pedroso; at the same time other Cuban poets who discovered the rhythm of Cuba's African background revealed a new horizon with the development of Afro-Cuban poetry. In 1927 the best elements of this new generation founded the magazine *Avance*, which soon became the forum for emerging intellectual currents.[7] Following this new trend of exploring Cuban social and cultural problems, the theater awoke from its languidness to present dramas with a nationalist flavor. Of the three plays which received national awards in 1928, two were devoted to problems of the land: *Alma guajira* (Peasant Soul) and *Tiempo muerto* (Dead Time —the name given to the period between sugar harvests, when Cuban peasants experience a drastic decline in work opportunities).[8] Finally, 1927 saw the publication of the book which probably had the greatest impact on the young generation, *Azúcar y población en las Antillas*, by Ramiro Guerra, a serious and scientific accusation about the dangers of latifundism in Cuba.[9]

The University

The University of Havana, naturally, was aroused early by these battering winds. In 1922 a group of students had founded the Manicatos (from an Indian word meaning "brave"), to develop sports at the University, and to challenge aristocratic

[7] *Avance* appeared in 1927 and died in the political crisis of 1930. The best writers on the island and many of Latin America contributed articles on diverse subjects. The first editorial of the magazine announced, "We unfold a blue flag, high and thin. For possible emergencies, a red pennant. What we don't carry is the white flag of capitulation." See Rosario Rexach, "La revista de *Avance*," in *Caribbean Studies*, III, No. 3 (1964), p. 6.

[8] See José Cid Perez, *Teatro cubano* (Madrid: Editorial Agüilar, 1962), p. 24.

[9] The book was originally a series of newspaper articles. A somewhat abridged edition was published in an English translation by Yale University Press in 1964. A book written by a Spanish journalist should be added to the list of influential works published in this period: Luis Araquistain's *La agonía antillana: El imperialismo yanky en el mar Caribe* (Madrid: Espasa-Calpe, 1928).

teams from private clubs.[10] Very soon this group advanced to more radical areas and began to propagandize for changes in the educational structure of the University. Julio Antonio Mella, one of its leaders and a sports hero (in basketball and rowing), quickly developed a sharp political sense and worked to widen the area of social struggle.

In that same year Dr. José Arce, Rector of the University of Buenos Aires and a defender of reformist ideas, arrived in Havana and was invited by the students to speak at the University. His discussions of the Argentine student movement and the process of reform initiated in 1918 at the University of Córdoba made a deep impression on the Cuban students.[11] In January 1923, under the leadership of Julio Antonio Mella (who was already influenced by Marxist ideas), the students forcibly occupied the University and demanded the dismissal of professors whom they considered anachronistic, inefficient, or corrupt, the modernization of textbooks, autonomy for the University, and free education for all.[12] After some conflict and discussion, President Zayas, always inclined to negotiate, yielded to the students' demands: by governmental decree a University Assembly—thirty professors, thirty graduates, and thirty students—was made responsible for the election of the Rector and the establishment of new regulations for the University. At the same time the Government granted legal authority to the recently formed Federación

[10] Letter of Eduardo Suárez Rivas (one of the founders of the Manicatos) to the author; interview with Dr. Juan de Moya (another founder) in Washington, Aug. 7, 1968.

[11] According to Raúl Roa, *Retorno a la Alborada* (Havana: Imprimex, 1963), p. 235, the role of Dr. Arce has been exaggerated. "His role was more of a detonator."

[12] Julio Antonio Mella, "La agitación universitaria de la Habana," *Juventud,* No. 6 (June 1925), p. 4.

Estudiantíl Universitaria (FEU—University Student Federation).[13] With this victory the students embarked on a growing role in the University and broadened the scope of their discussions. In October 1923 the First National Congress of Students was held in Havana; 128 delegates from all over the country attended. They not only adopted resolutions affecting educational problems, but also expressed their growing feelings of nationalism and radicalism: they adopted the name "National Revolutionary Congress of Students," vowed to fight for the realization of Bolívar's dream of a united Latin American republic, and condemned "all forms of imperialism, specially the intervention of Yankee imperialism in Cuban affairs." [14] On November 3, 1923, the José Martí Universidad Popular was created. It was an effort of Mella and other teachers and students to "involve" students in a social cause while arousing the political conscience of the workers whom they hoped to educate. They discovered, to their frustration, that the workers were more interested in learning the basics of geography, history, and mathematics than social or political theories,[15] but the Popular University did serve as a rallying point for young leftist intellectuals. In 1924 the students invited Víctor Raúl Haya de la Torre, then on his way to Europe, to speak at the University and applauded his proposal of "a common front against imperialism, and for Latin America." [16]

[13] *Gaceta oficial de la república*, March 22, 1933, p. 2.

[14] Julio A. Mella, *Documentos para su vida* (Havana: Comisión Nacional Cubana de la UNESCO, 1964), pp. 129–131. The book offers all the discussions and resolutions of that Congress.

[15] See the interview with Fernando Sirgo (one of the founders) in *Pensamiento critico* (Havana), no. 38 (April 1970, special issue), p. 31; Erasmo Dumpierre, *Mella* (Havana: Instituto de Historia, 1965), pp. 49–55.

[16] Dumpierre, p. 42. The anti-imperialist thesis of Haya de la Torre and his concept of an Indo-American revolution were not fully

It is true that the so-called "spirit of 1923" very soon cooled; through cajoling and pressure the government of Zayas managed to disperse the student rebels, opening the way for more moderate and amenable leaders. But some of the rebels, such as Mella, continued to espouse radical principles and tactics. Above all, their example of rebellion had galvanized the University, creating a tradition of opposition and political involvement. Those who followed the precursors of 1923 knew that one of the students' duties was to continue fighting for the reform of the University and, if needed, for a vast program of national regeneration.

The alertness of the University was shown even before the political horizon clouded in Cuba. On March 1, 1925, Mexican writer José Vasconcelos visited Havana. Juan Marinello saluted him as a teacher and as a revolutionary in a way that was symbolic of the new spirit and, to a certain extent, prophetic of things to come: "Professor, in the name of the youth who do not wish to die at the hands of either foreign or domestic enemies, but who are beginning to organize to combat them, permit us while we listen to you as a teacher, to salute you also as a precursor." [17]

Mella had proclaimed an anti-Machado attitude very early. On November 24, 1924, just after Machado's election as President, Mella wrote in the student magazine *Juventud:* "In a

---

shared by some Cuban students. Mella, especially, debated both points. Years later, in 1927, at the meeting of the Anti-Imperialist World Congress in Brussels, Mella, by then a full-fledged Communist, openly opposed Haya's ideas. After Haya founded his party APRA, Mella wrote a pamphlet "What Is ARPA?" (his use of "ARPA," the Spanish word for "harp," was intentional), in which, using Marxist arguments, he tried to present APRA as a reactionary party. See Julio A. Mella, *La lucha revolucionaria y el imperialismo* (Havana: Editora Popular de Cuba, 1960), esp. pp. 25–65.

[17] *Revista parlamentaria de Cuba,* IV (Mar.–Apr. 1945), 117.

democratic carnival, the people have gained another master. . . . Soon we shall see that he acts as his predecessors have acted." A few months later he was branding Machado "a tropical Mussolini."[18] On September 25, 1925, Mella was expelled from the University. Shortly thereafter he was imprisoned, accused of an act of terrorism against the government. Appealing to the conscience of the Cuban people, he began a hunger strike in jail.

Mella's dramatic gesture, which was opposed and criticized by the leadership of the Communist party, nevertheless had its desired impact. While well-known intellectuals and artists inside and outside Cuba pleaded in his favor, the students in the University organized a "Committee for Mella," whose secretary was Aureliano Sanchez Arango.[19] For the students, however, Mella was not the only cause for fighting. By governmental decree, Machado had reinstated all the professors purged by the students' rebellion of 1923. The moderate leaders of the FEU and the majority of the students had accepted the fact, but radical leaders organized meetings of protest and boycotted classes. Consequently, the students continued their struggle even after December 1925, when Machado freed Mella (who almost immediately left Cuba for Mexico). In an effort to restore calm, Machado announced that he wished to visit the University to explain his policy. Invited by the FEU, Machado managed to receive the acclaim and support of many students and faculty, in spite of some display of choleric temper when a small group of radicals shouted in protest.

[18] Dumpierre, pp. 38, 40.

[19] Interview with Sanchez Arango, Washington, Oct. 26, 1970. The Communist party ordered Mella to abandon his hunger strike as an individual initiative which lacked "social purpose." Mella refused, for he was "sacrificing himself for the benefits of the workers." See the declaration of a veteran of the Communist party, Blas Castillo, in *Pensamiento crítico*, No. 38, p. 49.

With Mella in exile, a conciliatory FEU in power, and a majority of students eager to finish their studies, an apparent calm returned to the University. The truce was broken by Machado's maneuvers to obtain an extension of his term. Immediately violence flared up again. In an effort to suppress the rebellion, the government issued a decree prohibiting "the existence and functioning inside the University of any association, group or organism with no specific educational or administrative purposes." [20] Thus, with the acquiescence of its leaders, the FEU ceased to exist legally. But this time the radicals had the backing of large groups of students. In an effort to find an organization to replace the FEU, Aureliano Sanchez Arango, Eduardo Chibás, Antonio Guiteras, and several others quickly convened a meeting of the directors of all the University's cultural and athletic organizations (the only ones still allowed to exist). When the directors of the organizations boggled at facing the situation, they were immediately deposed and replaced. In this way a new belligerent organization was created, called the Student Directory. Announcing an uncompromising anti-Machado attitude and appealing for a massive student struggle against the government, the Directory rapidly drew down on itself the action of both government and University authorities. Many of the founders were expelled, and a decree was passed giving full authority to the Rector "to take all necessary measures to re-establish order in the University." [21] But the stern measures were only partially

[20] Eduardo Suárez Rivas, *Un pueblo crucificado* (Miami: n.p., 1964), p. 34.

[21] Milo A. Borges, *Compilación ordenada y completa de la legislación cubana* (Havana: Editorial Lex, 1952), I, 662. The Student Directory answered with a manifesto accusing the government of trying "to subdue the last bastion of Cuban national dignity by reducing the university to a submissive military barrack" (Araquistain, p. 286).

successful. Recruiting new members, the Student Directory continued to exist and to fight. By 1928 the most radical elements of the University were sufficiently organized to sustain a long "war" against Machado.

Clearly, then, the University that was confronted by the illegal extension of Machado's powers was quite different from the somnolent institution that earlier had passively watched the political problems of Cuba. The shouting *muchachos* whom Wifredo Fernández had dismissed so lightly were a partial but decisive expression of new ideals and a new conscience. With radical, if vague, ideas at the beginning, willing to follow for a while the leadership of some members of the older generation whom they considered patriotic, these students were to show in a long and bloody struggle how passionate were their ideals for a new Cuba.

The students were not the only ones who fought and suffered Machado's authoritarian methods. Even before the University began to feel the heavy hand of the government, other sectors of Cuban society were paying a high price for their efforts to create a new and different kind of society.

Rise of Cuban Labor

In Cuba, a basically agricultural country, the strength of the proletariat had been slowly and sporadically growing since the second half of the nineteenth century. Its birth is associated with the first organizations of tobacco workers, *tabaqueros*, who, through their "readers," had early been able to develop a political conscience.[22] In 1866 the first Association of To-

[22] Tobacco workers labored in vast rooms. To entertain them during the long hours of manual work, one of the men was allowed to read books or newspapers aloud. Soon the method was used to explain and promote social theories, as those of Bakunin, Proudhon, and other anarchists of lesser importance. See José Rivero Muñiz, "La lectura en las tabaquerías," *Hoy*, May 1, 1943, p. 78, and Gaspar Jorge,

bacco Workers of Havana was created, and a newspaper, *La Aurora,* warily began to preach the need for union and organization of the proletariat. In 1883 for the first time, a small but significant strike occurred in Havana. That same year another newspaper, *El Obrero,* of more radical tendencies, appeared. Thanks to the energy of its founder, Enrique Roig, it began to spread anarchist ideas among tobacco workers, promoting violent action, which as usual produced the first great split among the small labor groups. In 1892 a Workers Regional Congress, held in Havana and attended primarily by tobacco workers, showed impressive gains for the anarchists. Three years later the War for Independence began, and the national cause attracted and consumed the best energies of the nascent Cuban proletariat.[23]

In 1898, when the peace was signed, the League of Cuban Workers became the most important of the new labor organizations, although the poet Diego Vicente Tejera, who had been promoting Socialist ideas from exile, vainly tried to rally the workers to his ephemeral Socialist party. Actually, from the beginning Cuban workers had been caught in the twilight zone brought about by the partial victory of the Cuban independence forces: their main concern was to fight for survival in a country progressively invaded by American capital and whose commerce was still largely in Spanish hands. Significantly, Article 1 of the League's program demanded the same guarantees for Cuban workers as were enjoyed by foreigners.[24] Some years later, when Spanish labor leaders accused the Cuban workers of ultranationalism and a lack of international

---

"Influencia del tabaquero en la trayectoria revolucionaria de Cuba," *Revista bimestre cubana,* Jan. 1937, pp. 110–115.

[23] Ramiro Guerra y Sánchez *et al.*, *Historia de la nación cubana* (Havana: Editorial Historia de la Nación Cubana, 1952), VII, 249–285.

[24] *Ibid.*, p. 294.

conscience, Carlos Baliño, the first important representative of Marxist ideas in Cuba, answered: "There are here labor unions so controlled by Spanish workers that only a few Cubans, and no Negroes, work in them. . . . Should native workers die of hunger in the name of a 'fraternity' based on the most unfair inequality?" [25]

After the advent of the republic and with a Constitution (1901) which, following the trend of the period, generally ignored social questions, the workers continued their struggle for organized labor and nationalistic objectives. In 1902, guided once more by the *tabaqueros*, the first general strike on the island was attempted. The failure of that strike, which almost all political forces opposed, represented a setback for the proletariat. But they recovered, and in 1907, when the *tabaqueros*, supported by several other labor groups, struck again demanding payment of their salaries in American and not in Spanish money (still in use as a medium of exchange), they were successful. This strike, which lasted 145 days, demonstrated the possibilities open to organized labor. In 1914 the first National Workers' Congress of the republican era was held, attended by about 1,200 delegates and representatives of labor organizations.[26]

In 1917 the railroad and port workers of Havana went on strike to obtain a raise in wages. A solidarity strike declared by many laborers in other industries forced President Menocal to appoint a commission which eventually dictated a resolution basically favorable to the strikers.[27] As a result of this

[25] *Documentos de Carlos Baliño* (Havana: Biblioteca Nacional José Martí, 1964), p. 61.

[26] José Rivero Muñiz, *El movimiento laboral cubano durante el período 1906–1911* (Las Villas: Universidad Central, 1962), pp. 72–80; Mario Riera Hernández, *Historial obrero cubano, 1574–1965* (Miami: Rema Press, 1965), p. 44.

[27] An excellent survey of this period is Barbara Ann Walker's "The Labor Policy of the Cuban Government since 1925" (Ph.D. diss.,

strike "Commissions of Intelligence for the Ports of Cuba" were created to solve labor problems, the first step toward the establishment of labor tribunals in sectors of labor other than tobacco.

In spite of several important gains in social legislation,[28] two basic weaknesses plagued the Cuban workers' movement. First, the process of organizing the workers in the sugar industry, the largest and most important industry of the island, was slow. The mills were far from the centers of population, employment was only periodic, and there were an influx of Haitian and Jamaican workers and a very low standard of living. Thus it was not until the 1920's that sugar workers began to organize. Second, the principal labor organization lacked both ideological programs and concrete objectives. Until 1924–1925 only the anarchists were really influential, but they were far from united and usually advocated isolated, violent tactics against management while opposing any participation in political or governmental organizations. This strategy prevented the workers from gathering much general support in the country.

The postwar economic crisis in Cuba intensified the political awareness of the proletariat. In 1920 the Federación Obrera de la Habana (FOH) was founded by Alfredo López and Enrique Varona, both of whom held anarcho-syndicalist con-

---

University of California, 1947), esp. pp. 20–35. The best book written on Cuban labor prior to 1959 is Efrén Córdova y Cordovés, *Derecho laboral cubano* (Havana: Editorial Lex, 1957).

[28] Among the most important were: the Law of January 26, 1909, which established an eight-hour day for government employees and workers in hotels, restaurants, and cafés; the Arteaga Law (June 1929) which prohibited the payment of wages, salaries, or any other remuneration in scrip, coupons, or any other substitute for money or legal tender; and the Law of December 8, 1910, regulating the minimum salaries of those employed by the national government, the provinces, or the municipalities.

victions. They were joined by several workers who would play a significant role in the labor struggles, among them, Antonio Penichet and Sandalio Junco. Against them, in continuation of the internal factionalism that divided the workers, the delegate of COPA (Confederación Obrera Panamericana) in Cuba, Juan Arévalo, used his strongest influence and propaganda. Under the aegis of FOH a Second National Workers' Congress was held in Havana. As a symptom of the changing times and the revitalization of nationalism, the delegates did not limit themselves to demanding social improvements for their class (similar wages for similar jobs, an eight-hour working day, and the like); they also strongly condemned "Yankee intrusionism" as represented by Enoch Crowder.[29]

Continuing these efforts, the railroad workers proclaimed a strike against the abuses of the Ferrocarriles Unidos (United Railroads) and the refusal of its administrator, Archibald Jack, to cease all work on Labor Day, May 1. The strike began in June 1924, lasted 21 days, and resulted in violence until then unknown in Cuba. Close to the town of Colón, workers sabotaged two bridges and paralyzed all transit. Several days later, as a result of the tough reprisal policy announced by President Zayas, one worker shot and injured Archibald Jack. The strike ended with a compromise.

After this strike the workers' movement gained momentum, at the same time becoming a source of growing concern to the authorities. In 1925 the anarcho-syndicalist leadership, realizing the regional and class limitations of the FOH (formed largely by *tabaqueros* and the maritime workers of Havana), founded the first national organization, the National Confederation of Cuban Workers (CNOC). But almost simultaneously the Communist party was born, and the anarcho-syndicalists met their first real challenge for control of the

[29] Riera Hernández, p. 50.

workers' movement. In that same year, Machado was inaugurated as President of Cuba.

Expanding the scope of its social demands, this growing but still feeble labor movement was the first target of Machado's authoritarian policies.[30] Because of the extremism of their propaganda and the violence of their tactics—the shooting of Archibald Jack had been only one of many violent acts—the anarcho-syndicalists were considered the most dangerous element, and they suffered the first repressive blows. A few months after Machado's inauguration, Enrique Varona, who was then organizing the railroad workers in the province of Camaguey, was shot and killed in the town of Moron. The following year, on May 25, 1926, Decree No. 649 authorized the Secretary of the Interior (whom Cuban Communists called, with some exaggeration, "the Cuban Stolypin") "or any other authority" to use the army or the Rural Guard against those who fomented or participated in strikes. The next month the entire directorate of the railroad workers' organization was arrested in Camaguey.[31] Some weeks later Alfredo López, the other important anarcho-syndicalist leader, was killed by the police in Havana.

[30] In March 1925, in an article in the Mexican Communist newspaper *El Machete*, Ricardo Marín wrote: "After having been in close touch with the majority of Cuban labor organizations, we are convinced that Cuban workers have not yet acquired the necessary conscience to orient their struggle in a clear and fixed direction." See Raquel Tibol, *Julio Antonio Mella en "El Machete"* (Mexico City: Fondo de Cultura Económica, 1968), p. 25. In November 1925, the CNOC recognized that "many of our resolutions have been paralyzed by repressive measures (of the government)." See "Confederación Nacional Obrera de Cuba," *Pensamiento crítico*, No. 38, p. 56.

[31] Calixto Masó, "El movimiento obrero cubano," *Panoramas* (Mexico City), No. 9 (May–June 1964), p. 74; Borges, I, 615; *Revista parlamentaria de Cuba*, VI (July–Aug. 1926), 206. Varona's murder was generally attributed to one of Machado's military aides.

With the anarcho-syndicalists repressed, the CNOC practically suppressed, and the FOH dissolved, Machado figured he had the labor movement well under control. The government then proceeded to form its own docile workers' organization, the Federative Union of National Workers (UFON), headed by a leader of dubious integrity and a radical past, Juan Arévalo.[32]

The government's stern measures against the workers' organizations, like those against the University, were only partially successful. Clandestine groups appeared and new leaders emerged. To fill the vacuum left by the decimated anarcho-syndicalists, the recently formed Communist party made its first bid for labor leadership.

The Cuban Communist Party

The Cuban Communist party was founded in Havana in August 1925. That one of its founders was Julio A. Mella reveals the link between the agitation in the University and the emerging Marxist group.[33]

The significance of this nascent Communist party should not be overestimated, however. Actually, its appearance had little impact upon Cuban society and politics; only ten persons were present at the forming of the party, and initially it had no more than eighty members. Only one of the founders had previous experience with Marxist theories and organizations—

[32] A socialist in his youth, Arévalo had tried to organize an uprising of sailors in 1917, when he was a leader of maritime workers. See Riera Hernández, p. 45. For a review of labor conditions in Cuba in the first two years under Machado, see Emilio Roig de Leuchsenring, *Los problemas sociales en Cuba* (Havana: Imprenta El Ideal, 1927), pp. 34–56.

[33] "Como se fundó el partido comunista de Cuba," *Hoy*, May 1, 1943, p. 45. Jorge Garcia Montes and Antonio A. Avila, *Historia del partido comunista de Cuba* (Miami: Ediciones Universal, 1970), pp. 57–59.

Carlos Baliño, by then a tired old man of seventy-seven.[34] The rest of the members, including Mella himself, as well as those who later joined the party, such as poet Rubén Martínez Villena, lacked basic doctrinal information. The theoretician of the party seems to have been a Polish immigrant, Fabio Grobart, who has played an important, though obscure, role in the party's history.[35]

This small party, which attracted intellectuals, middle-class professionals, students, and some workers, had formidable obstacles to face: the lack of organization and of political consciousness among the workers, control of the existing labor union by anarcho-syndicalists, the inexperience of its own leaders, and, after a short while, official repression. In 1927, after Baliño's death and Mella's exile, Rubén Martínez Villena became the party's most prominent figure.

In the spring of 1927, under Martínez Villena's initiative, the Grupo Minorista organized a tribute to Serafín Delmar, a Peruvian writer forced into exile in Cuba by the then dictator Juan B. Leguía. The Peruvian Chargé d'Affaires presented a formal protest for this act and accused Delmar and certain other exiles of plotting with Cuban Communists to overthrow

[34] Baliño, who had refused to join the Socialist Party founded by Tejera in 1901, managed in 1906 to organize a weak Cuban Socialist Party, which lasted less than four years. In 1919 he bitterly criticized the lack of unity among Cuban workers. See Baliño, *Documentos de Carlos Baliño*, p. 15; Blas Roca, "Recuerdos de Carlos Baliño," *Hoy*, Feb. 18, 1945, p. 4.

[35] Grobart (Abraham Simkowitz), who is still an active member of the Cuban Communist party, emigrated to the island in 1922. Many considered him an agent of the Comintern. At this time he was not elected a full member of the Central Committee, but only an alternate. See Pedro Serviat, *40 aniversario de la fundación del Partido Communista* (Havana: Editora Popular, 1963), pp. 104–106; "Mesa redonda sobre Mella," *Revolución*, March 25, 1964, p. 7; and Boris Goldenberg, "The Rise and Fall of the Cuban Communist Party," *Problems of Communism*, July–Aug. 1970, p. 64.

Machado's regime. The Cuban government took immediate action. All foreigners who had taken part in the "conspiracy" were arrested; some of them were deported, and many Cubans accused of participation were tried in what came to be known as "the Communist trial of 1927." Although there were no convictions as a result of this trial, the Communist party was declared illegal and was left, according to Grobart, "without leadership or organization. . . . Everything had to be rebuilt." [36] In 1928 the single party organ, the underground *El Comunista*, had a circulation of less than a thousand copies.[37] But the influence of the party in the radical atmosphere of Cuba went far beyond the number of its members. Following the pattern set in Europe by Willie Muzenberg, a series of peripheral organizations more or less connected with the party appeared: Liga Anti-Imperialista, Defensa Internacional Obrera, Liga-Anticlerical, and others. They served to continue the dissemination of Marxist propaganda on the island.

Throughout the 1920's Machado and his advisers—Fernández, Barraqué, and others—thinking in terms of the past, believed that opposition could be bought off, that the simple menace of American intervention could paralyze political antagonists, and that all problems could be solved by a secret and profitable transaction among politicians, as in the time of Menocal and Zayas. They did not realize until too late how different was the attitude of these new forces, who were willing to fight all the way to eliminate from Cuba what they considered, in Martínez Villena's phrase, "la costra tenaz del coloniaje" (the tenacious scab of the colonial heritage). And

[36] Fabio Grobart, "Recuerdos sobre Rubén, *Hoy*, Jan. 16, 1964, p. 3.
[37] *The Communist International* (London: Communist Party of Great Britain, 1928), p. 371.

for them Machado and his regime were its typical representatives.

But it took more than passionate intentions and radical declarations for these new forces to pose a serious threat to Machado's government.

7 *The Calm before the Storm, 1928-1929*

At the beginning the repressive measures against labor and the University, the protest of some intellectuals, and the opposition of a growing number of politicians did not visibly affect either Machado's popularity or his political grip. In 1928–1929, in spite of occasional disturbances, Machado appeared to be in full control of the national situation.

Before embarking on the adventure of constitutional modification and re-election, President Machado had paid a visit to the United States in 1927 and sounded out President Coolidge concerning U.S. plans. He was told by the President of the United States that "this was a question for the Cuban people and their government to decide." [1] After his return to Cuba, while preparing his program for the new elections, Machado had an opportunity to enhance the international prestige of his government by hosting the delegates to the Sixth International Conference of American States. Not only was the President of the United States his guest of honor, but on arriving in Havana the American delegate, Charles Evans Hughes, declared: "The American delegation considers it a privilege to be able to participate in the noble vision of President Machado." [2]

[1] *Foreign Relations of the United States, 1927* (Washington, D.C.: U.S. Government Printing Office, 1942), II, 527.

[2] *Diario de la Marina*, Jan. 17, 1928, p. 1.

Thus the American-Cuban friendship seemed extremely firm. During the Conference the Cuban delegation made every possible effort to prevent anyone from mentioning the name of Sandino (who was at the time fighting the American forces in Nicaragua), and refused to condemn the right of "intervention," although many Latin American delegates insisted. As the Cuban representative Orestes Ferrara explained, "We can't join the general chorus of non-intervention. . . . In my country the word 'intervention' has been a word of honor, a word of glory, a word of triumph, a word of liberty; it has been a word of independence." [3] Addressing the Conference, Machado himself defined the spirit of Pan-Americanism: "Pan-Americanism is the synthesis of all principles of good that rise from the lives of individuals to that of the State." [4]

Once the Conference was over, Machado turned his attention to the national political situation and the electoral process. On July 20, 1928, an Emergency Law was passed by the Congress prohibiting presidential nominations by parties other than the Liberal, the Conservative, and the Popular.[5] As a result, the National Union of Carlos Mendieta, the only political group in opposition, was barred from the race.

Machado, the only candidate of the three legal parties, published a platform prior to the election of November 1, 1928, explaining why "high patriotic duties and present circumstances" had forced him to make the sacrifice of running again. He also reviewed his past achievements: "In three years my government has produced more public works than all those that preceded me put together." In acknowledging the opposi-

[3] Quoted in Emilio Roig de Leuchsenring, *Historia de la Enmienda Platt* (Havana: Cultural, 1935), I, 283.

[4] "The Sixth International Conference of American States," *International Conciliation* (New York), No. 241 (June 1928), p. 279.

[5] *Gaceta oficial de la República de Cuba*, July 21, 1928, p. 1.

tion of the University, he expressed the dilemma of his government:

We have suffered some difficulties in our highest institution of learning; my government found itself caught between the opinion of the faculty and that of a rebellious group of students, between maintaining the University as a center of learning or allowing a few irresponsible youths to take possession of it in order to turn it into a place of enjoyment and of moral and material disorder. . . . I could not hesitate; I was obliged to reestablish the rule of law. . . . In this case, as in others, the dilemma presented forced me to decide between law and order . . . or license, compromise, abuse, scorn of authority. . . . I have not hesitated in regard to my attitude. I will never hesitate in the future. Our country will be free, but orderly and quiet.

He defended the soundness of his sugar policy, asserted his true concern for the workers, and ended with his traditional note of authoritarianism: "The spirit of order which is inherent in me does not permit me to temporize with the mob or with irresponsibility." [6] With the University tamed and the Unión Nacionalista paralyzed, the elections were held without serious problems, and Machado was duly elected for the term 1929 to 1935.

The American chargé in Havana refrained from congratulating Machado until he was instructed to do so. He thought "that this might be a suitable occasion to convey in a negative manner to the mind of General Machado the fact that the Government of the United States was not giving him personally the wholehearted support which he is apparently trying to have the people of Cuba believe he is receiving." [7] This opinion apparently was not shared by the majority of his

[6] Gerardo Machado y Morales, *Declarations Regarding His Electoral Platform* (Havana: Rambla, Bouza, 1928), pp. 4, 7, 9–10, 26.

[7] Chargé (Curtis) Dispatch, Nov. 6, 1928, U.S. Department of State Papers (DS/2713), National Archives.

countrymen living in Cuba (or by his government). The *Times* of Cuba, organ of the American colony there, presented a quite different viewpoint in July 1928: "The new Machado administration should be one of peace and prosperity for Cuba, and all elements, native and foreigners, should put forth their best efforts to make it so." [8]

Thus, nothing but official optimism surrounded Machado on the day of his second inauguration, May 20, 1929. With great solemnity the act took place in the unfinished but already impressive Congressional Palace—"a visible proof of Machado's dynamism," as one of the speakers remarked—before representatives of more than a hundred nations. That day, among many articles devoted to him, *El Heraldo de Cuba* favorably compared Machado with Cavour, Bismarck, Gambetta, and others.[9]

Certainly there had been trouble with students and workers. Just a few days before the inauguration a workers' meeting had to be interrupted by the police because of the fiery speech of a student named Gabriel Barcelo, whose revolutionary words were received with "thunderous applause." [10] And the leaders of Unión Nacionalista occasionally accused the government of being unconstitutional and threatened it with a popular rebellion. But these were considered minor incidents. As Machado's partisans never tired of repeating, the people loved and supported the President and the destiny of Cuba rested securely in his patriotic hands.

In May 1929, when his government asked him for a report

[8] *Times* (Havana), July 1928, p. 4.

[9] Viriato Gutierrez, "Machado el político," *El Heraldo de Cuba*, May 20, 1929, p. 6.

[10] *Diario de la Marina*, May 2, 1928, p. 3. Gabriel Barcelo had participated in the anti-Machado demonstration at the University in 1927. Arrested and deported in 1929, he continued the struggle against Machado and later became a member of the Student Left Wing and the Communist party.

on the political situation in Cuba, U.S. Ambassador Judah echoed that impression. He sent a long dispatch favorable to Machado, asserting that the President was "in complete control of all the political parties because all the constituted political parties support him and his policies." [11] The Ambassador failed to mention that several nonpolitical groups opposed the President, and that the formation of parties opposed to the government had been legally forbidden.

In mid-1929 the forces of opposition could still be classified in three main groups: (1) the slowly growing National Union of Carlos Mendieta, which rallied most of the old political figures who were against Machado; (2) the student groups in the University, already organized under the leadership of the Student Directory; and (3) several labor groups and the Communist party. By prestige and national reputation the first group was the most important and the one destined to guide the initial phase of the anti-Machado struggle. But there were no real contacts among them, nor were they fighting for the same goals or under the same conditions. Admonitions and friendly warnings were the usual government answer to the attitude of the political opposition. Disciplinary measures and, on rare occasions, short jail sentences were the punishment for rebellious students. Stern methods and occasional brutality were reserved for workers and Communists. In February 1928, Mella denounced from Mexico the abuses suffered by certain peasant leaders and the "disappearance" of two members of the Communist party, Claudio Bouzón and Noske Yalom.[12] Some months later he himself was assassinated in Mexico. Almost everyone in Cuba added his name to the list of those murdered by Machado's forces.[13]

[11] Dispatch, May 10, 1929, U.S. Department of State Papers (DS/2747), National Archives.

[12] Raquel Tibol, *Julio Antonio Mella en "El Machete"* (Mexico City: Fondo de Cultura Popular, 1968), p. 200.

[13] The responsibility for the assassination of Mella is not totally

It is important to bear in mind that in mid-1929 none of the forces opposing Machado had announced a concrete program of action or even the necessity of a revolution. The most aggressive declaration of the National Union party stressed that it was the patriotic duty of every Cuban "to fight for the re-establishment of freedom and legality in our country." [14] The students limited themselves to shouting "Down with the Dictator!" inside the walls of the University or in some public demonstration, and the workers fought basically to keep their organization alive. The Communists followed an isolated path.

Recovering from the blows of 1927, the Communists concentrated their efforts on reorganizing the party and expanding its influence in labor and intellectual circles. The task was far from easy. Internally, the small but growing party still suffered from ideological confusion and factionalism. A veiled criticism of the "intellectuals" of the party, whose most important figure was Martínez Villena, took shape in their demands for a "bolshevization" or "proletarization" of the lead-

---

clear. The Communist interpretation has always insisted on the traditional thesis, accepted by the majority of Cubans, that it was the work of Machado. Non-Communist sources have pointed out the possibility of a Communist reaction to an alleged antiparty attitude of Mella. See, for example, Robert Alexander, *Communism in Latin America* (New Brunswick: Rutgers University Press, 1957), p. 271; Victor Alba, *Esquema histórico del comunismo en Latinoamérica* (Mexico City: Ediciones Occidentales, 1960), p. 86; Julian Gorkin, *Como asesinó Stalin a Trotsky* (Barcelona, 1961), p. 204; and Natacha Mella's article (Julio's daughter) in *El Avance Criollo* (Miami), March 24, 1961, p. 31. More plausible is the fact that Mella had had some basic differences with the leadership of the party in 1925 and that he was temporarily expelled for "indiscipline" during his hunger strike in prison. Aureliano Sanchez Arango affirms that he saw the document of expulsion, signed by Dr. Bernal del Riesgo. Boris Goldenberg also mentions that point in his article, "The Rise and Fall of the Cuban Communist Party," *Problems of Communism,* July–Aug. 1970, p. 64.

[14] *Nuestro propósito* (Havana: Unión Nacionalista, 1928), p. 6.

ership. Aware of the danger of such friction, which also touched him personally, Mella opposed this emerging trend. "To promote division between intellectuals and workers inside the Communist Party," he wrote, "is to proclaim that it is not a revolutionary party. . . . Division? No! Never intellectuals versus workers, but good Communists against bad Communists." [15] But the internal struggle went on after his death.

In its anti-Machado stand, the party followed the radical tactics enjoined by the Sixth Congress of the Comintern (1928). [16] It refused to make any distinction between Machado and the forces that opposed him—students, liberal politicians, nationalistic bourgeois, anarchists, democratic groups. The party branded and condemned all as "lackeys of yankee imperialism" and called the workers to rally around the only true vanguard of the revolution—the Communist party. In 1928, in a typical declaration, the party proclaimed: "The struggle is without quarter! From the bourgeoisie, from 'democratic' governments we will only receive misery and death. The emancipation of the workers must be the task of the workers themselves!" [17] At the time of this declaration, the party was described by the Comintern as "a small sectarian group of no more than 250 to 300 members and having little connection with the masses." [18]

To the criticism of that fragmented opposition Machado always answered by downgrading the importance of the critics—"insignificant groups formed by ambitious and un-

[15] Tibol, pp. 246–247.

[16] For the effect of the Sixth Congress' decisions on the Latin American Communist parties, see Luis E. Aguilar, ed., *Marxism in Latin America* (New York: Knopf, 1968), pp. 30–36.

[17] "A Proclamation of the Cuban Communist Party," in Tibol, p. 337.

[18] *The Communist International before the Seventh World Congress* (Moscow and Leningrad, 1935), p. 494.

scrupulous persons"—and by pointing out his patriotic past and his accomplishments in the government. "Which actually proves nothing," commented the director of *Diario de la Marina*, "for a dictator is recognizable not so much for what he does, but for what he forbids others to do." [19]

But if Machado in 1929 could still regard the political situation in Cuba with relative confidence, there was another much more dangerous menace facing him—the declining trend of the Cuban economy. Actually, the island had never fully recovered from the crisis of 1919–1920. Between 1924 and 1927, Cuba maintained a high volume of sugar exports to the United States, but since prices had come down from 1923 levels, the total value of Cuban sugar exported to the United States fell to less than $2 million in 1926.[20] The recovery of many sugar producing countries after the war, the increase in U.S. sugar production, and an international trend toward protectionism kept the Cuban economy precariously balanced. To keep his program of public works active and to cope with the situation, Machado was forced to betray his electoral promise and to contract several loans with various American banks. By 1927 he had already received more than $100 million in such loans. But this did not alter the general trend of the Cuban economy. The decline was shown in the national budget: in 1925–26 the revenue budget of the state had been $84,791; in 1927–28 it was $80,988.[21]

In January 1929, the Cuban Ambassador in Washington, Orestes Ferrara, addressed a long and detailed report to the American government proposing a revision of the commercial

[19] José I. Rivero, "Impresiones," *Diario de la Marina*, May 20, 1928, p. 1.

[20] José R. Alvarez Díaz *et al.*, *A Study on Cuba* (Miami: University of Miami Press, 1963), p. 248.

[21] *Ibid.*, p. 217.

treaty in effect since 1903 between the United States and Cuba. With impressive figures and sound arguments, Ferrara recalled the sacrifices of Cuba for the common war effort during 1917–1918, the advantages for the United States of a prosperous Cuba, and the negative effects of American tariffs on the Cuban economy. Pleading for a better deal for his country, the Ambassador did not hide the gravity of the situation: "My government wishes to save from possible ruin the Cuban wealth which is, in part, wealth pertaining to American interests, and to favor further, in just reciprocity, exports from the United States to Cuba." [22]

Because the betterment of Cuban-American relations was considered essential, Machado's government was very sensitive to the propaganda which Cuban exiles began spreading in the United States. To curb that propaganda, a bill was introduced in the lower house of the Cuban Congress in March 1929, by which "any Cuban who seeks the intervention or interference of a foreign power in the internal or external development of the national life" was to be punished by life imprisonment.[23] Almost simultaneously, the government made a concerted effort to offer the impression of national support for Machado. A campaign was initiated in May urging all sectors of the population to express their solidarity with the President. Promoted by official groups and furthered by political pressures, this movement soon acquired vast proportions. In a common pronouncement, the representatives of nearly all the Cuban city councils proclaimed their support for a government that had restored peace and order in Cuba, strengthened national unity

[22] *Foreign Relations of the United States, 1929* (Washington, D.C.: U.S. Government Printing Office, 1943), p. 893.

[23] *Ibid.*, p. 895. Under American pressure, Machado vetoed the proposal.

and, above all, "opened new roads for Cuban economic development and progressive prosperity." [24]

With tragic irony, at the very moment these words were being published, an era of "prosperity" ended with the sudden collapse of the stock market in New York. That collapse and the ensuing measures of the American government to fight its consequences plunged Cuba's economy into its darkest period. As usual, the economic disaster had immediate and widespread political repercussions. It was then that the voices of protest against Machado and all that he represented found a receptive atmosphere, and the struggle against his government began to develop into a revolutionary movement.

[24] *Diario de la Marina*, Nov. 4, 1929, p. 10.

8 Depression and General Opposition, 1930-1933

Economic Crisis

The economic situation in Cuba from 1929 to 1933 was somber and desperate, and the spread of misery throughout all sectors of the population was inevitable. In 1928 the price of sugar was 2.18 cents per pound, a rather low price which had forced Cuba to readjust her economy but which still permitted a certain economic stability. In 1929, after the collapse of the market, the price dropped to 1.72 cents per pound. In 1930 the price was 1.23; in 1931, after the United States government had adopted the Hawley-Smoot tariff on sugar imports, the price declined to 1.09; and in 1932, in what seemed to be an irreversible trend toward total collapse, the price of sugar dropped to the all-time low of 0.57 cents per pound. In 1929 the Cuban sugar crop had a value of $225,100,000; in 1933 its value was $53,700,000, less than one-fourth of the 1929 total.[1]

This time Cuba could not rely, as she had at other times, on other products. Tobacco, for example, the second largest export product, also suffered a severe decline. In 1929 tobacco exports represented a total value of $43,067,000; in 1933 they reached only $13,861,000.[2]

[1] *Anuario azucarero* (Havana: Ministerio de Hacienda, 1959), pp. 37-38.

[2] José R. Alvarez Díaz *et al.*, *A Study on Cuba* (Miami: University of Miami Press, 1963), p. 362.

The results of this crisis were felt all over Cuba. In 1929 the government was still talking of expanding trade and industry; in January 1930 it announced a general reduction in the salaries of all public employees with the exception, naturally, of soldiers.[3] As early as March 1930, there were protests throughout the island because of the delay in paying the salaries of teachers and agricultural workers.[4] From then on it was common for all Cuban workers, public or private, to suffer delays in receiving their monthly check or to go for several months without receiving any payment. Prices declined for all products, and unemployment spread throughout the island, causing, in turn, political unrest. The observation of the U.S. Chargé d'Affaires in 1930 is significant, even when we take into consideration the social class with which he was in contact: "In every conversation I have had with Cubans and Americans who are opposed to the Machado administration I have asked the following question: If sugar were selling at three cents a pound, would the present political agitation continue? The answer has invariably been: No." [5]

Political Crisis

With the economic crisis affecting all aspects of Cuban life, it was evident that the wind was now blowing in favor of the

[3] *Diaro de la Marina*, Jan. 9, 1930, p. 1.

[4] *El País*, March 6, 1930, p. 1. One year later, on May 23, 1931, the government appealed to the people to accept the sacrifices made necessary by the drastic curtailment in public outlays. It was proposed to reduce the new budget 40 per cent below that of the preceding year. The salaries of civil employees had already been cut twice since July 1930. See Council on Foreign Relations, *The United States in World Affairs, 1931* (New York: Harper, 1932), p. 52.

[5] *Foreign Relations of the United States, 1930* (Washington, D.C.: U.S. Government Printing Office, 1945), II, 658. Many Cubans, especially "Machadistas," agree with Reed in considering the economic crisis the real cause of Machado's downfall; see, for example,

opposition. The government, far from realizing the necessity of flexibility, responded with more severe decrees. In January 1930 all public demonstrations by political parties or groups that were not legally registered were forbidden. Colonel Carlos Mendieta protested this measure and summarized the radical change in the political situation: "When the doors of legality are closed, the doors of violence are automatically open. . . . It is impossible to visualize what sooner or later is going to happen in this unfortunate country, victim of all misfortunes and subject to the affront of a new servitude." [6]

The doors of violence were indeed opened. In the following months a series of events changed the entire political situation and inspired a new national attitude. Examining the mounting symptoms of political unrest, from student protests to workers' strikes, Enrique José Varona wrote in the May 15, 1930 issue of *Avance*, "Full of lesson and hopes, the nation, in fact, has again realized its strength." Confronted by crisis on almost every front, the government was forced to move forward toward an acknowledged dictatorship.

On May 19, 1930, the Nationalists (members of Mendieta's Unión Nacional) held a meeting in the town of Artemisa, near Havana. According to government sources they did it in open defiance of the law, although the leaders of the party later insisted that they had authorization from local officers. In any case, when the meeting started, a group of soldiers, headed by a lieutenant, tried to interrupt the first speaker, Juan Gualberto Gómez, one of the most distinguished veterans of the War of Independence. A scuffle followed on the platform, a shot was fired, and the lieutenant fell. Immediately pandemonium erupted. The soldiers charged into the multi-

---

Rafael Guas Inclán, "Gerardo Machado," *Bohemia*, 30th anniversary special issue, 1938, p. 101.

[6] *Diario de la Marina*, Jan. 16, 1930, p. 1.

tude, firing their rifles. When the disturbance was over, eight persons had been killed and several dozen injured. The tragedy created a national commotion; many national leaders were arrested. "The events of Artemisa mean that politics is no longer possible in Cuba, the answer to brutality must be rebellion," proclaimed Ramón Zaydin as he went into exile.[7]

The government was still coping with the aftereffects of the Artemisa affair when, on May 28, less than ten days later, the railroad workers declared a general strike (which, apparently, had no relation to the political troubles but was a protest against the reduction of salaries). The army was ordered to take over the running of the trains, and several labor leaders were arrested. The following month, as a sign of the changing times, former President Mario G. Menocal came out of retirement and began to make public statements that could be interpreted as critical of the regime.[8] As a result, several members of the Conservative party (in which Menocal had always been a leader) showed a desire to abandon *cooperativismo* and move toward a policy of conciliation with the opposition.

Nevertheless, the government did not hesitate or show any sign of weakness. Machado proclaimed himself fully responsible for the acts of the army in Artemisa.[9] The strike failed to paralyze the country, and the bulk of Conservatives were kept in line.

The tough line of the government seemed to pay dividends. In June, U.S. Ambassador Harry F. Guggenheim, who had vainly tried to mediate between the government and the op-

[7] *Un pasado de lucha* (Havana: Edit Nueva Prensa, 1937), p. 97.

[8] This was the press's impression of his political reappearance.

[9] The Cuban Supreme Court declined to resolve the Nationalists' accusation against General Alberto Herrera (head of the army), "in view of the written declaration of the President, sent to this Tribunal, stating that he personally gave the order to suspend the meeting" (*Diario de la Marina*, May 30, 1930, p. 1).

position, reported to his government that "a calmer and more optimistic attitude toward Cuban economic and political conditions prevails."[10] Three months later Senator Clemente Vazquez Bello warned the opposition that "it was madness to defy this man [Machado] who is backed by the three existing political parties, the Congress, the people, and the glorious National Army."[11] The echo of those words was still in the air when the third group of antigovernmental forces intervened, opening a new and more dangerous political front. On September 30, 1930, the student movement erupted from the University into the national arena.

With the beginning of the new semester approaching, and with national political tension mounting, the Student Directory decided to organize a violent demonstration to disrupt the traditional ceremony of opening classes at the University. They didn't know that one of their members, José Soler, was working for the police and kept the government informed of all their plans.[12] Consequently, the Council of the University cancelled the ceremony and rescheduled it for November 10.[13] On the day the classes were to begin, September 30, the ar-

[10] *Foreign Relations, 1930,* II, 649–650. Guggenheim's mediation failed, according to him, "because of the obstinacy of Colonel Mendieta and his associates in demanding Machado's resignation." Mendieta, on his own, later explained that he was convinced that Machado's promises were only "an attempt to gain time to overcome the critical conditions of the moment."

[11] *Diario de la Marina,* Sept. 20, 1930, p. 19.

[12] José Soler Lezama, who was successively a member of the Student Directory, the Communist party, and ABC, was later (Sept. 1933) tried and executed by the Student Directory. This dramatic episode of the revolution of 1933 is the subject of *El Acoso,* an excellent novel by Alejo Carpentier.

[13] *Diario de la Marina,* Sept. 21, 1930, front page. The history of the conspiracy and the events that followed is gathered from newspaper information and from direct accounts of Juan Antonio Rubio Padilla, Carlos Prío, and other participants.

riving students found the University guarded by police. The leaders of the conspiracy refused to enter; they gathered outside with other group of students and began a street demonstration. They announced their purpose to march to the residence of philosopher Enrique José Varona. The police blocked the streets and the inevitable confrontation occurred. Several arrests resulted, plus serious injury to one policeman and two students. The following day one of the students, Rafael Trejo, died in the hospital.

The death of Trejo and the national commotion that followed marked a turning point in the struggle against Machado. The next day the government suspended constitutional guarantees, announced that there were in the University groups that "follow orders from Moscow," and the president warned that he would act "without weakness or hesitation." [14] But manifestations of protest and proclamations of solidarity with the Student Directory poured from every corner of the island. Enrique José Varona publicly condemned the outrage, and after him University faculty, high school students, the Bar Association, politicians, and others expressed their support for the students. In the Chamber of Representatives, Aquilino Lombard expressed the general concern by pleading: "Let us cease the policy of 'cooperativism,' for the house is crumbling over us and we must stop it from falling." [15] General Menocal, encouraged by the evident expansion of the anti-Machado feeling, rejected a last appeal from Wifredo Fernández—in an article in *El País* entitled "Detente Caudillo!" (Halt Leader!) —and proclaimed that there was no possibility of conciliation with the government.

[14] *Ibid.*, Oct. 2, front page. There were some reports in the press that members of the Communist Youth did participate in the student demonstration.

[15] *Ibid.*, Oct. 4, front page.

The students, suddenly part of the national scene, found themselves a rallying point for diverse forces, the vanguard of a national struggle. "The shots were not aimed at Trejo but at our liberty!" wrote an indignant Varona; "Forward, boys," exhorted Pablo de la Torriente Brau; "Forward! . . . In Cuba today dignity belongs to young people. . . . Let us cleanse our republic once and for all. . . . Forward, toward a new era of liberty and justice!"[16] Not quite ready for that formidable role, the students nevertheless understood its implications and accepted its responsibilities. "It is not the student group that has invaded the political arena," they proclaimed; "it is politics that has infringed upon student life."[17] To meet the historical challenge, the Student Directory stressed its independence from the political parties and announced to the nation the immediate publication of its own program. After frantic work, on October 29, the Student Directory published its "Minimum Program" and announced its decision to intervene directly in the political struggle.

The document reads partially as follows:

> After the initial moments of just indignation over the death of our *compañero*[18] Rafael Trejo, the moment has come to proclaim our ideals and objectives, and our future plan of action to face present injustice.
>
> Our last protest, drowned in blood by the police, was only one more phase of the movement which for more than seven years has been dwelling at the University. Here, as in many other areas, Cuba is only reacting to the pressure of international circumstances. Whoever has paid attention to the social evolution of

[16] Varona in *El País*, Nov. 9, 1930; Brau, "Arriba muchachos," *Pensamiento crítico*, No. 38 (April 1970), p. 108.

[17] *Diario de la Marina*, Oct. 27, 1930, front page.

[18] The Spanish word *compañero* has different emotional implications from its English counterpart "companion." Here it means something close to "comrade-in-arms."

the postwar era, and especially to that of the Hispanic-American community, knows how a general task of renovation has been largely accomplished by student masses. Convinced that the University has been a place for the perpetuation of the most monstrous inequalities, knowing that teaching has been exclusively devoted to the function of providing degrees—degrees that have become powerful weapons to maintain old injustices—aware that present education is useless, when not damaging (uselessness and damage sharply criticized by our Martí), along the entire continent the new American student has accepted the hard mission of transforming the nature of "official education." . . .

The students of Havana University—whom the Student Directory is honored to represent—are fully aware of the dangerous compromise which has been thrown on their shoulders by present circumstances. As in other countries, the Cuban student must now engage in political work. If the University is today a reactionary and militarized center, it is because reaction and militarism are the characteristics of the present Cuban government. . . . We demand for our people the liberties that the oligarchy has suppressed . . . for we clearly realize that a "new" University cannot exist while a new type of state does not exist. Calmly but energetically, the Cuban student will fight for the deep social transformation that our present moment requires. . . . It is urgent that the University become the voice of the new politics, and stop being the field of play for old politicians.

The indispensable vindications that we demand are:

a) Investigation of the events of September 30 and punishment of those responsible.
b) The immediate resignation of Secretary of Education, Dr. Averhoff, and his expulsion from the University [where he was a professor] for his responsibility in the tragic events.
c) Expulsion of the present Rector of the University, Dr. Ricardo Martínez Pietro.
d) Immediate demilitarization of all educational centers of the republic.

e) Recognition of the right to form a national federation of all university and national student associations.
f) Participation of the students in the government of the University.
g) Total reinstatement of the students expelled from the University because of the protest of 1927.
h) Absolute autonomy for the University in academic, administrative and economic affairs.[19]

After the publication of the program, the opposition forces grew in size and aggressiveness. Many Cubans, young and old, within and outside the University, had found a martyr in Trejo and a new and radical voice in the Student Directory. Early in November the government prohibited a ceremony to commemorate the death of Trejo. On November 9 the old philosopher Varona once more raised his voice in protest. On November 11 students led violent demonstrations in Pinar del Río, Santa Clara, and several other cities. In Santiago de Cuba they tore down busts of Machado, Governor Barcelo, and Mayor Arnaz. Injuries, killings, and arrests accompanied this wave of national protest.

At the end of November all schools were closed in Cuba; a law was passed punishing even those who "spread false rumors"; several newspapers—including the *Diario de la Marina*, the oldest and most respected of them all—had been forced to suspend publication; and the army was patrolling the streets of the most important cities. In vain the government,

[19] *Diario de la Marina*, Oct. 29, 1930, p. 19. The document was signed by: Carlos Prío Socarrás, Manuel Varona Loredo, Augusto V. Miranda, Jústo Carillo Hernández, José Sergio Velásquez, Raúl Ruiz Hernández, José Morell Romero, Alberto Espinosa Bravo, and Francisco Suarez for the Faculty of Law; Rubén León García, José Leyva, Carlos Guerrero, Fernando López, Fernández, Juan Antonio Rubio Padilla, Rafael Escalona, and Roberto Lago for the Faculty of Medicine; Ramón Miyar, Carlos M. Fuertes, Ramiro Valdes Daussá, Rafael Sardiñas, and Antonio Viego for the Faculty of Letters.

in a belated effort to calm student unrest, offered autonomy to the University and forced the resignation of the rector. The students, emboldened by the national response to their cry of protest, answered by demanding Machado's resignation. On January 4, 1931, the entire membership of the Student Directory was arrested and imprisoned. The moment for compromise had passed: the hour of violence had come

On December 28, 1930, as a further proof that the opposition to Machado was now not only horizontal (over the entire nation), but also vertical (including all classes), the most aristocratic of Cuban clubs, the Havana Yacht Club, was closed by the police on the allegation that it was being used by "conspirators" and enemies of the government.

In spite of the force and extent of the students' actions and protests, at the beginning of 1931 they were neither the leaders of the anti-Machado struggle, nor the government's main concern. Machado was still more alarmed by the maneuvers of the old *caudillos*, Mendieta and Menocal, than by the noisy deprecation of the youth.

For their part Mendieta and Menocal were operating according to the old rules of the Cuban political game. Their tactic seems to have been twofold: to organize a classical military uprising in the *manigua* (Cuban term for the open country), while encouraging all types of actions and rumors to discredit the government; and to exert increasing pressure on the American Embassy to encourage the United States to intervene and unseat Machado, or at least to declare its disapproval of Machado's policies, and thereby weaken and discourage Machado's partisans and force him to reach a compromise with the opposition.[20]

[20] On October 6, Mendieta visited the American Embassy to request application of the "preventive" policy and to invoke the Platt Amendment for the restoration of a constitutional government in

From the beginning, then, there were basic disagreements between the old and the new factions of opposition. Tactically, the younger generation felt that the heroic times of the fight in the *manigua* belonged to a past buried by the development of modern weaponry; they preferred to rely on hit-and-run strikes in the cities, on bombs that began to shatter the tranquility of Havana's nights, on urban terrorism and violence. In terms of objectives, Mendieta, Menocal, and their followers regarded violence as a means to convince the American government of Machado's failure and the need to replace him. For the new groups, even if at the beginning they showed only mild disapproval of the tactics used by the old politicians, one objective of their struggle was to put an end to the Machado regime, as well as to dependency on and submission to the United States. When Mendieta reported to the Nationalists his visit to the American Embassy, the representative for the students declared that they did not approve the position taken toward the American government.[21]

Position of the American Embassy

Caught in the middle of a mounting political crisis, the American Ambassador and his entourage were forced to ponder every word and every gesture. Every declaration or even whisper of the American Embassy (or the American government) was immediately analyzed and used by both the government of Cuba and the opposition. In September 1930,

---

Cuba. The following day Menocal, while lunching with the American Ambassador, "denounced the U.S. Government for its policy of non-intervention" (*Foreign Relations, 1930*, II, 667–668). Throughout this entire period, Menocal always bragged about his contacts and his prestige among soldiers and officers of the Cuban army. Because of that, and for his superior military rank, he assumed the position of being the real leader and spokesman of the opposition.

[21] Interview with Rubio Padilla and Prío.

Chargé d'Affaires Reed complained in a report that exaggerations in the publicity circulated in the United States of every Cuban incident "only serve to exasperate the Cuban authorities and to encourage the Government's enemies to look to the United States for assistance in turning out President Machado." He added that the Nationalists "neither expect nor desire American intervention in the sense of a temporary occupation," but only wanted the American government to put enough pressure on Machado to force a "given course of action," with the hope that this would be more than enough to ruin him politically.[22] Probably as a result of that report, on October 2, 1930, Secretary of State Stimson held a press conference. When asked if the American government would land forces in Cuba in the event of a revolution, he was careful to answer that the American forces had never landed in Cuba when there was any regime in existence, but only when there was no government. Furthermore, he added, these were only the precedents under whose guidance the government would have to act should action become necessary. He said that there was always danger in intimating that the United States would not intervene, for it was possible that a junta might take that as encouragement to revolt. "Every case in the future will be judged on its merits and a situation might exist which would distinguish it from the preceding ones." [23]

The hint was readily accepted in the governmental circles of Cuba as definite proof of American support for Machado. As usual, the government raised the ever present ghost of American intervention. "The irresponsible ones who plan violent struggle are summoning the foreigners," stated Wifredo Fernández. "The hope inspired by the sugar stabilization plan and the growing realization that your policy is not to meddle or

[22] *Foreign Relations, 1930*, II, 657. [23] *Ibid.*, pp. 663–665.

interfere with the affairs of the Cuban Government have created a distinctly better atmosphere here," reported the American Ambassador to the Secretary of State on October 13.[24]

The events of the following weeks forced the Ambassador to change that optimistic outlook. On November 16 he reported that "circumstances had been altered by events of the last few days, and General Menocal undoubtedly has hope of arousing public opinion in the United States to interfere in Cuba." The day before he had recognized the impact of student action: "It seemed at one time as if my good offices would be helpful in arranging a modus vivendi between Government and opposition, *since the latter was in mood for compromise.* The situation changed rapidly, however; the student agitation became critical, public opinion was inflamed." [25]

While the internal conditions in Cuba forced the Ambassador to send gloomy reports, the propaganda of Cuban exiles and the news published in the United States were also affecting American policy toward Cuba. In January 1931, Assistant Secretary of State White reported in a memorandum to Stimson that "Machado is getting more dictatorial every day." [26] Shortly afterward, Stimson called Orestes Ferrara, the Cuban Ambassador in Washington, to express his concern about the events in Cuba, hinting that the continuation of such a situation meant that the Cuban government was unable to fulfill the conditions of the Platt Amendment, and adding finally that the thing that he most wanted to avoid was "a revolution with its concomitant, a possible intervention on our

[24] *Excelsior* (Havana), Oct. 7, 1930, p. 4; *Foreign Relations, 1930,* II, 667.

[25] *Ibid.*, pp. 672, 675 (italics mine).

[26] Memorandum, Jan. 17, 1931, U.S. Department of State Papers (DS/2951), National Archives.

part."[27] This declaration is extremely important, for it expresses two points of cardinal significance in the changing outlook of American diplomacy: a growing concern about Machado's capacity to control the situation, and a desire to find a formula that could simultaneously solve Cuba's political problem and avoid a revolution.

This modification of the American attitude toward Machado's government was immediately detected by the opposition forces and encouraged a more open and definite attack. The principal figures of the government and almost all of the anti-Machado forces waited for Menocal and Mendieta to act. These two had the prestige, the economic resources, and, supposedly, the necessary contacts inside the army. The coup against Machado was to be attempted in their way.

Last Attempt of the Old Guard

While stepping up their propaganda campaign against the government—innumerable leaflets were distributed, rumors of conspiracies and impending insurrections multiplied—the opposition to Machado opened the year 1931 with an intelligent legal battle: three points of unconstitutionality were presented to the Supreme Court with the purpose of establishing the illegal methods of the regime. These charges cleverly focused attention on a great financial blunder of the government. Trying to avoid a decline in revenues, the government on January 29, 1931, issued an Emergency Tax Law by which a series of new taxes were created and several old ones increased. The law was a heavy burden on a society in critical economic condition and provoked immediate resistance and criticism. Furthermore, the law failed in its purpose: in the fiscal year 1930–31, the revenues of the Cuban government were $59,739,000;

[27] *Foreign Relations of the United States, 1931* (Washington, D.C.: U.S. Government Printing Office, 1946), 54

the following year, after the Emergency Tax Law, revenues declined to $46,940,000.[28] By using this unpopular law as a means to call attention to the unconstitutional acts of the regime, the opposition won vast and enthusiastic support among all levels of the population.

To ease the tension, the government offered in May to reduce the terms of all recently elected congressmen from eight years to four, and to appoint a "national cabinet" which would include members of the opposition. At the same time that Machado was adopting a much more conciliatory attitude toward the opposition, he asked the American Ambassador for help in getting an extension of credit for the $20,000,000 debt with the Chase Bank. Politely the Ambassador answered that it would be better "not to broach the matter until the situation developed a little more favorably."[29] The months of April and May passed with a series of fruitless conversations between the government and the opposition in an attempt to reach a compromise. On one side, the most important leaders of Congress refused to accept a shortening of their term, and many of Machado's advisers insisted that a compromise was a demonstration of weakness that would destroy the government. On the other side, Menocal and Mendieta, secure in their popularity and certain that the decisions of the Supreme Court would be in their favor, refused to accept any solution that did not include the immediate resignation of Machado.

On June 30, 1931, the Supreme Court rejected all the arguments presented against the Emergency Tax Law and thus, with one dissenting vote, closed the possibility of shaking the government on unconstitutional grounds. The legal battle ended in defeat for the opposition.

[28] Rolegio Pina Estrada, *Los presupuestos del estado* (Havana: Ministerio de Hacienda, 1936), p. 137.

[29] *Foreign Relations, 1931*, II, 46.

Impatient as usual, the younger members of the opposition increased their demands for action and pressed for a military battle against the government. With no more legal maneuvers available, and with a sort of green light from the American Embassy to act against the government, the old leaders had no recourse but to fight the battle they had been promising from the beginning. In exile in Miami, Menocal promised the students, in the words of Rubio Padilla, that "in less than two months Mendieta, himself, and many other leaders of the War of Independence would be fighting in Cuba, and tyranny would be defeated." [30]

In July, Cuba was seething with rumors of an imminent revolution. Machado sounded extremely confident: "I am not alarmed," he told diplomat Manuel Márquez Sterling, "by the possibility of a revolt. . . . I doubt the force and the success of the revolution if it ever breaks. The peasants do not want or support it, and the Negro, whom I have done so much to dignify, would side with me. The loyalty, discipline and courage of the army are in my opinion beyond doubt. I am ready for any event." [31] Everybody waited for the announced action. In August 1931 the old *caudillos* fought their battle.

The result was a miserable fiasco. Menocal and Mendieta

[30] Interview with Rubio Padilla.

[31] Manuel Márquez Sterling, *Las conferencias del Shoreham* (Mexico City: Ediciones Botas, 1933), p. 123. In view of the events of 1959 in Cuba, and some of Castro's propaganda, these words of Machado, expressing his confidence in the support of the peasants and the colored population, the same sectors which Castro always boasted to have gained for his cause, deserve special attention. At least in 1931 Machado's judgment of the situation was much more accurate than that of the opposition (as we will immediately see); and until 1933 several sectors of the opposition complained that the Cuban colored population was neutral or backing Machado. On the other hand, there were no important peasant uprisings against Machado's government.

went to the open country in what was to be a coordinated movement with certain sectors of the army, a landing of forces in Gibara in Oriente Province, and a rebellion in the navy. The history of this episode—known as Río Verde—is still very confused, but evidently everything went wrong. No one rebelled in the army, the landing in Gibara took place so late it was only an isolated episode, easily controlled by governmental forces, and the navy remained immobile (later one of the captains of the cruiser "Patria" was accused of betraying the plans). On August 14, four days after their rebellion was initiated, Menocal and Mendieta were captured in a swampy area in Pinar del Río Province.[32]

The governmental circles were jubilant. The storm had dissipated after no more than a sprinkle. For several days *El Heraldo de Cuba* ridiculed "the inglorious finale" and the "lack of vision of those who can't really read the signs of our time." Ambassador Guggenheim noticed the change in the President. Before Río Verde, Machado had spoken with the American Ambassador of accepting constitutional reforms and even the possibility of stepping down in September 1932. On September 2, 1931, however, the Ambassador was reporting: "I saw President Machado again . . . after his return from a short holiday. He was in a very aggressive mood and disavowed that he had been in agreement in regard to announcing at this time his intention of retiring in September 1932." Two months later, resuming his usual defiant tone,

[32] A sympathetic, although unclear, account of the events can be read in Alfredo Lima, *La odisea de Río Verde* (Havana: Cultural, 1934). See also Emilio Laurent, "Datos esenciales de la expedición de Gibara," *Bohemia*, Aug. 20, 1934, pp. 24–50. Laurent, Sergio Carbó, and Carlos Hevia were the civilian leaders of the forces landed in Gibera.

Machado announced that he would stay in office until May 20, 1935: "not a minute more or a minute less." [33]

Conversely, with their leaders in prison and their hopes crushed, the opposition—at least the Nationalists and the followers of Menocal—began to soften their tone. After Río Verde, many of the articles that were allowed to be published and meetings with officials of the American Embassy were directed to obtaining amnesty for the prisoners.

But not all forces were affected in the same degree by the failure of Río Verde. The younger groups had had reservations about a triumph that would begin with a rebellion in the *manigua*, and the disaster of Río Verde seemed to prove them right. Furthermore, with Mendieta and Menocal out of the picture, they felt free now to carry out the struggle in their own way and with their own forces. As one of the participants in the events of the period wrote, "When Mendieta and Menocal climbed the gunboat that took them prisoners, the prestige and the dominance of a generation, now broken and defeated, climbed with them." [34]

It was time for the new generation to act.

[33] *Foreign Relations, 1931,* II, 73; *Diario de la Marina,* Dec. 23, 1931, p. 4.

[34] Enrique Fernández, *La razón del 4 de septiembre* (Havana, 1950), p. 21. The author of this pamphlet was Undersecretary of Government and War during the revolutionary government of Grau San Martín in 1933. He wrote this essay in 1934. Many members of the "generation of 1930" consider it one of the most lucid and penetrating analyses of the revolutionary situation of 1933. Fernández was assassinated by Batista's police in 1935, when organizing a general strike against the government. He died at thirty-four.

9 New Tactics and New Programs

In January 1931 the majority of the Student Directory leaders, both the official members of 1930 and the representatives of previous Directories (1927, 1929) who were accepted as permanent members, fell into the hands of the police, who had been looking for them. They were sent to prison, where they remained until March.

In prison, waiting for an amnesty, they devoted as much time as possible to reading and discussing the current political situation. It was then that ideological differences appeared and a political split occurred. A group with definite Marxist tendencies and, perhaps, a higher level of political consciousness broke away from the Directory and founded the Ala Izquierda Estudiantil (Student Left Wing).[1]

Scarcely less dogmatic than the Communists (with whom they maintained close contact), this group represented a further radicalization of the student position. Followers of Mella and of what they considered a true revolutionary doctrine, rhetorical and passionate, they soon had their own publication, *Línea*, and began to criticize other revolutionary groups, including, at times, the Student Directory, as petit-bourgeois and

[1] Some of its more important members were Aureliano Sánchez Arango, Raúl Roa, Piro Pendás, Manolo Guillot, Carlos Martínez, Gabriel Barcelo, Pablo de la Torriente Brau, and José Chelala Aguilera.

"opportunistic." From a theoretical point of view the Student Left Wing accused the Directory of not being really anti-imperialist but only anti-Machadist, for not recognizing that the proletariat and the peasants were the only true revolutionary forces in Cuba, and for trying to form a united front of all the forces in opposition without realizing the reactionary character of many of those forces.[2] On the subject of tactics, the Student Left Wing insisted that students should play the role of allies and not leaders of the proletariat, and that terrorism and direct actions were less important than the education of the masses.[3] Rather ineffectual as social revolutionaries —their "alliance" with workers and peasants remained theoretical—the Student Left Wing participated actively in the struggle against Machado, helped to weaken the Student Directory and, later, augmented the ideological confusion of the revolutionary forces.[4]

[2] See Manifiesto programa del Ala Izquierda Estudiantil," in *Pensamiento crítico*, No. 38 (April 1970), pp. 123–129. The Manifesto was published in January 1931.

[3] Interview with Cárlos Martínez and Piro Pendás; also the declaration of Pedro Vizcaino in *Pensamiento crítico*, No. 38, p. 155; Raúl Roa, "Carta a Jorge Mañach," in *Retorno a la Alborada* (Havana: Imprimex, 1963), pp. 22–38. Some years before, Julio Antonio Mella had outlined the role of "secondary forces" of the students in the revolutionary struggle. He also dismissed, with a certain scorn, the revolutionary importance of rebellious youth: "where serious revolutionary principles are involved, the question of the youth is basically a literary topic. The workers laugh at this question, seeing how many leaders are trying to 'save' them, while collecting a good price for their role" (*La lucha revolucionaria y el imperialismo* [Havana: Editora Popular de Cuba, 1960], pp. 27, 102).

[4] The Student Left Wing was far from a united group with a common program. By 1933 several splits and instances of frictions on theoretical and practical points had scattered many of the original members. Apparently the most debated—and for many, unacceptable —point was that of not joining other groups in the common struggle against Machado.

Prompted, perhaps, by the necessity of discussing and clarifying their own political position and, certainly, by the political vacuum after the failure of Río Verde, the Student Directory increased their radicalism and their anti-government activity. Earlier demands for concrete political reforms (elections, freedom of expression, autonomy for the University) were expanded to encompass "the necessity of radical and total transformation of the social structure of Cuba." Taught by those characters who are the common precipitate of every period of violence (the lumpen revolutionaries), they learned how to make explosives and bombs—noisy and harmless petards thrown in a hurry from a balcony or a roof at first, and later, when the struggle became bitter and merciless, well placed and deadly bombs, which awoke Cuba to an era of terrorism. After 1931, so-called "action groups" multiplied everywhere.

The ABC

While the students were increasing their militancy, an important new political organization was forming. In October 1931, in the office of a well-known lawyer, Dr. Juan Andrés Lliteras, a group that had been meeting there since 1930 to discuss politics decided that the fiasco of Río Verde demanded immediate action. The principal figure of the group was Dr. Joaquín Martínez Saenz. Adopting his plan, they agreed to organize a secret cellular society, terrorist in nature, with the aim of punishing the principal members of Machado's government for their bloody deeds against the opposition. Each cell would be formed of seven members, and each member would be responsible for a new cell of seven members, and so on. Each cell member knew only his own leader and the other six members comprising the cell of which he was the leader. This structure prevented the collapse of the organization whenever the police arrested one or several of its members. The directing cell was known as A, the second level of cells as B, the third level as C, and so on. The entire organization was known as the ABC.[5]

Almost immediately the leaders of the ABC invited some young intellectuals—Jorge Mañach and Francisco Ichaso among them—to join the organization and to write a revolutionary program.

The success of the organization was impressive. Enveloped in an aura of mystery, the ABC expanded rapidly through the island. It appealed to many social sectors, but most of its recruits were young, middle-class people who wanted to act against the government but were unsympathetic to the Student Directory and rejected the ideas and tactics of the Communists and other leftist organizations. On the other hand, its reputation as an underground organization allowed the ABC to be credited with almost every act of violence carried out against the government.[6]

In 1932 the ABC was strong enough to issue its Program Manifesto. Written almost entirely by Mañach, Ichaso, and Martínez Saenz,[7] this program Manifesto was probably the most serious study of Cuba's problems written during this entire revolutionary period. Many of its ideas were later adopted by other groups.

In the spirit of the new revolutionary atmosphere, the docu-

[5] Interview with Dr. Juan Lliteras, Jr., Feb. 22, 1964, in Washington, D.C.

[6] Eduardo Chibás, one of the student leaders, complained later that several terrorist actions of the students were attributed to the ABC; see Jaime Suchlicki, *University Students and Revolution in Cuba, 1920–1968* (Coral Gables, Fla.: University of Miami Press, 1969), p. 29.

[7] Letter from Martínez Saenz to the author, Feb. 16, 1965. The author submitted to him two questionnaires which were answered in two letters dated Jan. 25 and Feb. 16, 1965.

ment began by stating that the purpose of the ABC was "not only to get rid of the present tyrannical regime but also of the causes that had determined its existence." Consequently they announced their intention to fight for new men, new ideas and tactics, reconquest of the land, political liberty, and social justice.[8]

After reviewing the history of the economic, political, and social causes for Cuba's tragic situation, they singled out the most serious one—the economic displacement of Cubans in their own land—and proceeded to offer solutions.

The remedies were not strikingly radical. Quite the contrary, for the ABC took pride in displaying a sober realism:

> It is not a question of mobilizing naïve enthusiasm in favor of a solution for Cuba so extreme as to be illusory. . . . In politics, to look too far away is as dangerous as to look only at the feet. . . . Whether we like it or not, Cuba is a young American republic, without an economy of her own, placed in the economic orbit of the United States. . . . The program of the ABC is far from being a liberal program, and is still less a conservative one. Totally dominated by a principle of economic determinism, and because of many of its recommendations, our program is an avant-garde program. But it does not pretend to go beyond the real possibilities of Cuba. It does not encourage easy illusions, nor does it try to incite one social class against another in a nation where all classes are needy, and where it is urgent to create national union. In short, it does not speak of totally socializing an economy which is still to be conquered.[9]

The remedies offered by the ABC's Program are too numerous to list completely. In the economic field the most significant were the encouragement and protection of small rural

[8] *Doctrina del ABC* (Havana: Publicaciones del Partido ABC, 1942), pp. 3, 30.

[9] *Ibid.*, pp. 30–31.

properties, the gradual destruction of *latifundios* through increasing taxation, the passage of laws to limit the right of companies to own land and the adoption of measures to nationalize land, nationalization of those public services that had created a monopoly; and social legislation for the protection of workers (old-age pensions and insurance, legal protection of labor unions, an eight-hour day, the right to strike, special tribunals for labor disputes).

For political advances the ABC advocated the right of women to vote, autonomy for the University, and the creation of special tribunals to deal with the misuse of public funds. Other proposals, such as substituting for the Senate a "functional chamber" and eliminating the right of illiterates to vote,[10] provoked some criticism and raised accusations of "fascist" and "reactionary" from opponents both in and out of the government. Quoting paragraphs of the program, usually out of context, ABC's enemies tried to present it as a totalitarian and racist organization.[11]

Role of the Communist Party

In the meantime the Communist party continued its struggle to follow the tactics outlined by the Comintern Congress of 1928. Throughout this period the Cuban Communist party seems to have been forced, like its comrades on the continent,

[10] *Ibid.*, p. 33.

[11] It should be mentioned that the ABC explicitly condemned Communism and fascism as "systems that exclude all political liberties" (*ibid.*, p. 35). To the charge of discrimination they answered: "The ABC wants a radical rectification of Cuban life and the Negro is part of our people. . . . The exploitation of the Negro is a result of deep causes which are affecting our entire nation. The ABC does not make distinction between Cubans with white hands and Cubans with black hands. The ABC asks only for Cubans with clean hands" (*Diario de la Marina*, Aug. 2, 1933, p. 10).

to follow a fighting strategy for which it was far from ready. The 12th Congress of the E.C.C.I. (held in Russia in 1932) admitted that in Latin America, as in India, "the development of the revolutionary crisis is retarded primarily by the low degree of organization of the proletariat, and the immaturity of the Communist parties." [12] Nevertheless, these parties were instructed to fight, alone and on their own, simultaneously, American imperialism, fascism, socialism, deviationism, and all "reformist" movements that had appeared on the continent. They were commanded to maintain "under all circumstances their political and organizational independence, fighting to win the masses for their program, systematically criticizing the vacillations and inconsistencies of the petit bourgeois leaders who may be at the head of such movements and waging a merciless struggle against the bourgeois landlords, demagogues, allies of foreign imperialism, who are trying to exploit these movements for counter-revolutionary and fascist ends." [13]

As a result, a small party whose entire membership "could fit in one room" in 1927 [14] refused to cooperate with other revolutionary groups and hurled accusations of "fascist," "lackey of yankee imperialism," and "traitor" in every direction, from Machado down to the ABC and the Student Directory. Anyone who disagreed with this tactic—as did Sandalio Junco, the Cuban delegate to the Congress of Latin American Communist Parties in Buenos Aires in 1929—was expelled from the party as renegade and Trotskyite.

[12] William Simmons, "The Expanding Inter-Imperialist War in South America," *The Communist* (New York), XI (1932), 1081.

[13] O. Rodríguez, "The Growth of the Revolutionary Upsurge in the Caribbean," *ibid.*, p. 722.

[14] Joaquín Ordoqui, quoted in Andrés Suarez, *Cuba: Castroism and Communism, 1959–1966* (Cambridge: M.I.T. Press, 1967), p. 1.

After 1930, the increasing illness of party leader Rubén Martínez Villena (who had tuberculosis) forced him to seek a cure in Russia; his absence facilitated the "proletarization" of the party and opened the way for new leaders like Blas Roca, César Vilar, and Joaquín Ordoqui, who were less intellectual and closer to labor groups. The party expanded its anti-imperialist propaganda and its penetration of worker organizations, repudiated terroristic activities,[15] and concentrated on sudden street demonstrations (*mítines relámpagos*), the organization of the clandestine CNOC (National Confederation of Cuban Workers), and the promotion of general strikes. They were partially successful in organizing one on March 20, 1930, but it lasted only twenty-four hours. They tried again in December 1932, with even less success. Nevertheless, the party propaganda inflated these attempts and exaggerated their influence on the Cuban people. Even Martínez Villena, writing from Russia, was overenthusiastic. He described a situation where the soldiers "refused to shoot at the workers," downgraded the role of the ABC and the students, and placed all hopes on the "revolutionary conscience of the masses":

> Basically politics is concerned with masses. It is not a question of individuals. Basically in Cuba it is a question of oppression and of imperialistic exploitation. When the Cuban masses launch a revolutionary struggle against imperialism, this fact overshadows all others. It is for this reason that the strike in the sugar mills presents the most eloquent reply to the arguments of all the enemies of the Cuban revolution, that is, to all the enemies of the people, from Machado through the theoreticians of the ABC and

[15] *El País* (Havana), Sept. 21, 1933, in an article "Las izquierdas en Cuba," quotes Gretta Palmer, who wrote for the *New York World Telegram* on the "moderation" of the Communists in their anti-Machado struggle. Martínez Villena is reported as saying that the party "never realized terroristic activities in Cuba."

of the bourgeois-landlord opposition all the way to the renegades from the Communist Party.[16]

By deriding "bourgeois nationalism" at the very moment a wave of nationalism was sweeping the island, and by their unrelenting attacks on all political groups fighting against Machado—some of whom had strong anti-imperialist feelings—the Communist party contributed also to the dispersion and confusion of the revolutionary forces, and perhaps missed an opportunity to become the leaders, or at least to be in the vanguard, of a revolutionary movement. In 1935, when the "popular front" approach was adopted by the Comintern, the Cuban Communist party, changing its tactics, tried to approach many revolutionary groups and form a United Front. But by then the situation had changed drastically; the revolutionary government of 1933 had toppled, and Batista held power with a new and firm hand.[17]

Terrorism and Repression

While the ABC, the students, and other groups were stepping up their fight against Machado, and while Menocal and Men-

[16] "The Rise of the Revolutionary Movement in Cuba," *The Communist*, XII (1933), 565.

[17] In 1934, after the downfall of the revolutionary government of Ramón Grau San Martín, the party still insisted that "the fundamental danger lies in the influence of the bourgeois-landlord parties of the 'Left,' and their reformist, anarchist, and Trotskyite agents" ("The Present Situation, Perspectives and Tasks in Cuba," *The Communist*, XIII [1934], 1163). One year later, having been severely criticized by the Comintern, the party proclaimed that it was "ridding itself of the mistaken idea which restricted its initiative, the idea that the proletariat is opposed by one reactionary front composed of all parties from the ABC to the Guiteras group." (Guiteras was a member of the Student Directory and the Grau government and organizer of a group called "Young Cuba.") They also conceded that "the underestimation of the national question which exists in the ranks of the

dieta, freed by the government at the beginning of 1932, hurried to the American Embassy to ask the United States to "settle the chaotic conditions in Cuba,"[18] the government tightened its repressive measures. A special force called "the Porra," placed beyond the control of the army and the police, was organized to combat street demonstrations and to dispose of the enemies of the regime. Censorship of the press became the rule rather than the exception, and on February 17, 1932, a law was passed amending the military code in order to invest the military courts with exclusive jurisdiction over crimes that were thought related to terrorist activities.[19] On June 21, 1932, the Congress authorized the President to suspend constitutional guarantees for two years if necessary. "The apparent purpose of the measure is to serve notice to the opposition that the Machado Government intends to continue to proceed with a strong hand," commented Reed.[20]

The opposition took notice and answered accordingly. While Mendieta was being arrested and sent to prison for conspiracy and Menocal took the road to exile, the famous or infamous Captain Calvo, chief of the so-called *expertos* (the special repressive corps), on July 9, 1932, became the first well-known governmental fatality when he was shot from a passing automobile. Two months before, a lieutenant who had participated in the affair of Artemisa was blown to pieces while opening a present scented with perfume sent by mail. After the death of Calvo, terrorism and brutality became the usual weapons of both government and opposition. Bombs ex-

---

party should be finished with once and for all." See V. Cortes (Blas Roca), "For the United Front in Cuba," *The Communist International*, June 5, 1935, pp. 656–657.

[18] *Foreign Relations of the United States, 1932* (Washington, D.C.: U.S. Government Printing Office, 1948), II, 542.

[19] *Gaceta oficial de la Republica*, Feb. 17, 1932, p. 6.

[20] *Foreign Relations, 1932*, II, 550.

ploded in central places of Havana, killing and injuring many persons; bursts of machine gun fire spread terror in the streets; in many ingenious and terrible ways soldiers, officers, and functionaries received the deadly message of the opposition. On the government's side, homes were searched by the police, prisons were filled with young people, the *ley de fuga* became the common destiny of many prisoners, "shot while trying to escape," and the names of men like Arsenio Ortiz and Captain Ainciart acquired a somber and frightening ring.

As is usual in this kind of struggle, the opposition suffered the more severe losses. It is true that by the end of 1932 every important functionary of the government was forced to live in fear and seclusion, the international press commented on the "terrible" conditions in Cuba, and the opposition to Machado was general and active. But the price paid by the opposition was impressive, and there were no signs of relief.[21]

In September 1932, Clemente Vázquez Bello, the President of the Senate and a close friend of Machado's, was gunned down in his car.[22] The usual wave of brutal repression followed, and among its victims were three brothers who be-

[21] For melodramatic accounts of terrorism in this period, see Carlos Peraza, *Machado: Crímenes y horrores de un régimen* (Havana: Cultural, 1933), and "Los Asesinatos cometidos por el gobierno de Machado," *Bohemia*, Aug. 26, 1934, pp. 139–151. As in the case of every dictatorship, the tales of horror spread by Machado's enemies have to be cautiously studied. Exaggerations and false rumors are common. Hugh Thomas, for example (p. 857), accepts the story of four students thrown into the sea to be eaten by sharks. The story is quite dubious. At least one of those he mentions as devoured by sharks, Manuel Cotoño, was alive and well in Mexico in 1941.

[22] The terrorist plan, simple and brutal, extended beyond this act. They had previously dynamited what was to be his grave site in order to blow up Machado and the cabinet members, as well as all bystanders, when they assisted at the burial. A sudden decision of Bello's widow to have him buried in his native Santa Clara, not in the Havana cemetery, frustrated this barbaric plan.

longed to a very well-known Cuban family, the Freyre de Andrade. In December of that year the Cuban and the international press reported that small bands of revolutionaries were operating in Oriente Province.[23]

At the end of 1932 the government released some prisoners and took steps toward reconciliation with the opposition. The government news organ, *El Heraldo de Cuba*, quoted Juan Gualberto Gómez, a prominent leader of the National Union, as saying there was no reason why the factions that opposed Machado could not try to find a way of talking with the government and solving the crisis. But the principal leaders of the political opposition—Menocal and Mendieta—refused to accept what they considered a maneuver of the government.

The government's attempts and the opposition's response were basically due to the apprehensions and hopes brought about by new factors that had just come into the picture—the victory of Franklin D. Roosevelt in the presidential elections of 1932, and the announcement of a new policy of the United States at home and abroad.

[23] See Charles W. Hackett, "Guerrilla Warfare in Cuba," *Current History*, July 1933. Actually, the only group of relative importance was headed by self-made "captain" Blas Hernández, who with a band of 30 or 40 men managed to evade the persecution of the Rural Guard in Santa Clara Province. After the downfall of Machado, Hernández was killed in the attack against Atarés Fortress in Havana, where he was fighting with the ABC against the revolutionary government.

10 The Mediation of Sumner Welles

In the first months of 1933 a remarkable change could be noted in the Cuban government propaganda. Evidently realizing the growing efforts of its enemies to discredit Machado in the United States and to pressure the Roosevelt administration into taking strong measures against Machado,[1] the government press began to play more and more on the note of "nationalism." Forgetting all about the conciliatory role of Cuba in the Sixth International Conference of American States in 1928 and the declarations of Machado and Ferrara in favor of U.S. intervention, *El Heraldo de Cuba* stressed the point that Machado represented the dignity and the sovereignty of Cuba while, as the newspaper put it, "the opposition in Cuba favors intervention." [2] Each declaration of the Roosevelt administration reaffirming the Good Neighbor Policy and the desire of nonintervention in Latin America was hailed as a triumph for Machado and a setback for his "anti-Cuban" enemies. When

[1] It should be remembered that the "old" leaders wanted only, as Ramiro Guerra put it, for the United States to "exert its moral authority to bring about a just revision of the procedures of governing the island" (Ramiro Guerra y Sánchez *et al.*, *Historia de la nación cubana* [Havana: Editorial de la Nación Cubana, 1952], VIII, 78).

[2] April 9, 1933, p. 1. As we have previously seen, this statement, if applied to the leaders of the "old" opposition—and some of the "new"—was basically true.

in April, Cordell Hull declared that the United States was in favor of respecting the national rights of all Latin American republics, *El Heraldo de Cuba* published a headline typifying its new tactic: "The opposition to the Cuban Government yesterday received a mortal blow. Hull says that he will not intervene. . . ." [3]

In the meantime, the Government of the United States was confronted with quite a dilemma in Cuba. Sumner Welles later expressed part of it when he wrote:

> To President Roosevelt two facts were clear. First, that while the existing treaty with Cuba gave this country the right to intervene, any such intervention would be contrary to the general line of inter-American policy which he had set for himself. Second, that a state of affairs where governmental murder and clandestine assassination had become matters of daily occurrence must be ended.[4]

There were other considerations that Welles did not mention. The economic crisis in Cuba had affected all the American investments on the island, and those affected interests had good connections in the Roosevelt administration. Three members of the "Brain Trust" were officials in the American Molasses Company, which in turn controlled the Sucrest Corporation, a refining company using Cuban sugar.[5] Another inter-American conference had been scheduled for December 1933 in Montevideo and, considering the criticism that the Americans had received in Havana in 1928 because of the policy of intervention, the American government was very eager to avoid any situation in Cuba which would force it to take drastic measures.

[3] April 16, 1933, p. 1.
[4] *The Time for Decision* (New York: Harper, 1944), p. 194.
[5] Robert F. Smith, *The United States and Cuba* (New Haven: Yale University Press, 1961), p. 142.

In April 1933, Sumner Welles, then Assistant Secretary of State, was appointed Ambassador Extraordinary and Plenipotentiary from the United States to Cuba. From the beginning his mission was surrounded by expectation and mystery, and gave rise to rumors among all Cuban groups. The government press, accepting the official interpretation of the U.S. State Department, insisted that the Ambassador basically had a mission to restore good economic relations between Cuba and the United States and that his appointment had no political significance.[6] Behind the façade there was more concern. Government circles did not know Welles (they had been expecting John Cudahy[7]), nor did they have a clear idea of the instructions he had received.[8] Furthermore, in the very month of Welles' appointment a revolutionary junta had been created in exile in the United States which included representatives from all the principal factions of the opposition, from Menocal and Mendieta to the ABC and the students. For the first time since the beginning of the struggle, the opposition could present the semblance of a united front against Machado. The possible influence of this junta on the recently appointed Ambassador was a source of concern to Machado.[9]

[6] Cuban Secretary of State Ferrara, for example, expressed his assurance on April 21 that Welles was a regular ambassador, not a special envoy (*Heraldo de Cuba*, April 21, 1933, p. 1).

[7] *Ibid.*, April 8, p. 1.

[8] See Alberto Lamar Schweyer, *Como cayó el presidente Machado* (Madrid: Espasa-Calpe, 1934), pp. 58–60. The author, a member of Machado's inner clique, wrote his book in exile. He provides a clear insight into the position and actions of the Cuban government at the time.

[9] *Ibid.*, pp. 41–42. The junta was actually formed in March 1933 in Miami, but the first notice of it appeared in the Cuban press in April. It was organized by the Conservatives, headed by General Menocal; the Nationalists of Carlos Mendieta; the Liberals, represented by Miguel Mariano Gómez; the ABC; and the Association of University Professors. The president was an eminent scientist, Dr. Carlos de la

Welles' instructions were both broad and precise. One historian has suggested that the degree of independence enjoyed by Welles was so great that he was allowed to write his own instructions, but subsequent events and Hull's own statements seem to indicate that Welles received fairly specific directions for his conduct from Hull.[10]

These instructions included a brief and remarkably clear analysis of the situation in Cuba: "The conditions, highly unsatisfactory and even alarming as they may be, do not constitute a just basis for the formal action of the Government of the United States looking towards intervention." The instructions covered four areas: (1) The following suggestions that the Ambassador was to present to the President of Cuba were to be considered as friendly advice and expressions of concern. (2) The Cuban Government should realize that it was essential to take measures to avoid terrorism and especially excesses by the armed forces of the republic. (3) The United States government desired to offer its services as mediator between Machado and the opposition, the chief objective being "the negotiation of a definite, detailed and binding understanding" between those forces that "will lead to a truce in the present dangerous political agitation . . . until such time as national elections can be held in Cuba." (4) It was "the earnest desire of the Government of the United States to assist

---

Torre. The Student Directory and some other organizations, like the OCRE (Organización Celular Revolucionaria), had observers, but did not form part of the junta.

10 See Bryce Wood, *The Making of the Good Neighbor Policy* (New York: Columbia University Press, 1961), p. 59. As will be seen later, one of the main reasons for the confusion of the Cuban government was its idea that Sumner Welles was exceeding his instructions. Cordell Hull affirms in his *The Memoirs of Cordell Hull* (New York: Macmillan, 1948), I, 313, that he was the author of Welles' instructions.

in every feasible manner in the consideration of measures intended to ameliorate the distressing economic situation now existing in the Republic of Cuba." [11]

According to the letter of those instructions, and probably also according to their spirit, Welles' mission was eessentially to gain a truce in the political struggle until a legal government could be elected, while trying to find remedies for Cuban economic conditions. But apparently the Ambassador was not a man to be confined by instructions. Perhaps his direct access to the White House or his own character or both gave him a remarkable independence and decisiveness.

Sumner Welles arrived in Havana on May 8, 1933. On May 11 he presented his credentials to Machado and three days later he reported to his government: "If the present acute bitterness of feeling against the President persists or becomes intensified . . . it would in all probability be highly desirable that the present chief executive be replaced, at least during the electoral period." This represented a departure from the initial plan, which said nothing about replacing Machado. As if concerned with this and other innovations that he was about to make, the Ambassador ended his report by saying: "It will be this policy that I shall attempt to carry out unless I am instructed to the contrary. I beg to request that a copy of this telegram be sent to the President for his information." [12]

The Ambassador's expanded policy was implemented swiftly. By May 22 he was already reporting on his contacts with the leaders of the opposition and his hopes for their cooperation.[13] Once assured on that point, the Ambassador decided to make his formal proposal of mediation to the Cuban President. But first he added another element to his strategy—economic

[11] *Foreign Relations of the United States, 1933* (Washington, D.C.: U.S. Government Printing Office, 1952), V, 283, 284–285.
[12] *Ibid.*, p. 290. [13] *Ibid.*, p. 292.

pressure. "It is obvious to my mind that no accommodations or concessions, financial or economic, should be made to the Cuban Government until a positive understanding is had as to the course the President will be willing to pursue." [14] So, apparently, even before making any proposal to Machado, the Ambassador was leaning toward an anti-Machado stand, and was willing to exceed his instructions and put pressure on the Cuban government to force it to accept a mediation that according to the general interpretation of both factions, government and opposition, was inevitably going to work against Machado.

The attitude of the Ambassador—his immediate and friendly contacts with opposition groups, especially with the leaders of the ABC—produced an open split in the ranks of Machado's enemies. Almost all of them, after making strong declarations against American intervention, accepted the mediation of the Ambassador.[15] Only the Student Directory (which hesitated for two days), Menocal, and the Ala Izquierda Estudiantil refused to accept it, with the argument that it was a new form of American control.[16] The Communists, of course, condemned the Ambassador and those who condoned his intervention, as "enemies of Cuba and lackeys of Yankee imperialism." Significantly enough, for the first time in its history the

[14] *Ibid.*, p. 296.

[15] The OCRE, for example, proclaimed in New York on May 28 "its refusal to accept the intervention of any foreign ambassador in the solution of Cuban problems" (*La Prensa* [New York], May 28, 1933, p. 2). A month later the OCRE was participating in the mediation.

[16] Student Directory members in Cuba were willing to accept Welles' mediation, but a stern telegram sent by those in exile decided them against it (interview with Carlos Prío Socarrás and Rubio Padilla). This point was corroborated by some of those who were in Cuba (interview with Felipe Pazos and Jústo Carillo, Feb. 12, 1965, in Washington, D.C.).

government press printed the arguments of Communist leader Martínez Villena, who denounced the "false opposition and the lackeys of Wall Street." [17] Even within the ABC, acceptance was not general. In open protest against the decision of the leaders, a group split and formed the ABC Radical, which condemned the interference of the American Ambassador.

Nevertheless, with the support of the most representative forces of the opposition, on June 2, 1933, Sumner Welles offered his good offices to President Machado.[18] At the same time he was taking steps to avoid any interference from those who, like Menocal, had not accepted his mediation and were still talking of armed insurrection.[19]

Machado's position was very difficult. Raised on the conviction that American lives and properties in Cuba were "sacred," and that American support was essential to any president who wished to remain in power, he had gone to every extreme to gain and maintain that support. From siding with the United States on every point of the agenda during the Sixth International Conference of American States, to continuing to pay the foreign debt when Cuban people were starving, Machado had shown an unswerving loyalty to American interests, and he was, as he himself recognized later, "blind" to the possibility of an American Ambassador working against him.[20] On the other hand, it was clear to everyone in the

[17] *Heraldo de Cuba,* May 10, 1933, p. 1.

[18] *Foreign Relations, 1933,* V, 299.

[19] Welles asked several times that measures be taken to stop the sending of weapons from the United States to Cuba. See, for example, his report of June 6, *ibid.,* p. 304.

[20] *New York Post,* May 25, 1934, p. 3. When Manuel Márquez Sterling resigned as Cuban Ambassador to Mexico in September 1932, he accused the government of following "a ruinous economic policy" by insisting on paying the foreign debt; see *La Prensa,* Sept. 14, 1932, p. 3.

"I must be judged in the light of these convictions, shared by the government that to accept the mediation was to present an appearance of weakness and encouragement to the opposition. But an open refusal was a direct challenge to the United States which Machado was far from willing to make. With Welles' assurances that his only intention was to seek a "constitutional" solution, the best road seemed to be, as Rafael Guas Inclán later reported, "to accept the mediation while maintaining open all possibilities of maneuver." [21]

A balanced study of the governmental press of those critical days, of the opinions Machado expressed later, and of the statements of persons who were deeply involved in the events seems, then, to sustain the thesis that, when confronted with the mediation of Sumner Welles, Machado based his conduct on the two fundamental assumptions, first, that he could not afford a direct confrontation with the American Ambassador, and second, that, no matter what the appearances, the American government was basically friendly and willing to support him, as it always had. Consequently, when Welles began to show a pro-opposition attitude, Machado believed that it was due to Welles' personal decision rather than to the policy of the American government.

So the offer of mediation was gracefully accepted the very day it was made. But the Ambassador's request was only the first of many. Slowly but steadily, Welles pushed the government toward other concessions: reform of the constitution, restoration of the vice-presidency, relaxation and eventual abolition of press censorship, guarantees for those who were

---

majority of Cubans," wrote Machado after his downfall; see "Fugitive Tells His Own Story," *New York Post*, May 24, 1934, p. 3. The *Post* ran a series of five articles, from May 22 to May 26, in which Machado gave his version of the downfall of his government.

[21] Interview with him in Miami, Aug. 15, 1967. Guas Inclán was at the time President of the Chamber of Representatives.

in exile or taking part in the mediation, and freedom for political prisoners. Machado yielded to almost all of these demands. Lee McBain, of Columbia University, was invited by the government to come to Cuba and assist in the reform of the electoral code; and the President began to issue a series of decrees dealing with the other requests. As a result, the press began to write with more freedom, and several groups of anti-Machadistas returned to Cuba.

After the ABC, the OCRE, the Nationalists, the Women in Opposition, the University Professors, and the High School Professors had officially accepted the mediation and nominated their delegates, Machado designated three representatives of the political parties that supported his government to represent it in the mediation. On July 1, 1933, in an atmosphere of expectation, the first meeting of all the delegates took place in the American Embassy. The Ambassador read a message from President Roosevelt to both groups which ended: "The representatives of all factions may rest assured that the moral support of the American people will be behind these attempts at the peaceable adjustment of Cuban problems through the orderly procedure of constitutional government." [22] The reference to "constitutional government" was not altogether pleasant to the opposition, but the Ambassador was enthusiastic. It was true, as he reported to his government, that the opposition had already split into two sectors, the radicals and the conservatives, but he added:

In the former category is of course the ABC. Fortunately, however, the representatives of that organization are both intelligent and well-disposed. . . . [so] I am happy to state that there is very evident on both sides not only a conciliatory disposition

[22] Telegram, June 21, 1933, U.S. Department of State Papers (DS/3556), National Archives.

but an apparent feeling of expectancy that these negotiations will have a successful outcome.

So optimistic was his report that on July 7, Acting Secretary of State Phillips asked Welles: "Could you give me any idea how much longer you feel that, in justice to the work which you are now doing, you should remain in Havana?" [23]

But the optimism was short-lived. The mediation, as a political instrument to solve the Cuban crisis, had little chance of success. Its failure may be attributed to three factors which were present from the beginning.

First, Machado was not a man to yield easily or completely to pressure. He had retreated to a degree, he had accepted some conditions, but he was playing for time, seeking any opportunity to paralyze or destroy the mediation. Long before him, under similar but less favorable circumstances, Zayas had won against Enoch Crowder. From Ferrara to Wifredo Fernández, all members of his government were convinced that a break would eventually come to allow Machado to survive the crisis.[24]

Second, the factions that took part in the mediation were, with the exception of the ABC and the National Union, representative of minor groups or disorganized forces. Some of these groups, like the Women in Opposition, had been formed hastily and specifically to participate in the mediation and, consequently, had no real popular support. For their part, the ABC and the National Union were separated by a deep ideological and generational chasm. The ABC was supposedly a revolutionary organism with a far-reaching program; Cosme de la Torriente, the representative of the National Union, had, according to Welles, expressed himself as "positively op-

[23] *Foreign Relations, 1933,* V, 317.
[24] Interview with Guas Inclán in Miami.

posed to revolution."[25] The ABC had condemned the entire political past of Cuba and was thinking in terms of a new constitution with radical changes; Cosme de la Torriente had repeatedly stated that his party was in favor of a "return to the Constitution of 1901."[26]

Third, in addition to these internal difficulties, the mediation effort had to face the angry criticism of those opposition groups who had not accepted it and who, raising the banner of radical nationalism, condemned those who participated in it for yielding to Yankee imperialism.

Why, then, did the ABC, the only truly new political and supposedly revolutionary faction at the conferences, accept the mediation? Basically, because the leadership was more realistic than revolutionary, more pragmatic than radical. Having accepted the unavoidable fact of the American presence in Cuba, and fearing worse measures if the crisis deepened, they proclaimed "their anti-interventionist position," and at the same time their "willingness to tolerate North American help only in order to replace the present government." As Martínez Saenz expressed it: "We tried to follow the pragmatic policy of doing what each circumstance allowed us to do. The ABC used every opportunity to act, within the margin of its possibilities, for the integral renovation of Cuba." On the other hand, they had strong doubts about the capacity of the opposition to overthrow Machado. The mediation was, thus, the lesser of the evils, "a formula of transit to restore normality and to provide the atmosphere for carrying out the basic programs of reform."[27]

[25] *Foreign Relations, 1933,* V, 295.

[26] *Diario de la Marina,* July 2, 1933, p. 3.

[27] *Denuncia,* May 10, 1933, front page; letter from Martínez Saenz to the author, April 26, 1966; *Diario de la Marina,* July 5, 1933, p. 1. "Without the mediation," wrote Carlos Saladrigas later, "Machado would still be in power" (*El País,* Oct. 21, 1933, p. 12). Mar-

Their arguments were valid and reasonable, but not unanswerable. In their first public manifesto, the ABC Radical, the group that had broken from the party because of the mediation, retorted:

> By saying that with this act we have avoided intervention we are only recognizing that intervention. We have only spared Cuba the landing of the marines, but a simple menace has forced us to accept the responsibility for acts dictated by others, and has made us look as if we are freely accepting what in reality is an imposition.[28]

At the conference table, the opposition sectors felt that, since the mediation was the creation and responsibility of the Ambassador, and since his prestige was involved, they could threaten him with their withdrawal from the talks every time the government refused or delayed some concession. On July 10 the ABC refused to continue to participate in the talks because the government would not free an ABC member in whose house a cache of weapons had been discovered by the police. Immediately the Ambassador visited Machado and obtained the prisoner's release.[29] On July 17 both the ABC and the Women in Opposition announced their intention to withdraw unless a law of amnesty was passed freeing all political prisoners. Once more the Ambassador put pressure on Machado, adding this time that full constitutional guarantees should be re-established in the province of Havana.

---

tínez Saenz expressed himself in similar terms in a letter in *Alma Mater*, Dec. 15, 1933, front page.

[28] Quoted in Enrique Fernández, *La razón del 4 de septiembre* (Havana, 1950), p. 31. Fernández' own judgment was harsher: "The Mediation betrayed every revolutionary aspiration and ideal . . . it divided and confused the revolutionary groups . . . it was treason against Cuba. . . . The Mediation was the Río Verde of the ABC" (*ibid.*, pp. 31–33).

[29] *Foreign Relations, 1933*, V, 321.

Machado was already reaching his limit. Apparently the Cuban Ambassador in Washington, Oscar B. Cintas, had informed Machado several times that Welles was exceeding his powers [30] and that the Cuban President could fight back. So the President, knowing the weakness of the opposition as represented in the mediation and believing that the position of the Ambassador was not quite firm, decided to resist. He had already agreed that the opposition could study a project for the reform of the Constitution, but when on July 21 the Ambassador insisted on the restitution of guarantees in Havana, the President answered in a stern tone: "The re-establishment of the guarantees is a prerogative of the President of Cuba and will be done when the President considers it necessary." [31] It was the beginning of a formal crisis in the mediation.

The moment of truth came five days later. According to Welles' reports, it took him by surprise. On July 26 the government approved a law giving general amnesty to all prisoners. The law had been constantly demanded by the opposition, but its provisions were so general that it included members of the police, the army, and the "Porra." Various sectors of the opposition, headed by the Women in Opposition, proclaimed their dissatisfaction and called for the immediate suspension of talks. The following day President Machado paid an unexpected visit to the Congress and, in an atmosphere rife with tension, proclaimed:

> The mediation of Mr. Welles cannot damage our sovereignty, because it is a result of his spontaneous desire and not of any instructions received from the Government of the United States. If it had been otherwise, I would never have accepted it.[32]

[30] Lamar Schweyer, p. 105; *Foreign Relations, 1933*, V, 334.
[31] Lamar Schweyer, p. 106.
[32] *Diario de la Marina*, July 27, 1933, p. 1.

The President reiterated that he would remain in office until May 20, 1935. On July 27, Welles reported the event to the State Department and added:

If an appropriate opportunity is presented to comment on President Machado's speech it would be helpful if the Department would state that while of course my tender of good offices has been spontaneous as stated by President Machado, it could not have been made other than with full authorization of my Government.[33]

Although the talks continued, for all practical purposes the mediation was dead. It was now a struggle between Sumner Welles and President Machado, a battle fought with all kinds of diplomatic and nondiplomatic weapons in Havana and in Washington. On August 4 the Liberal party delegates asked the Ambassador to suspend the mediation negotiations, while almost at the same time the Cuban Ambassador in Washington increased his complaints about the attitude of Welles. The reaction of the American Ambassador was to widen his contacts with the opposition groups and with members of the army, and to spread word of impending disaster for Cuba if a drastic decision was not made: more than once, to high members of the Cuban government, the Ambassador spoke of "the necessity of intervention." [34] At the same time, Welles repeatedly asked for a formal declaration of support from the Secretary of State.[35] At times the tone of his demand sounded desperate. When Machado reassured the Senators and Representatives that Welles' plans had no support from Roosevelt—and the

[33] *Foreign Relations, 1933,* V, 330.

[34] See, for example, Orestes Ferrara, "La misión de Welles," *Politica, V* (March 1942), 76, and the testimony of Guas Inclán, and of Machado himself in the *New York Post* articles.

[35] See his telegram of Aug. 7 in *Foreign Relations, 1933,* V, 336.

absence of any public statement backing the Ambassador seemed to show that Cuban Ambassador Cintas was not entirely wrong—Welles sent another urgent cable to Secretary of State Hull: "I understand that you are seeing Cintas at noon tomorrow. I beg that you inform him that I am acting in every detail with your fullest authorization and approval." [36] The rest of the telegram concerned the necessity of telling Cintas that the attitude the Ambassador had adopted, including the threat of direct intervention, was not a bluff.

Actually the Ambassador's position had changed from that of a "friendly mediator" to one openly demanding Machado's resignation, a form of ultimatum that President Machado was resisting, convinced as he was that Roosevelt would never order the landing of troops in Cuba. And even after a meeting between Ambassador Cintas and President Roosevelt, in which the latter indirectly supported his Ambassador's demands for Machado's resignation and hailed it as "a noble act," [37] it seems as if the diplomatic battle was not entirely won by Sumner Welles. On August 11, Cordell Hull wrote to the American Ambassador in Cuba:

> Out of the mass of information which has been sent to the United States from Cuba, some misapprehension has arisen as to what you are doing, and there has been some adverse comment, both here and in Latin America, that the United States is attempting to coerce rather than to persuade.[38]

More pressing still for Welles was the warning to him that Cordell Hull in his coming press conference was going to clarify that "it was a mistake to speak of a 'Welles plan,' as the plan under discussion is a Cuban plan, agreed upon by Cubans and put forward by yourself on their behalf." [39]

Fortunately for the Ambassador, at the very moment in

[36] *Ibid.*, pp. 339–340. [37] *Ibid.*, p. 348. [38] *Ibid.*, p. 354.

[39] *Ibid.* A factor to keep in mind when studying this confrontation

which the mediation faltered and these misapprehensions were expressed, a decisive factor had appeared in the picture, a factor which, even if unforeseen by the Ambassador and the majority of the opposition leaders, was going to give them the opportunity for a final victory over Machado.

---

of interests and personalities is that the relations between Cordell Hull and Sumner Welles were, according to many testimonies, less than cordial. For example: "It was not always easy to work with Cordell Hull. Men like Assistant Secretary Moley and Under Secretary Welles never quite succeeded. . . . [Hull] preferred shirtsleeves and old friends to morning coats and suave diplomats" (E. Wilder Spaulding, *Ambassadors Ordinary and Extraordinary* [Washington, D.C.: Public Affairs Press, 1961], p. 252).

II
The Downfall of Machado

While the mediation evolved into open warfare between Machado and Sumner Welles, and the different factions of the opposition were clarifying their positions in that battle, a minor event occurred in Havana which would in a few days become the most powerful weapon of the opposition. On July 25, 1933, exasperated by a tax imposed on omnibus fares by the Mayor of Havana, José Izquierdo, and by the Mayor's order that every omnibus was to obtain gasoline only at the garages of the Sinclair Oil Company, with which he had an agreement, the workers of several unions of bus drivers declared a strike.[1] Apparently, the Communists moved in to help the strikers swiftly and efficiently; their two most experienced men were Rubén Martínez Villena, who had just returned from Russia, extremely ill with tuberculosis, and César Vilar. On August 1, because of a clash between police and workers, according to some,[2] or because of a pact between the workers

[1] The complete history of the general strike is still uncertain. In addition to the published sources I have used materials from interviews with César Vilar (Havana, July 6, 1959) and Eusebio Mujal (Washington, D.C., Feb. 2–3, 1963). Both played important roles in labor struggles in Cuba. Mujal, a former Communist, was later the Secretary-General of the CTC (Confederation of Cuban Workers). The author has received two memorandums from labor leaders who were involved in the strike but who prefer to remain anonymous.

[2] Charles A. Thompson, "The Cuban Revolution: Reform and Reaction," *Foreign Policy Reports*, XI (Jan. 1, 1936), 254.

and Frank Steinhart, the owner of the Havana Electric Railway Company, who was anti-Machado,[3] the streetcar workers joined in the strike, followed quickly by stevedores and newspaper employees. On August 4 the strike had become general and the capital was nearly paralyzed.

Sumner Welles was so involved in his political campaign against Machado that he seems at the beginning not to have realized the implications of the strike. In fact, when he first mentions it in his reports, he attributes it to probable government complicity aimed at stopping the mediation.[4] Certain sectors of the opposition, especially the ABC, seem also to have regarded the strike as a menace to the mediation, and tried to stop it.[5]

But if the Ambassador did not realize the importance of the strike, Machado did. Interrupting a fishing trip, he issued strict orders to the police to avoid any clash with the workers, and called the Communist leaders of the CNOC (National Confederation of Cuban Workers) to an urgent meeting. He offered them legal recognition and official support if they agreed to call off the strike. Possibly dazzled by this sudden opportunity to assume power, or interpreting the situation according to the party's own propaganda—if Machado's enemies were as reactionary as the dictator, why not profit from the government's weakness to advance the cause of the proletariat

[3] César Vilar was supposedly present at the meeting.

[4] *Foreign Relations of the United States, 1933* (Washington, D.C.: U.S. Government Printing Office, 1952), V, 335. It is possible that there was some truth, at least initially, in Welles' judgment. On August 2, *Diario de la Marina* pointed out the danger of the strike and accused the authorities "because they not only did not stop the movement at its beginning but have let it expand dangerously." This attitude of the government could also be attributed to the desire of avoiding any clash with the workers.

[5] See Antonio Penichet, "La tragedia íntima de la huelga que derrocó a Machado," *Bohemia*, Aug. 26, 1936, pp. 58, 142.

and the Communists?—the most influential leaders of the party resolved to accept the offer. But it was not easy to convince the workers. To avoid further discussions, Martínez Villena and Vilar referred the final decision to the Central Committee of the Communist party in Cuba. Even there they met opposition. The representatives of the Third International advised the Cuban members to reject any deal with Machado and to continue the strike until the government collapsed. Deriding them as "Abecedarios" (members of the ABC), Villena denied them the right to vote on an internal affair of the Cuban Communist party, and blended passionate dialectic with stern disciplinary methods to obtain a favorable decision. When the Secretary-General of the party, Jorge Vivó, insisted on the right of the delegates of the Third International to vote, Martínez Villena demanded and obtained his immediate demotion. The Committee then decided to accept Machado's offer and to call off the strike.[6]

For once the Communist leaders had completely misjudged the tension of the moment and the will of the masses. They were accused of "treason" by Sandalio Junco, Marcos García Villarreal, and other leaders of labor organizations, and even the rank and file resisted the order to return to work.[7] But be-

[6] For these events, see "Entrevista con Blas Castillo," *in Pensamiento crítico*, No. 38 (April 1970), pp. 197–199. Blas Castillo is a veteran Communist who was present at these meetings. Hugh Thomas seems to believe that the pact between Machado and the Communists took place after the sugar strike and after weeks of discussion (*Cuba, the Pursuit of Freedom* [New York: Harper & Row, 1971], p. 605). Actually the events of the August strike took the Communists by surprise, the decisions were taken on the march, and the pact with Machado did not last more than seventy-two hours.

[7] In 1934, the CNOC recognized its mistake and the negative effect it had among the workers. According to their explanation, the anarchist tendencies that had survived inside the group blinded the leadership to the real implications of the general strike. See "El movi-

fore the matter could be decided, an underground radio station controlled by the ABC Radical announced that Machado had resigned and called the people to a public demonstration. In spite of an immediate denial by the official radio station, a mob surged into the streets and tried to march toward the Presidential Palace. They were met by police fire. When the demonstration ended, about twenty persons had been killed by the police and several others injured.

This massacre changed the political situation. It was then, according to Lamar Schweyer, that Machado and his followers realized that they could not win,[8] that Ambassador Welles now had a strong weapon to back his argument for Machado's resignation. It was also then that all maneuvers to stop the strike failed; rather, the strike extended now to almost every sector of Cuba. By August 9 the whole island was

---

miento obrero de 1925 a 1933," in *Pensamiento crítico*, pp. 193–194. The Cuban Communist party similarly declared in 1934: "As yet the Party has not completely liquidated the opportunistic and anarcho-syndicalist influences which were in evidence during the general strike of August and which blinded our Central Committee to the perspective that the general strike opened up the road toward the agrarian anti-imperialist revolution and to the overthrow of Machado" (*The Communist*, XIII [1934], 885). Analyzing the weakness of the Cuban Communist press of that period, a Russian, P. Bijowsky, was more blunt in his comments: "A serious political mistake in the paper [the Cuban Communist organ] is that it did not carry on an explanatory campaign regarding the opportunist mistake made by the Central Committee of the Communist Party of Cuba at the time of the development of the August struggles against Machado. At that time the C.C. considered that armed struggle against Machado would lead directly to imperialist intervention, and that the proletariat in Cuba was not ready for this struggle, and so called on the workers to stop the general strike at a time when it had already grown into a spontaneous armed insurrection" (*The Communist International* [New York], April 5, 1934, p. 260).

[8] Alberto Lamar Schweyer, *Como cayó el presidente Machado* (Madrid: Espasa-Calpe, 1934), p. 140.

affected. On August 10, in an effort to appeal to nationalism, the Conservative party followed Machado's suggestion and adopted a resolution supporting the mediation but condemning "foreign intervention" and denying that it had ever "asked the President to shorten his period of office by one minute." [9]

The following day Sumner Welles, his position strengthened by the general strike, by the impact of the massacre, and probably by the assurance of an anti-Machado stand from several high-ranking officers of the army,[10] presented his plan to President Machado: (1) an immediate leave of absence for Machado; (2) the immediate resignation of all his Cabinet, with the exception of General Herrera, who would then become head of the government (according to the Cuban Constitution one member of the Cabinet could substitute for the President, and Herrera seemed capable of controlling the army); and (3) the acceptance of this proposal as if it were on the initiative of the Cuban President.[11]

This last point indicates both the skill and the position of the American Ambassador. He was forcing Machado out—according to the President, Welles threatened him with "drastic actions" if the plan were not accepted—but he was keeping to the end the appearance of a neutral mediator. The dialogue between the Ambassador and the Secretary of State Orestes Ferrara, as quoted by Machado, deserves recording:

[9] The complete text is in *ibid.*, pp. 156–157.

[10] Mario Riera Hernández in *Histórico obrero cubano, 1574–1965* (Miami: Rema Press, 1965), p. 83, contends that Welles, through the American Military Attaché Gomperlick, had been inciting the officers to rebel since July. The contact of the Ambassador with the rebellious officers and their quick acceptance of his suggestions seem to verify that assertion. Lamar Schweyer, p. 172, and Machado himself in the *New York Post* articles, also mention the participation of the Ambassador.

[11] *Foreign Relations, 1933*, V, 355.

Ferrara: Then you are laying down an ultimatum and threatening intervention to remove a president elected at the polls?

Welles: Who is speaking of an ultimatum?

Ferrara: Then President Machado may remain in office?

Welles: No, his withdrawal is indispensable.[12]

In the meantime, an anti-Machado conspiracy that was taking shape in the army was forced into the open. When General Herrera, who had been invited to participate in the conspiracy, tried to disarm the officers involved, they answered by taking possession of certain military barracks and proclaiming a rebellion against the government. Knowing that the backing of the army was essential, Machado, who never lacked physical courage, went on the morning of August 12 to visit the Columbia Military Barracks to assess the situation in the army. There a group of officers, headed by Colonels Julio Sanguily and Erasmo Delgado, Brigadier Lora, and Captain Mario Torres Menier, informed him that to save Cuba from intervention he should resign.[13] Deprived of united support from his basic source of power, the President accepted the inevitable and went back to the Presidential Palace to execute the plan of Sumner Welles.

By then, the rebellious officers had changed their minds. In spite of General Herrera's unwillingness to join their conspiracy, they had accepted him as the proposed President *ad interim*, but now, facing a mounting national crisis, they began to feel that Herrera had been too close to Machado to guarantee stability and, much more essential, too close to save the army from the accusation of "Machadism." Fully aware that

[12] *New York Post*, May 25, 1934, p. 4.

[13] For these events see the detailed account of retired Colonel Horacio Ferrer, one of the conspirators: "El General Herrera, al traicionar al ejército, precipitó la caida de Machado," *Diario de la Marina*, Aug. 23, 1933, p. 4.

they had only administered the *coup de grâce* to a collapsing regime, the rebellious officers began eagerly to display their patriotic nationalism [14] and to insist on a "clean" figure to act as provisional President. Sumner Welles then proposed Carlos Manuel de Céspedes, who had been Cuban Ambassador in Washington and Paris, and was, according to Welles, "a most sincere friend of the United States." [15] The officers and the representatives of the opposition who had taken part in the mediation accepted the proposition. That afternoon Machado asked for a leave of absence, and his entire Cabinet resigned, with the exception of Céspedes, who had been hastily designated Secretary of State. Machado then took a plane for Nassau in the Bahamas. Céspedes became President.

So finally the battle had ended. It was, apparently, a complete victory for Ambassador Welles. Machado had been ousted, a revolution had been avoided, the substitution of power had followed a constitutional pattern, and the new

[14] Lt. Col. Erasmo Delgado and Capt. Torres Menier went so far as to declare that they "believed that the intention of President Machado was to provoke the intervention [of the Americans], and we decided to avoid it at any cost" (*Diario de la Marina*, Aug. 13, 1933, p. 2). This desire to escape any share in Machado's crimes was to prove disastrous for the new officers of the army. Hesitating to take any action to impose their authority, they allowed disorder to grow among the troops. The sergeant's revolt of Sept. 4, 1933, was to be the result.

[15] *Foreign Relations, 1933*, V, 359. Cosme de la Torriente suggests in his book, *Cuarenta años de mi vida* (Havana: Editorial Siglo XX, 1939), p. 318, that Céspedes had been selected by the principal factions of the opposition. I tend to believe the more common opinion that Welles, who as early as 1920 had suggested Céspedes as a possible provisional president, was the one who made the selection. Colonel Ferrer declared that "the Ambassador, much before August 11, had suggested the candidacy of Dr. Carlos Manuel de Céspedes"—a declaration, by the way, which seems to confirm that Welles had previous contacts with the rebellious officers (*Diario de la Marina*, Aug. 23, 1933, p. 4).

President was a good friend of the United States. While cheering Cubans went out into the streets to celebrate—and also to take revenge on the lives and property of well-known Machadistas—the Ambassador sent an exultant report to Washington. Remembering the apprehensions of Cordell Hull, whose message had been received the preceding day, Sumner Welles took pains to stress that "the solution which has now been elaborated and which I have every confidence will be acceptable to the enormous majority of the Cuban people has been worked out solely by the Cubans themselves and represents in my judgment the expression of the volition of nearly the totality of the Cuban people." [16] That night the Ambassador received a telegram which frankly stated: "The President and Secretary have asked me to express their warm congratulations to you and their appreciation *of what you have done*." [17]

[16] *Foreign Relations, 1933,* V, 359.
[17] *Ibid.,* p. 360 (italics mine).

12 Failure of the Provisional Government, August 12—September 4, 1933

As was natural after so long a struggle, the atmosphere in Cuba after August 12 was marked by flare-ups and violence. Captain Ainciart and many other hated members of Machado's armed forces were tortured and killed in the streets, houses were burned, statues were demolished. A flow of exiles poured into the island, exalting their own participation in the fight and calling for "revolutionary reforms." Labor began to reorganize and to present demands. The air was charged with radicalism.

Welles could not quite understand this attitude. For him everything had been solved and the struggle had ended. Knowing better than anyone else how the provisional government had been established, he found these revolutionary gestures unwarranted: "They are taking the attitude that a triumphant revolution has placed the Government in power and that they are consequently entitled to dictate the policies of the Government."[1] Apparently the Ambassador was forgetting that the returning exiles, the majority of whom belonged to student groups, had been fighting against Machado

[1] *Foreign Relations of the United States, 1933* (Washington, D.C.: U.S. Government Printing Office, 1952), V, 366.

long before he arrived as a mediator and that many of them had been imprisoned and persecuted for their cause. He did not seem to recall that some of them had not accepted the policies of a government which was born from a political maneuver they had rejected. Possibly he did not know that in June 1933 *Alma Mater*, the official organ of the students, had said:

No, Mr. Sumner Welles, Cuban students don't sell their souls to the Devil: they don't want the mediation. We have begun a duel to the death which cannot be stopped at the first drop of blood. . . . The American State Department has never "mediated" in any nation to truly protect the rights of men. . . . Forget about us, Mr. Welles, and organize your mediation without us, the youth, for we are not willing to be accomplices in a pact with crime.[2]

In such circumstances what was needed was an energetic government which could work with speed and show that old grievances were going to be corrected and a new justice was on its way. Instead, in the middle of a revolutionary situation, the government of Céspedes looked anything but revolutionary. The provisional President of the Republic was a man unknown to the Cuban people, and he lacked the presence, oratory, and decisiveness to cope with the difficult moment. The rest of his cabinet, with the exception of those who were members of the ABC, belonged in the same category. The Secretary of War and the Navy, at a time when the restoration of discipline in the army demanded a strong hand, was Demetrio Castillo Pokorny, a mild man, a retired diplomat who had participated in the Honest Cabinet that Crowder had imposed on Zayas in 1922. The Secretary of Communica-

[2] Quoted in Julio César Fernández, *En defensa de la revolución* (Havana: n.p., 1936), pp. 99–103.

tions was Dr. Nicasio Silveiro of the OCRR (a fragment of the OCRE that had split over the mediation), a gentleman with no political or truly revolutionary experience. The only known qualification of the Secretary of Agriculture was his friendship with Miguel Mariano Gómez. It was natural that the people jokingly called this group "el gabinete de las sombras" (the cabinet of shadows).

Only the members of the ABC could have given Céspedes' government the revolutionary momentum it urgently needed, but the ABC failed in this first test of its political capability. They made one of the most dangerous mistakes any revolutionary group can make—to participate in a government over which they did not have complete control. The leaders of the ABC had acknowledged this need for control when, on August 13, the Ambassador had invited them to take part in the provisional government; they demanded four secretaryships: *Gobernación* (Interior), *Hacienda* (Treasury), *Agricultura* (Agriculture), and *Guerra y Marina* (War and Navy). They thought that with these four positions, which controlled the armed forces, the police, the national budget, and the agrarian administration, they could push their revolutionary program and carry out quickly the measures that were needed. According to the testimony of some of the leaders, the Ambassador agreed to grant them four ministries. But when they were called to Céspedes' home at 2:00 A.M. on August 14, the provisional president was already announcing his cabinet, and only two positions were given to the ABC: Secretary of Justice (Carlos Saladrigas) and Secretary of the Treasury (Martínez Saenz). The three members of the ABC that were there—Saladrigas, Martínez Saenz, and Lliteras—hesitated. They realized how dangerously weak their position would be. Finally Saladrigas urged them to accept. As a result, the most powerful of the political organizations that had participated in the mediation, the only representative of the new generation, became a minor factor in a weak government.[3]

Another factor that hindered the efficiency of the ABC was a growing friction between Martínez Saenz, the leader of the party, and Carlos Saladrigas, the second in command. This antagonism paralyzed many decisions and provoked an open crisis in the party in November 1933, after the downfall of Céspedes' government.

Of course, it would not be fair to the ABC to saddle it with responsibility for the failure of the Céspedes government. In fact, it is doubtful that the provisional government could have survived, even with full control. The problems were enormous. But there is no doubt that a certain passivity in making decisions along with a lack of energy and leadership on the part of the government precipitated the final crisis. Céspedes and Sumner Welles seem to have believed that by maintaining the appearance of normality, normality would be restored.[4] And so while the press and the radio were clamoring for reforms and, above all, for the elimination of persons and institutions that had survived from the Machado regime, the Provisional President was sworn in before the Supreme Court (the same Supreme Court that had rejected all legal arguments against Machado). The President retained the Congress and left the majority of positions in the bureaucracy and in the

[3] The report of these events was given to me in an interview with Dr. Lliteras, and confirmed personally by Dr. Martínez Saenz. Furthermore, in their declaration of November 3, 1934, the ABC indirectly recognized the mistake by saying: "The Government [Céspedes' government] without proper tools had to act as arbiter without authority and power." See *Doctrina del ABC* (Havana: Publicaciones del Partido ABC, 1942, p. 65). Jorge Mañach stressed that "the ABC never had control of the armed forces; if it had, we probably wouldn't be as we are now" (*El País*, Oct. 16, 1933, p. 2).

[4] On August 20 Welles declared to the press: "For Cuba the essential thing now is to keep public order," (*El País*, front page).

army untouched. To the man in the street, jobless and impatient, it looked as though the government of Céspedes were doing nothing to solve the basic problems of Cuba.[5]

The weakness of the government was conspicuous in a very dangerous area—discipline of the army. As we have seen, the army's role in the ouster of Machado had provoked a deep crisis. Many of the officers who remained in their positions had been loyal to Machado to the end; others had acted too late to save themselves from being accused of being Machadistas. On the other hand, the soldiers were in the streets and had fraternized with the people. The moral authority of the officers was thus undermined, and most of them were unwilling to give orders or to take any step that might provoke a hostile reaction. To solve the problem, the government recalled to active service several retired officers and appointed them members of a special military court, which was entrusted with the task of purging the Machadistas. But these officers, the most distinguished of whom was Colonel Horacio Ferrer, although free from the imputation of collaboration with the dictator, lacked contact with or prestige among the troops. To make matters worse, the only officer with true authority, Colonel Julio Sanguily, became gravely ill and had to be hospitalized. Communists, members of the Student Directory, the ABC Radical, the Student Left Wing, General Menocal, and others tried to incite officers against the government by spreading rumors about reduction in salaries and new regulations governing promotions.[6]

[5] On August 15, the Cuban press was reporting that "there are reasons to believe that the spectacular flight of Machado was made with the cooperation of high officers of the new regime" (*Diario de la Marina*, front page). In that same issue (last page) Raúl Maestri stated, "the worst enemy of revolution is inertia."

[6] Ricardo Adam y Silva, *La gran mentira* (Havana: Editorial Lex, 1947), p. 163, on the crisis in the army; also Eduardo Suarez Rivas,

On August 24, Sumner Welles, who a few days before had suggested to his superiors that he should be recalled and Jefferson Caffery appointed in his place, spoke with dismay about a "general process of disintegration" that was going on in Cuba.[7] That same day the Student Directory issued their Manifesto-Program to the Cuban people.

The Program was a severe denunciation of the provisional government, the ABC, and the whole political power structure. It began by accusing the groups in power of a triple treason: (*a*) to the Revolution by sanctioning the illegal prerevolutionary political structure, (*b*) to Cuba by openly admitting that her people were incapable of determining their nation's destiny, (*c*) to Latin America by approving Yankee meddling and penetration. The Student Directory then appealed to all Cubans to fight for a true revolutionary program and offered their own as the only possible one. It contained these basic points:

1) Liquidation of all political groups and forces that had helped Machado's tyranny.

2) Establishment of a provisional government whose members would be selected by the Student Directory and whose urgent objectives would be:

a) restoration of order and individual rights,

b) punishment of criminals and those responsible for Machado's dictatorship,

c) freedom of expression,

d) promulgation of a constitution that would be re-

Un pueblo crucificado (Miami, 1964), p. 45; and interview with Prío, Padilla, and Jústo Carrillo. The revolutionary groups approached basically young officers; Menocal tried his influence among senior officers (R. Hart Phillips, *Cuba: Island of Paradox* [New York: McDowell, 1959], pp. 62–63).

[7] *Foreign Relations, 1933,* V, 367, 371.

sponsive to the new needs and aspirations of the Cuban people,

e) the holding of elections in two years, to give the nation a truly representative government,

f) establishment of a basis for agrarian reform, and initiation of the study of basic institutions for a national economy,

g) a thorough housecleaning in all branches of the administration,

h) autonomy for the University and educational reforms,

i) social reforms demanded by public opinion, and

j) a new diplomacy with cultural goals.

3) Politically, this government should proceed to:

a) make a new electoral law,

b) grant all citizens the right to vote at eighteen,

c) grant women the right to vote, and

d) encourage the free formation of political parties, with the exception of the three (Liberal, Conservative, and Popular) which had cooperated with Machado.

4) Provision for reforms:

a) only Cuban citizens would be permitted to own more than five *caballerias* of land; [8]

b) a progressive tax would be levied on the rent of owners of land in excess of five *caballerias;*

c) individually owned land would be limited to 100 *caballerias;*

d) land would be expropriated and distributed; and

e) the right of Tanteo would be reserved for the state in every acquisition of land. (The so-called "right of Tanteo" meant that the state had the right to buy any land at the same price that was established by the owner at the time of sale. It was a legal method by which the state could avoid a traditional system of taxes or the payment of debts, through the selling

[8] A *caballeria* has 33 acres.

of large portions of land to another company or a subsidiary at very low prices.)

The Program also devoted full attention (twelve articles) to social legislation and educational problems, and ended with a passionate appeal to all Cubans, especially to the army, to adopt a true revolutionary attitude and fight for a new Cuba, free from latifundism, oppression, and "friendly" intervention.[9]

Only then, after losing two weeks and creating the impression that it had been prompted into action by the Student Directory, did the provisional government of Céspedes decide to move: it abolished the Constitutional reform of 1928, declared the legal termination of Machado's presidential term, and called general elections for February 24, 1934. The ABC, according to its members, pressed for more reforms, among them nullification of Machado's Amnesty Law and confiscation of all property belonging to the members of his government.[10]

But they never had the time to implement these reforms. Already on August 26, 1933, a so-called "Junta de los Ocho," formed by dissatisfied sergeants, began to meet in the enlisted men's club at the Columbia military barracks. The result was the formation of the Columbia Military Union. The program

[9] The Program was signed by Carlos Prío Socarrás, Manuel A. de Varona, Augusto V. Miranda, Jústo Carrillo, Raúl Ruíz, José Morell Romero, Sara del Llano Clavijo, Rubén de León, José Leyva, Rafael Escalona, Juan António Rubio Padilla, Roberto Lago Pereda, Carlos Guerrero, Fernando López, Clara Luz Durán; Ramiro Valdes Daussá, José A. Viego, Inés Segura Bustamante, Silvia Martel Bracho (*Directorio estudiantil al pueblo de Cuba* [Havana: Imprenta Marta Abreu, 1933]).

[10] Decrees that would make these reforms into law were ready to be signed when the government of Céspedes was toppled, according to the ABC; see "El ABC ante la crisis cubana" in *Doctrina del ABC*, p. 264.

of this junta aimed at organizing the lower ranks of the army in order to obtain better conditions and better opportunities for promotion. Soon, realizing the disorganization and weakness of the high-ranking officers, they began to plot a general insurrection.[11]

At the same time the Student Directory, the Ala Izquierda Estudiantil, and the ABC Radical were stepping up their activities against what *Alma Mater* repeatedly called "the government of Mr. Welles." [12] Early in September 1933 while the Céspedes government was confronted with internal discord between the ABC and the other groups and was making some feeble attempts to speed up certain reforms, two general movements of opposition were taking form, one military and one civilian. There was no real communication between them, but by a sort of natural gravitation they were ready to work in a common effort against the provisional government.

It is a curious fact that one of the members of the Columbia Military Union, Sergeant Fulgencio Batista, was a member of the ABC.[13] Apparently, Batista tried to establish contact with Martínez Saenz and other leaders of the party to ask their support in an attempt to overthrow Céspedes. But because of their antimilitaristic principles,[14] or perhaps because they did not realize the importance of the movement, Martínez Saenz and his friends turned down the offer. The sergeants, then, had

[11] The junta was formed by Sergeants Pablo Rodríguez, Fulgencio Batista, Eleuterio Pedraza, and others, and joined later by Lieutenants Manuel Benítez and Francisco Tabernilla. All of them later reached high positions in the army. See Aristides Sosa de Quesada, *4 de Septiembre de 1933* (Havana: P. Fernández, 1938), pp. 43–46, 58.

[12] *Alma Mater*, Aug. 26, 1933, p. 1.

[13] Batista confirmed this seldom-mentioned affiliation when he declared that he "no longer belonged to the ABC" (*El País*, Oct. 21, 1933, p. 1). He probably joined after the downfall of Machado.

[14] This is the reason given by Martínez Saenz in his letter to the author of April 26, 1966.

no recourse but to act on their own and accept the backing of whoever came to their support.

The sergeants' coup took place on September 4, 1933. The high-ranking officers were so demoralized and disorganized that the insurrection met with almost no resistance. Proclaiming that they were acting "for the improvement and just vindication of the soldiers of the Cuban Army," in a matter of hours the sergeants were in full control of Columbia headquarters and most of the other military barracks of the capital. Immediately they established contact with other garrisons in the interior of the republic, which quickly joined the rebellion.[15]

As soon as they learned of the revolt, several leaders of the Student Directory rushed to the Columbia barracks. The first to arrive were José Leyva, Ramiro Valdes Daussá, Juan António Rubio Padilla, Carlos Prío Socarrás, Rubén de León, and Jústo Carrillo. They joined the sergeants and talked them into widening the movement. Because of their action, a military rebellion inside the army was transformed into a general movement against the government of Céspedes and everything it represented. In the words of Enrique Fernández: "They transformed an insubordination into a revolution."[16] They were also accepting the historical responsibility of backing open intervention of the army in a political struggle.

[15] *El País*, Sept. 5, 1933, p. 4. Apparently the sergeants were prompted into action by the rumors of a conspiracy of senior officers who, backed by Menocal, were plotting to overthrow Céspedes. See Phillips, pp. 88–89, and Batista's statement in the *New York Times*, Oct. 14, 1934, p. 3. According to Dr. Juan de Moya, who was then the liaison between the ABC and the Student Directory in Santiago de Cuba, in that city the revolt of the sergeants occurred simultaneously with, and independently from, the events in Havana.

[16] Fernández, p. 40. Many of the members of the Student Directory had spent the night in a secluded place, where they were trying José Soler Lezama for treason—and finally executed him.

A Revolutionary Junta was formed immediately in Columbia, a proclamation was issued to the nation, and, following Uruguay's example, a Pentarchy (government with five members) was announced.[17] At 1:00 P.M. on September 5, 1933, President Céspedes was informed of the movement and of his deposition. With his Cabinet he abandoned the Presidential Palace at once. That very day the popular newspaper *La Semana* printed a headline that rapidly became the symbol of the movement: "Paso a la Auténtica Revolución" (Open the way for the authentic revolution). The provisional government had ceased to exist.

[17] The idea of a collective executive to correct the abuses of power of a "strong" president had been explained and defended at the University by Dr. Arturo Mañas, a distinguished Cuban professor and lawyer, whose theory had deeply impressed the students (interview with Felipe Pazos, Washington, D.C., Dec. 6, 1969).

13 The Revolutionary Government

Significance of the Movement

On assuming political power, the Revolutionary Junta issued a proclamation:

The revolutionary group of Cuba composed of enlisted men of the army and the navy and of civilians belonging to various sectors headed by the University students' group declares:

First, that it has constituted itself in order to carry out, in full, the revolutionary program for which the great majority of the Cuban people are striving and will continue to strive within the bounds of modern democracy and based purely on the principles of national sovereignty.

Second, this program in brief is as follows:

1) Economic reconstruction of the national and political organization on the basis of a constitutional convention to be held immediately.
2) Immediate elimination and full punishment of all those responsible for the previous situation. . . .
3) Strict recognition of the debts and obligations contracted by the republic.
4) Immediate constitution of adequate courts to insist upon the responsibilities above mentioned.
5) Reorganization . . . of all services and national activities, achieving a rapid return to normality.
6) Finally, the execution of all the measures not foreseen in this document necessary to begin the march toward the

> creation of a new Cuba founded upon an immovable foundation of justice and of the most modern concept of democracy.[1]

The proclamation was signed by Sergeant Fulgencio Batista as "Revolutionary Chief of all Armed Forces of the Republic," by several members of the Student Directory including Carlos Prío Socarrás, Rubio Padilla, and Jústo Carrillo, and by the members of the newly appointed Pentarchy: Dr. Ramón Grau San Martín, Sergio Carbó, Porfirio Franca, Guillermo Portela, and José Irisarri.

The coup of September 4 inspired various currents of enthusiasm, nationalism, hope, and fear. Everyone realized that a radical step had been taken and that the future held both opportunities and dangers. In the midst of the initial exhilaration, an ominous note was sounded. On September 7, the Cuban press published an impressive list of American warships which, headed by the dreadnought "Mississippi," were supposedly on their way to Cuba.

To understand the events that followed, the ups and downs of this new revolutionary period, it should be remembered that the group which was now in power—more accurately, the group that was trying to obtain power—did not represent a political party or even a well-structured organization like the ABC; the students, for example, fell into the contradiction of proclaiming themselves "nonpolitical" at the very moment they were assuming political power. The power behind the Pentarchy was basically a heterogeneous alliance of several factions which, by a sudden turn of events, found themselves bound together by common revolutionary ideals, by their natural desire to enjoy power, or by the force of circumstances. One of the members of the Pentarchy, for example,

[1] *El País*, Sept. 5, 1933, p. 1.

whose name was proposed and approved because it gave a certain respectability to the new government, banker Porfirio Franca, never took office or even appeared at the meetings. Others, like Portela and Irisarri, had accepted the responsibility of power reluctantly and were ready to resign at any moment.[2] Some factions that joined the movement in enthusiastic approval of the "authentic revolution," like the ABC Radical, had their own programs and objectives and would take independent roads as soon as they felt excluded from the important government positions.

The two most important elements in the new government, the Student Directory and the army, were participating for very different reasons. For the students this was the opportunity to apply all the ideas of reform and revolution that had been developing since they began their fight in 1927. They were a bunch of boys, eager to act, impatient for radical reforms, but without clear and concrete political ideas or

[2] The career of a man like José Miguel Irisarri, which spanned the years from this revolutionary period to Castro's government, can serve to illustrate the vicissitudes of recent Cuban political history. A distinguished lawyer, Irisarri was imprisoned in 1931 because he protested certain political frauds. Impressed by his political knowledge and his radicalism, the students turned to him for guidance. After his release in 1932, he wrote their Program-Manifesto (1933), stressing anti-imperialism and agrarian reforms, and became a member of the Pentarchy. But Irisarri always shunned the spotlight. After his resignation he continued to work in the Department of Agriculture of the revolutionary government. When that government toppled, he joined Antonio Guiteras' Young Cuba organization to fight against Batista. When Batista was properly elected president in 1940 and many political groups including the Communists decided to cooperate with him, he became Minister of Finance in Batista's cabinet. Afterward he occupied administrative positions of the second rank during the government of Carlos Prío Socarrás and Batista. At the time of his death he held a minor position in the National Bank and was working, as silently and hard as ever, for Castro's government.

even a common ideological background. They all shared a profound feeling of nationalism, a general desire to wipe out all the evils of the past and build a new Cuba, but they had not worked out any clear programs for destruction and reconstruction. Consequently, disagreement and divisions were to appear almost immediately.

The sergeants represented quite a different position. They were of humble origin and had no strong political ideas or convictions. Men that until recently were obeying orders now commanded entire provinces or enjoyed high positions in the army. Their basic concern was to remain there, to cling to their authority and their newly acquired power. They spoke of revolution, of national programs and objectives, but they were ready to crush ruthlessly anyone or anything that might endanger their position, be it the antirevolutionary forces they had just deposed or their radical allies, the students. Their recognized chief was Batista, by far the most intelligent and politically minded of them all; but, at least at the beginning, his authority was based more on partnership than on personal power. As one analyst of the situation has explained it, the army was now divided into a kind of feudal zone system under several leaders. "To be obeyed, Batista had to guarantee others their freedom to command." [3] Furthermore, the discipline of the army had received another blow with the sergeants' revolt. For a time, the authority of the self-promoted colonels and captains depended upon a precarious factor—the willingness of the soldiers to obey.[4]

[3] Carlos González Palacios, *Revolución y seudo-revolución en Cuba* (Havana: Editorial Lex, 1946), pp. 78–79.

[4] One episode illustrates the lack of discipline in the army. On September 23 Batista ordered a truck of food sent to the former army officers who were surrounded where they were concentrated in the National Hotel. When the truck arrived, in spite of Batista's written instructions, the soldiers refused to let it pass. When one corporal

The initial dichotomy between the students and the army, plus the fragmentation within each group, gave the revolutionary government the appearance of chaos, disorganization, and lack of central authority. During almost this entire revolutionary period, when no one seemed to be capable of commanding real obedience, the question that was repeatedly asked in all sectors eventually appeared in *El Mundo* (September 23): "Who is ruling Cuba?"

Nevertheless, a government that, according to the American Ambassador, could not last more than a few days, stayed in power for more than four months, carried out the most radical and profound process of transformation in the history of the republic, and established the basis for the political forces that ruled Cuba for the next twenty years.[5]

The best explanation for the popularity of this revolutionary government, for its capacity to survive, for its deep impact on all aspects of Cuban life, is that its principal leaders —Grau, Guiteras, and certain members of the Student Directory—instinctively understood the almost universal desire of the Cuban people. For a brief historical moment they were the hope and the symbol of the forces of nationalism, patriotism, and reform that had begun to appear in Cuba as early as the first cry of protest of the Thirteen in 1923. For four months they were, in the words of Ortega y Gasset, "the interpreters of history."

On September 10, 1933, a cartoon appeared in *La Semana* and was reproduced and posted in almost every Cuban town.

---

ordered a soldier to obey, the soldier answered: "If you come closer, corporal, I'll shoot you." The truck returned unloaded to the barracks. See *El Mundo*, Sept. 23, 1933, p. xxi.

[5] Of the figures who emerged from this period, Batista ruled Cuba from 1934 to 1944, followed by Grau San Martín (1944–1948), Carlos Prío Socarrás (1948–1952), and Batista again until 1959.

It accurately expressed the new sense of dignity and real independence that Cubans were enjoying. It pictured an American tourist looking at a high pole with the Cuban flag flying on top. The tourist was asking a Cuban, "How come your flag is smaller now?" The Cuban answered, "It's not smaller, Mister, it's just that it's flying higher!"

A Strange Triumvirate

After three convulsive days, in which the Student Directory and the other revolutionary factions tried to reach an understanding with the ABC and with the other political forces displaced by the revolt of September 4,[6] the inability of the Pentarchy to act decisively was so evident that the students decided to adopt the presidential formula. The majority of them supported Ramón Grau San Martín, a well-known physician who had opposed Machado from the beginning (he was the only professor who voted against conferring on Machado the title of Doctor in Honoris Causa in 1926), who had suffered imprisonment and exile, and who had acted with the students on every occasion, before and during the Pentarchy. Taking a more moderate position, the other three members of the Pentarchy (excluding Porfirio Franca, who never appeared) defended the idea that the provisional president should be a nonpolitical figure who could receive the support of the students, the army, and the rest of the political forces that had been with Céspedes and were now moving toward opposition. On the night of Sep-

[6] On September 5 the ABC issued a proclamation "declining all responsibility for the revolt" and assuming an attitude of "expectant vigilance." On September 7 its representatives, Lliteras and Martínez Saenz, together with delegates of Menocal and the National Union, had a meeting with the students, but no agreement was reached. See *Doctrina del ABC* (Havana: Publicaciones del Partido ABC, 1942), pp. 259–262.

tember 8, the Student Directory decided to give a vote of confidence to the four Pentarchs to select the man; their only condition was that he should not be a representative of the old order.[7]

The next day one of the students, Rubio Padilla, learned accidentally that the Pentarchs planned to meet in the Presidential Palace to choose Gustavo Cuervo Rubio as president. Cuervo Rubio was a respected physician considered by many to be nonpolitical, but some members of the Student Directory knew of his close relations with Menocal. Another urgent meeting was convened, and while the members of the Pentarchy were deliberating on the third floor of the Presidential Palace, the Student Directory met in a turbulent assembly on the second floor. The Directory now had more than thirty members, since it had decided to let all those who had ever been members of the body participate in the sessions. A commission composed of Rubén de León, Rubio Padilla, and Carlos Prío went up to inform the Pentarchs that they were no longer Pentarchs and did not have the right to select the president. The Student Directory, on its own authority, appointed Ramón Grau San Martín as the head of the revolutionary government.[8]

With the disappearance of the Pentarchy, Grau and the students proceeded to select the revolutionary cabinet: José Barquin, a public accountant known for his honesty, as Secretary of the Treasury; Carlos Finlay, son of the physician who

[7] Eduardo Chibás, "Ramón Grau San Martín" in *Bohemia*, 30th anniversary special issue, 1938, pp. 62, 63, 94.

[8] Juan António Rubio Padilla, "Como nació y fué asesinada la comisión ejecutiva," *Bohemia*, Sept. 30, 1934, pp. 46–47. Dr. Rubio Padilla and Dr. Prío Socarrás gave the author a full account of the events in the interviews cited earlier. José (Pepelín) Leyva also offers the same version in *Pensamiento crítico*, No. 38 (April 1970), pp. 207–208.

had helped discover the cause of yellow fever, as Secretary of Sanitation; Eduardo Chibás, the father of the student leader, as Secretary of Public Works; and Dr. Antonio Guiteras Holmes, a former member of the Student Directory, as Secretary of Agriculture and Commerce. Two members of this government were to emerge as the centers of power, the ones who would carry on the fight for a revolutionary program: President Grau San Martín and Antonio Guiteras. With them, but following an independent course, ex-Sergeant, now Colonel, Fulgencio Batista completed the strange triumvirate, the dramatis personae around whom events and decisions were to revolve.

Under an outward appearance of very gentle manners Ramón Grau San Martín hid a strong character and the capacity to make decisions and keep them. He also had a dramatic instinct for the right gesture, a political consciousness of being on stage. On September 10, when he was to be sworn in as President of the Republic, the members of the Supreme Court gathered in the Presidential Palace to administer his oath. At the last moment, Grau decided to disregard the old magistrates and take the oath on the balcony, in front of the populace, who, as he proclaimed, constitute "the real basis of our power." Leaving the embarrassed functionaries behind, he went to the balcony, where amid the cheers of the multitude he swore "to fulfill the program of the Revolution." [9] From then on he never hesitated to take the course he considered best, no matter what the consequences. A distinguished physician and University professor, Grau seems to have had few definite political convictions, but once he sided with the students and became a revolutionary leader he fought bravely—and with considerable opportunism—to

[9] *El País*, Sept. 10, 1933, p. 1. Also G. Rodríguez Morejón, *Grau San Martîn* (Havana: Ediciones el Mirador, 1944), pp. 67–68.

keep that public image. For him the three basic characteristics of the revolutionary program were nationalism, socialism (non-Marxist), and anti-imperialism.[10]

Antonio Guiteras Holmes was quite a different person. Born of a middle-class family, he had been involved in political struggles since his high school days.[11] He studied pharmacy at the University of Havana and was a member of the Student Directory of 1927. Expelled because of the student protest of 1927, he became a salesman of medical products and traveled throughout the island. In 1931 he was implicated in the Río Verde affair. In 1932 he organized an attack on a military barracks in San Luis (Oriente Province). Captured by the army, he was sentenced to eight years in prison. Then freed by the general amnesty of 1933, he was attempting to organize a conspiracy against the Céspedes government when the sergeants' revolt of September 4 occurred. In Oriente he heard the news of his appointment as Secretary in the new government, and rushed back to Havana. He was 27.

Guiteras was a man of extraordinary courage, laconic, idealistic, and determined, but his political ideas, like those of most of his fellow revolutionaries, are hard to classify or define. According to some members of the Student Left Wing, Guiteras was impressed by Marxist and Trotskyite ideas. According to others, he accepted only anti-imperialism from Marxism.[12] A true revolutionary to the end, he was

[10] See Ramón Grau San Martín, *La revolución cubana ante América* (Mexico City: Ediciones del PRCA, 1936), p. 104.

[11] According to his close friend Túlio Díaz Rivera, who sent me a memorandum on the subject, when Guiteras was studying in the High School Institute of Pinar del Río, he was already actively participating in anti-Zayas and nationalistic demonstrations and strikes.

[12] Interviews with Porfirio Pendas, Washington, D.C., May 12, 1967, and with Carlos Martínez, Washington, D.C., Feb. 12, 1968. Both men were founders of the Student Left Wing.

fervently nationalistic, radical, and convinced of the necessity of cutting deep into the economic and political structure of Cuba. For him, imperialism was the root of all evils. He wrote later:

> Our program could not simply stop with the principle of non-intervention. It had to go to the root of our evils: economic imperialism. . . . For us that struggle, together with the growing belligerency of the proletariat, was in reality the Revolution.[13]

These two men, backed by an ever-diminishing group of students, were the architects of this revolutionary movement. Together with Prío, Padilla, Rubén de León, and a few others who remained to the end, they fought for their ideas until the last moment of the revolutionary government. Grau was the symbol, Guiteras was the force and the soul of the struggle.

Fulgencio Batista y Zaldívar was another type of character. A man of obscure origins (there are even doubts that he was born in Cuba), he was, as a sergeant-stenographer, better informed about the internal situation of the army than the other members of the triumvirate. At the same time he was better-read than his fellow sergeants, and when he found himself on the crest of a turbulent period, he knew how to make the most of his possibilities. Contrary to a common belief, he was not the organizer of the military coup of the sergeants. But Pablo Rodríguez, the real organizer of the group, and the other sergeants needed a man with oratorical skill to move the soldiers to action. That was Batista's opportunity. Before the other sergeants realized it, he had moved swiftly from spokesman of the group to leader.[14] As soon as

[13] "Septembrismo," *Bohemia*, April 1, 1934, pp. 30–32.

[14] Ricardo Adam y Silva, *La gran mentira* (Havana: Editorial Lex, 1947), p. 171. Also the apologetic book of Edmund A. Chester, *A Sergeant Named Batista* (New York: Henry Holt, 1954), p. 61.

he gained national status, his companions had to remain in the shadows of his figure. Astute, alert, free from any ideological ballast, he opened all his senses to the changing political atmosphere. Surrounded by new and old politicians who were more cultivated than he, confused by a deluge of doctrines and programs he could not fully grasp, heading an unruly and unreliable army, he depended for survival on his capacity to detect rapidly which was the most powerful current and which the most propitious moment for changing his course. He listened to everybody, reassured all forces, appraised friends and enemies, and was always ready to jump in any direction, depending on the circumstances. Pablo de la Torriente Brau, a member of the Student Left Wing and a bitter opponent, paid Batista this reluctant homage:

> If we deny his personal courage, we can't deny his other qualities for leadership. He has the imagination of a stenographer, that is, a capacity to quickly interpret a confusing sign, a senseless paragraph or, if applied to politics, a difficult situation. On the other hand, he has the attributes of a demagogue: he is a good speaker, a man of projects, he knows the secret of the smile and the handshake. He constructs, steals, and improves himself. . . . No doubt he is facing a difficult situation, but we should not forget that in Cuba today he is perhaps the man with the best political skills, that he knows how to solve problems, and that when measuring his forces he never forgets to also measure those of his enemies.[15]

Distrusted from the beginning by many revolutionaries, especially by Guiteras, who saw in him a potential and dan-

[15] Pablo de la Torriente Brau, "Algebra and Politics," a letter to Raúl Roa dated June 13, 1936, published in *Islas*, April–June 1968, pp. 243–244. This letter, an intelligent analysis of Cuban political factors, contains also this remarkable insight on Batista's character: "He belongs to that category of men who, in case of a revolution and if given enough time, would have a plane ready to fly"—exactly what Batista did 22 years later, in December 1958.

gerous enemy, Batista maneuvered swiftly to establish his authority in the army, while looking everywhere for less turbulent and more manageable political allies. He also knew how to bide his time.

Increasing Radicalism

Quickly and firmly, but with no apparent method, the revolutionary government began to display its program of national reforms. On September 10, Grau announced the abrogation of the Platt Amendment; on September 20, Decree No. 1693 established the eight-hour day for workers. That same day, Decree 1703 required all professionals (lawyers, physicians, architects, and so on) to become members of their respective professional organizations in order to continue practicing. On October 2, the Department of Labor was created; seven days later Decree 2059 proclaimed the autonomy of the University of Havana. (On January 2, 1934, a new decree providing free registration for low-income students opened the University to all social classes.) On October 18, Decree 2232 declared illegal the importation of workers from Haiti and Jamaica, and orders were given to begin deportation of those workers who had been brought in illegally. On November 18, the Decree for the Nationalization of Work (2583) made it obligatory for at least 50 per cent of employees in all industry and commerce to be Cubans.

In a deluge of decrees, the government created the first *colonos* association, granted the peasants permanent rights to the land they were occupying, announced the beginning of a program of land distribution, reduced the interest on loans and penalized usurers, dissolved all political parties that had cooperated with Machado, gave women the right to vote, and reduced electrical rates by 40 per cent. From labor to commerce, from peasants to teachers, all sectors of Cuban society felt the impact of the new legislation. Under the slogan

"Cuba for the Cubans," the government was trying, as President Grau put it, to "liquidate the colonial structure that has survived in Cuba since independence." [16]

It was not an easy task. Deprived of any real propaganda media through which to explain and defend its measures, without time to clarify or deny the wave of alarming rumors that was sweeping the island, proclaiming its honest revolutionary intentions in a general chorus of revolutionary stridency,[17] the government found that each new law produced confusion, expectation, and polemics. Naturally, the economic sectors were the most alarmed over the speedy transformation of the political and social structure. As early as September 18 the Cuban Economic Corporations, in a manifesto addressed to President Grau, expressed their deep concern with the impact of so many laws and projected laws on the economic stability of Cuba.[18] According to them, the government needed to study and analyze each law more seriously before passing it. The Student Directory's answer was typical and simple: support the revolutionary government because it represents the best possibility for social justice and economic expansion in Cuba.[19]

On the other hand some labor movements, many of them

[16] *Diario de la Marina*, Dec. 7, 1933, front page. For the laws of the revolutionary government, see José Enrique Sandoval, *Indice cronológico de la legislación social cubana* (Havana: Rambla, Bouza, 1935); Carlos Hevia, "Leyes económicas del gobierno revolucionario," in *Bohemia*, Aug. 19, 1934; Rodríguez Morejón, pp. 3–7; and Grau San Martín, "El nacionalismo auténtico y sus leyes," *Bohemia*, Aug. 26, 1934.

[17] Only the newspaper *Alma Mater*, directed by Julio César Fernández, was the closest thing to an official organ of the government. There were more than twenty radio programs of different revolutionary organizations; see José Perez Acosta, *La radio en Cuba, 1920–1940* (Havana: P. Ruiz, 1948), p. 115.

[18] "El comité conjunto de las corporaciones económicas expresa sus orientaciones," *El Mundo*, Sept. 18, 1933, p. 1.

[19] *Diario de la Marina*, Sept. 23, 1933, front page.

under the influence of Communists, were demanding more changes, waving red banners, and speaking of "soviets in Cuba." Their statements increased the fears of the middle class and extended the accusation of "Communist" to many members of the government. Simultaneously though in quite different tones, the Communists, the Student Left Wing, and the Anti-Imperialist League denounced the government as reactionary, rightist, and a lackey of Yankee imperialism.

In spite of everything, Grau, Guiteras, and the students moved on toward more radical reforms. An American observer tried to express in Cuban terms their feelings and objectives:

> This is Cuba's golden hour for social revolution. Foreign dominance, political corruption, and political intervention have created a servile state. We live in a land no longer our own. We must regain our heritage, reform our financial system, expropriate lands, clip the wings of foreign capital, and build a free republic.[20]

There was much to be done, and the instability of the situation engendered fear that the time would be all too short.

Growing opposition, increasing alarm, disconcerting criticism from both Left and Right, and uncertainty of the best course to take, as well as the firm anti-Grau attitude of the American Embassy, made many revolutionaries hesitate. On October 24, the ABC Radical withdrew its support from the revolutionary government. Two days later the organization Pro Ley y Justicia, formed by students who favored direct and violent action, proclaimed disagreement with Grau's government because of its "submission to the army."[21] On No-

[20] Hubert Herring, "Can Cuba Save Herself?" *Current History*, Nov. 1933, p. 152.

[21] The declaration of ABC Radical appeared in *El Mundo*, Oct. 24, 1933, front page. A copy of the proclamation of Pro Ley y Justicia exists in the U.S. National Archives, Proclamation to the Cuban

vember 5, after several meetings that were rife with dissension, the Student Directory made the dramatic decision to dissolve.[22] Their explanation to the Cuban people was an attempt to cover up their internal division and to disguise their own anxieties: "When the fourth of September coup occurred, by assuming the responsibility of its leadership we avoided military dictatorship." They justified their political action, reasserted their revolutionary fervor, and concluded: "Now that the revolutionary government is consolidated, the duty of the students is to return to the University." [23] This was, at best, wishful thinking. The most serious trials of the revolutionary government still lay ahead. By dissolving, the Student Directory reduced the possibilities of consolidating the government, but its dissolution did not imply lack of individual support for the government.

When some of the measures of the revolutionary government began to affect American companies directly, the ranks of the government's supporters grew even thinner. A bitter Guiteras wrote later:

When our terrible blows began to break the gigantic machinery which choked us, the Cuban people, as many others in Latin America, came on the scene to fight, but the clamors of all the servants and lackeys of that machinery sent back our collaborators one by one. They preferred the defeatist exclamation, "This way we will never be recognized by the Americans!" or the even more frightening, "The Americans will land, we won't be able to sell our sugar." I saw them in their moment of retreat, for they

---

People, October 26, 1933, 837.00/4344. The document is signed by Guillermo Ara, Manolo Castro, Antonio Hernández, Manuel Romero, and others.

[22] *Alma Mater*, Nov. 5, 1933, front page. For further comments on the motives of the Student Directory, see pp. 191–192 below.

[23] *Diario de la Marina*, Nov. 6, 1933, p. 2.

always came to see me, trying to convince me that we should diminish the attack, that we should compromise.[24]

"Compromise, compromise, is always the advice of those false revolutionaries who never understand the real lesson of Danton: that in Cuba, as in any other place, what a revolutionary needs is audacity, audacity and more audacity," commented Pablo de la Torriente.

But for many Cubans it was not really a problem of audacity versus cowardice. It was "a matter of knowing where radicalism ends and irresponsibility begins." [25] And certainly the appearance of the government, with the coming and going in the Presidential Palace of armed young men shouting for the urgent enactment of some decree, was not reassuring. The improvised speeches from balconies and the declarations that appeared in every part of the island helped to convey the impression of irresponsibility. *El Mundo*, for example, early in October carried an article that called for the transformation of the entire Cuban educational network into a system of "proletarian education." Many concurred with Martínez Saenz that this government was no government at all but only "a student oligarchy"; Sumner Welles called the situation "passive anarchy." [26]

In November the government began to deal directly with American business interests. As loans from the Chase National Bank had become very unpopular, Grau San Martín decided to suspend payment on them. Later, to resolve some labor and economic disputes, two sugar mills of the Cuban-American

[24] "Septembrismo," *Bohemia*, April 1, 1934, pp. 30–38.

[25] Jorge Mañach, "Respuesta a una encuesta," *El Mundo*, Oct. 2, 1933, p. 4.

[26] Gilberto Perez del Castillo, *El Mundo*, Oct. 5, 1933, p. 2; Joaquín Martínez Saenz, "Como se fundó el ABC," *Bohemia*, Oct. 1, p. 53; and Oct. 15, p. 38.

Sugar Company were seized.[27] In December, to avoid the legal way in which American and Cuban companies tried to escape from paying any taxes by selling their sugar mills or land at very low prices to another company, often a subsidiary, the Cuban government proclaimed *el derecho de tanteo* (the right of estimate), that is, the right of the state to be considered a potential buyer in any of these transactions at the price fixed by the company that was selling.[28] "I must stress the significance of this law," wrote Grau San Martín later, "for it gave us the opportunity of recovering for the state an extension of land equivalent to a million acres, among the best in the country, with all the railroads that belonged to Cuban Cane, at the price of only four million dollars." [29] In January 1934, a workers' strike paralyzed the Cuban Electric Company, a subsidiary of the American Electric Bond and Share Company, and Decree 172 placed the company under temporary government control.

These and many other laws modified the political and social structure of Cuba and opened the way for more radical transformation, but they could not solve the two most urgent problems: economic crisis and political instability. Quite the contrary, each new measure made certain sectors fearful of more radical change and increased their demands for order and security. As usually happens, the more strident the opposition was and the more reduced its own base of power, the more radical the government became. In the last days of November, the Uruguayan Ambassador, Fernández Medina, made an attempt to mediate between the opposition and the

[27] Charles A. Thompson, "The Cuban Revolution: Reform and Reaction," *Foreign Policy Reports,* XI (Jan. 1, 1936), 267.

[28] Carlos Raggi, "El derecho de tanteo," *Legislación obrera cubana,* III (April 1946), 46–51.

[29] Ramón Grau San Martín, *La revolución cubana ante América,* pp. 95, 41.

revolutionary government. He proposed a plan whereby Grau would continue as provisional president until the spring of 1934, when he would resign and transfer the presidency to a substitute, selected in a joint session of the Cabinet, with a Council of State composed of representatives of all important political and nonpolitical groups of the republic.

The plan failed because of the intransigency of both parties. The lack of American diplomatic recognition and the evident difficulties of the government encouraged the opposition to reject any compromise, while they waited for the inevitable collapse of the revolutionary regime. The radical elements of the government, headed by Guiteras, considered that this plan, supposedly backed by Sumner Welles, was a second attempt to create a mediationist atmosphere: to accept it would be tantamount to betraying the Revolution. When the opposition began to speak of a general strike, Guiteras challenged them to try it: "A general strike is impossible," he declared, "because all leftist labor organizations, with the exception of the Communist Party, are supporting the government." [30] When even Grau San Martín showed inclinations to accept the Uruguayan Ambassador's plan, Guiteras and his friends provoked a crisis in the government. Secretaries Guiteras (Interior), Moreno (Public Works), Fernández Velasco (Communication), Carlos Hevia (Agriculture), and Enrique Fernández (Subsecretary of the Interior) demanded that (1) all foreign meddling cease, (2) the activities of the Tribunal de Sanciones, created to punish ex-Machadists and counterrevolutionaries, be speeded up, (3) all revolutionary laws be enforced, especially the reduction of electrical rates, and (4) the Cabinet be purged of all members who were not truly revolutionary or leftist.[31]

[30] *Alma Mater,* Dec. 7, 1933, front page.
[31] *Alma Mater,* Dec. 12, 1933, front page.

The President yielded, all contact with those opposing this group was abruptly stopped, and a policy of shifting to the Left was announced. "The Left has destroyed the attempts of a second mediation," *Alma Mater* announced jubilantly. As a consequence, governmental radicalism increased. Guiteras proclaimed that the government would "pass a law prohibiting latifundio. Foreign companies who have illegally acquired vast possessions that belong to the Cuban state are going to be deprived of them. Those lands and many others belonging to the State will be distributed among Cuban families." "The Columbus Cemetery will be expropriated because the Archbishop, besides enjoying an irritating privilege, is charging excessive prices for the ground." [32] Later, Guiteras made a still more dramatic announcement: "The government will inaugurate a socialist policy. . . . This is another step against the bourgeoisie. . . . The distribution of 10,000 *caballerías* of land among the peasants will not imply giving them title to the property but only the usufruct of the land. We will avoid the creation of a rural bourgeoisie, the famous *kulaks* so fiercely attacked by the Soviets. We will try to create cooperative farms instead." [33]

But radicalism and zeal could not stop the erosion of the revolutionary forces, or disperse their enemies, or solve Cuba's desperate economic problems. Furthermore, the shift to the Left augmented the growing split between the government and the armed forces that supported it. The *coroneles* were increasingly alarmed by the government's extremism. Feeling more secure in their position, having defeated all attempts to overthrow the government,[34] they began to apply their own brakes to the situation. Even *Alma Mater* was forced to recog-

[32] *Ibid.*, Dec. 16, Dec. 15, Dec. 18, 1933, front pages.

[33] *Ahora*, Dec. 19, 1933, front page.

[34] See pp. 187–188, 194–196.

nize the contradiction: "While the people parade in front of the Presidential Palace, while the Left wins on the high levels, the army is arresting labor leaders." [35] At the beginning of January 1934 it was evident to many that this tragic cleavage would be the tomb of the revolutionary government. "Of all the evils which menace the road of the republic at the beginning of a new year," warned *Bohemia*, "none is as dangerous as the predominance of militarism." [36] A few days later, supported by a vast common front of antigovernment forces, Batista's army took the decisive step of presenting an ultimatum to President Grau. The fragile alliance of students and soldiers came to an end. The revolutionary government was doomed.

[35] *Alma Mater*, Dec. 19, 1933.

[36] Jan. 7, 1934, p. 31 (editorial). A few days before, Miguel Angel Queredo, *Bohemia's* editor, had pointed out that Batista's military loyalty to his "fellow sergeants" forced him to betray the revolution. See his "Glosando las declaraciones de un coronel," *Bohemia*, Dec. 10, 1933, p. 33.

14 Enemies of the Revolutionary Government

As in any revolutionary period, which opens the way for a multiplicity of ideological positions and for inflammatory rhetoric, in Cuba there were at this time those who complained that the government was doing too much and those who protested that the government was doing too little.

The Left

The groups and individuals of the Left belonged with those who protested that too little was being done. Either because of a mechanical application of party strategy or because of exaggerated extremism, they opposed the revolutionary government and demanded more and more drastic measures.

The Student Left Wing maintained a position of criticism toward Grau from the beginning, although they were divided into several factions, some of which were already in open and violent disagreement with the Communist party.[1] As early as September 22, 1933, the organization was protesting governmental intervention—the purging of professors—in certain Havana schools and proclaiming its own revolutionary objectives.[2] From then on the accusation of "betrayal of the ideals

[1] Interviews with Porfirio Pendás and Carlos Martínez. For an example of criticism of this type, see Raúl Roa, "Reaction versus Revolution," *Retorno a la Alborada* (Havana: Imprimex, 1963), pp. 22–38.

[2] *El País*, Sept. 22, 1933, front page.

of the Revolution" or "false revolutionaries" were common charges against the government by some of the leaders of the movement.

But the Student Left Wing, formed by students who had moved away from the Student Directory, represented a minority group, vocal in its opposition but with little capacity to cause trouble. They were the most important of a rash of leftist groups that appeared in Cuba at the time; they took impressive names, but had no mass support.[3]

More important, of course, was the attitude of the Communist party. The revolutionary coup of September 4, 1933, did not alter their inflexible strategy of condemning all groups as enemies of the people. For the Communists, not only was the ABC a fascist organization, but the government of Grau San Martín was a "bourgeois-landlord government . . . placed in the presidential chair by the petit bourgeoisie and by the army . . . a government which defended the interests of the bourgeoisie, the landlords, and the imperialists."[4] Consequently, when in his efforts to rally popular support around the revolutionary government Antonio Guiteras tried to talk with the leaders of the party, César Vilar, then the Secretary-General, refused even to see him.[5] Open opposition to the government was the accepted tactic. The party moved to stir discontent in the country and among the workers in the city. Some sugar mills were seized (a "soviet" was proclaimed in

[3] From the manifestoes of the period may be gathered this partial list: Bolshevik Leninist Party, ABC Socialist, Cuban Aprista Party, Proletarian Revolutionary Association, Revolutionary Nationalist Party. Many of them disappeared without leaving a trace.

[4] "The Communist Party and the Cuban Revolutionary Situation," *The Communist*, XII (1933), 875–887.

[5] Pedro Vizcaino in *Pensamiento crítico*, No. 38 (April 1970), p. 278. Vizcaino was a member of one of the "action groups" of the Student Directory. In 1933 he joined the organization Pro Ley y Justicia.

the Mabay mill, in Oriente Province), a red flag was raised over the former offices of the *Heraldo de Cuba*, and a rash of local strikes were promoted all over the island. Guiteras then appealed directly to the workers:

In our capitalist system, no government has been so ready to defend the interests of workers and peasants as the present revolutionary government. Nevertheless, induced by American companies, the workers are unconsciously helping in trying to topple the government. . . . It is essential that the worker become aware of the reality we are facing today. It is impossible for the masses to gain political control; thus, instead of opposing this revolutionary government they should cooperate with it to obtain the satisfaction of the most immediate demands of the workers, and to avoid being an instrument of imperialist companies. *The National Confederation of Workers will be responsible before History for the setback that the masses will suffer if we give the Americans a pretext to intervene.*[6]

The answer of the party was to increase its disruptive activities, and to proclaim, through its Anti-Imperialist League, that "the social revolution was on its way." [7] Actually, the party was far from being ready to promote or initiate a social revolution. With its prestige damaged by the "mistake" of August, and with small and poorly organized cadres, the Communist party played into the hands of the enemies of the government, hindered Guiteras' plans, and strengthened the position of moderates and anti-Communists. On September 29, the Communist party tried to organize a demonstration to honor Julio Antonio Mella, whose ashes had been brought back from Mexico, but the police and the army used weapons to disperse the crowd.[8] During the latter part of September the strike

[6] *El País*, Sept. 16, 1933, front page (italics mine).

[7] *El Mundo*, Sept. 18, 1933, p. 11.

[8] *Alma Mater*, Sept. 30, 1933, p. 1, suggested that the first shots were fired by snipers.

wave began to recede,[9] and the nationalist stand of the government began to pay dividends among the masses of workers, who increasingly moved toward cooperation with the revolution. In November the labor situation on the island was almost normal.

The party, however, did not modify its position. They opposed the Decree for the Nationalization of Work on the grounds that it was a "chauvinistic, petit bourgeois measure to divide the working class." [10] And in January 1934, when the revolutionary government was fighting for its life against its own army as well as American pressure, Juan Marinello, in an open letter to a Cuban worker, upheld the party's line that Grau's administration was not a revolutionary government but only a bunch of opportunists issuing reform measures that were never applied, or fascist decrees to stop the progress of the proletariat.[11]

It can be safely concluded that, while somehow dividing the proletariat and augmenting the political disharmony of the period, the actions and criticisms of the Left never posed a grave threat to the revolutionary government.

The Right

The term "Right" is used here in its widest connotation and applied to those groups in Cuba who after September 1933 for one reason or another were fighting to re-establish a pre-revolutionary situation, be it the Constitution of 1901, the provisional government of Céspedes, or a coalition government headed by some of the old leaders such as Menocal or Mendieta.

On September 10, 1933, after Grau San Martín was desig-

[9] *Problems of the New Cuba* (New York: Foreign Policy Association, 1935), p. 184.

[10] "Jornadas obreras," *Trabajo*, Sept. 1934, p. 23.

[11] See his "Letter to a Tampa Worker," *Bohemia*, Jan. 7, 1934, p. 20.

nated provisional president, the ABC moved from expectant vigilance to open opposition. Following them, the National Union, the partisans of Menocal, and the former army officers began to take positions against the revolutionary government. The OCRE and the OCRR were already in the process of disintegrating and did not count as important factors. The Women in Opposition had completely disappeared.

All these factions turned more or less desperately toward Welles, asking for American support in the oncoming struggle. Their first objective was, apparently, the restoration of Céspedes as President of the Republic. The first group to move was the former officers of the army, who gathered in the National Hotel waiting for an opportunity to act. On September 10 they publicly declared that if the United States recognized the government of Grau they would decline any responsibility in the course of events, but if recognition did not come they would try to reinstate Céspedes.[12] At the same time, they sent Colonel Horacio Ferrer to Welles to ask that "a sufficient force of American Marines be landed to disarm the soldiers and the innumerable civilians who are armed." The Ambassador refused even to hear such a petition.[13]

All attempts on the part of the government and the army to reach an agreement with the officers failed. Encouraged by their contacts with the ABC, the National Union, and Menocal, and probably also by Sumner Welles, who had moved to the National Hotel, the officers even defied an order from the government recalling them to active duty.[14] On

[12] *El País*, Sept. 10, 1933, p. 1. The *New York Herald Tribune* (Sept. 11, p. 1) reported that Colonel Ferrer had assured that the officers would never "serve under any chief who was not recognized by Washington."

[13] *Foreign Relations of the United States, 1933* (Washington, D.C.: U.S. Government Printing Office, 1952), V, 418.

[14] Edmund A. Chester, *A Sergeant Named Batista* (New York: Henry Holt, 1954), p. 102. It was more than ironic that the same

October 2 the army attacked the National Hotel and in the ensuing battle fourteen officers were killed (some of them after surrendering), seventeen wounded, and the remainder taken prisoner. As a group, the former officers of the army disappeared. The sergeants, by now colonels, were beginning to be in full control of the troops.

As a result of this failure by the supporters of Céspedes, the hopes of the counterrevolutionary forces moved toward Mendieta as a prestigious figure capable of attracting mass support. The American Ambassador began to sound out Batista on his political position, assuring him that in the Ambassador's judgment Batista "himself was the only individual in Cuba who represented authority." [15] But of these relations between the Ambassador and Batista more later.

With the officers out of the picture, it was the turn of the ABC, potentially the government's most formidable antagonist. The transformation of the ABC from a secret organization into a massive political instrument had been rapid and impressive. Its brief period of power, during Céspedes' government, permitted further expansion. True, it had been easily deposed, but the ABC fell with dignity and restraint, announcing that they preferred to renounce power rather than provoke a bloody confrontation among revolutionaries. And the new situation, so charged with danger and discord, permitted the ABC to become a rallying force for all those who were or pretended to be revolutionaries but who opposed the turbulent radicalism of Grau's government. Furthermore, the open blessing of the American Embassy, while it hurt the ABC's nationalistic image, made many important political sectors re-

---

officers who had toppled Machado's government "to avoid American intervention" were now defying the government in the hope of bringing American intervention.

[15] *Foreign Relations, 1933,* V, 470.

gard the ABC as the most fitting instrument to restore order in Cuba and to obtain immediate U.S. diplomatic recognition.

The government, aware of these possibilities and trying to avoid a direct confrontation with the ABC, the Nationalists, and other minor political groups, made an effort to find a conciliatory formula. On October 19, Grau invited Dr. Fernando Ortiz to become a member of the cabinet and to propose a political solution that could unite all revolutionary groups. Dr. Ortiz accepted only the second part of the invitation. His formula for union was to keep Grau as provisional president while changing the structure of the government so as to include representatives of all important political groups, thus working toward a genuine "national" government. Grau and the students accepted the plan, and even Welles considered it a "reasonable compromise." [16] But in spite of some promising initial meetings, the formula failed because of mutual suspicion and past resentment and the internal fragmentation of almost every group involved.

On the government side, the widening split between the radical minority that shunned compromise and the majority that wanted it embittered discussion and hampered agreement. In search of his own path, Batista, whose disagreement with Grau and the radicals was by then obvious, secretly offered the opposition a more convenient solution—the substitution of Colonel Carlos Mendieta for Grau.[17] Encouraged by the students' dissension and by Batista's attitude and sensing that their opportunity was fast approaching, the ABC rejected Ortiz' plan and, without entirely trusting Batista, moved to back Mendieta as provisional president.

At the end of October, hope for a conciliation had died,

[16] *Ibid.*, p. 493.

[17] In October, Batista had already had several more or less secret meetings with representatives of the ABC and the Nationalists.

terrorism in Havana increased, and the two most important sectors of the anti-Machado forces—the students and the ABC—were openly attacking each other. According to the editors of *Bohemia* it was then and there, with the failure of Ortiz' plan, that the revolution lost its last opportunity to consolidate a powerful, civilian government, capable of checking the emerging power of Batista and the army.[18] By October 29, the ABC Radical had withdrawn its support of the government, and Batista had reached an agreement with the ABC and the Nationalists to force Grau's resignation and proclaim Mendieta as president. The revolutionary government seemed at the brink of total collapse. Its condition appeared so critical that Welles wrote confidently: "The general public expects the fall of the government tonight or tomorrow, although the change will not in my opinion take place before the middle of the week." [19]

Once more the Ambassador's confidence proved wrong. Ten days later Grau was not only still in power, but the leaders of the ABC were in exile and the Nationalists had been temporarily forced to abandon all demands to replace the revolutionary government. The government was saved by two decisive factors. One was Mendieta's hesitation to accept the presidency against the will of the students.[20] The other was the drastic action taken by the radical elements in power.

When the students learned of Batista's imminent agreement with the opposition, they decided to force the issue and take the offensive before Batista was ready. They convened an urgent meeting of the Revolutionary Junta (the initial Junta formed on September 4), and sent some of the most loyal

[18] "Historia de la revolución," *Bohemia*, Aug. 26, 1934, p. 101.

[19] *Foreign Relations, 1933*, V, 503.

[20] Mendieta exasperated his potential allies by insisting on convincing the student of the necessity to replace Grau. He wanted to restore peace and order in Cuba without using force, and balked at the prospect of violent student opposition.

revolutionaries—Rubén de León, Carlos Prío, and Antonio Guiteras—to probe the loyalty of several military commanders of Havana District. They soon discovered that Batista, in his conspiratorial haste, had failed to inform many officers of his political plan. Consequently those officers, always suspicious of any change in the political situation, not only disassociated themselves from the conspiracy, but offered their services to the revolutionary government. Two governmental decrees were prepared at once: one ordered the arrest and court-martial of Batista as traitor to the government, the second named Major Pablo Rodríguez, supposedly the real organizer of the 4th of September military coup and a man loyal to the government, as commander-in-chief of the army. On the evening of November 3, armed with these decrees and the decision to kill Batista on the spot if he offered any resistance, the students, Grau, Guiteras, certain other government members, the principal military commanders of Havana District, and the members of the Revolutionary Junta (Irisarri, Portela, and Carbó) met at Carbó's house and waited for the arrival of Batista.

Unaware of the real purpose of the meeting, Batista came with only one military aide. As soon as he entered, according to some of those present at that highly dramatic meeting, he sensed the mortal danger he was facing. When Grau accused him of treason, he admitted his faults, recanted his political sins—which he attributed to his "naïveté"—and offered his loyalty to the revolutionary government. Then, to the surprise and indignation of some revolutionaries, Grau not only accepted his apologies but even confirmed his confidence in him. With evident relief, Batista returned to his commanding position at the military barracks of Columbia.[21]

Grau's move demoralized his allies. The military officers

[21] The events of this meeting were recounted in interviews with Prío and Rubio Padilla, who were present, and confirmed by Sergio

who had openly backed an anti-Batista movement now faced the prospect of continuing under Batista's command. Their survival would depend on their loyalty not to the government but to Batista. Angry and confused by Grau's attitude, the group of students that had been acting on his behalf had only two alternatives: either to denounce Grau and assume the initiative, or accept his action and follow a course which to them seemed disastrously wrong.[22] But to move against Grau —kill Batista on their own, as Guiteras proposed—they needed the consensus of the entire student body. An urgent meeting of the Student Directory was convened the following day at the Presidential Palace. The session was presided over by Ramón Miyar, who apparently belonged to the "moderates." The decision to act not only against Batista, but against Grau, was too much for the majority. In spite of the pleading of the minority of radicals, after a turbulent session the Student Directory decided to avoid censuring the government or taking a definite stand by dissolving itself. As we have already mentioned, their excuse was that the revolutionary government was finally consolidated in power. Actually what they accomplished was to deprive the government of its last semblance of organized support.

Carbó, in whose house the event took place. The meeting and the attitude of the army officers are also mentioned in *Foreign Relations, 1933*, V, 511–512. Pablo Rodríguez confirms the facts in his statements in *Pensamiento Crítico*, No. 38, pp. 226–227.

[22] There is no accord among those involved on the reasons for Grau's action. According to Prío and Carbó, Grau thought that Batista had been scared enough to cease his antigovernment activities and that, as he told Prío: "We already know Batista; his successor is going to be as bad if not worse than him." Rubio Padilla and others had a different interpretation; for them the basic reason was Grau's desire to free himself from the Student Director and to assert his political independence. Knowing the political opportunism which Grau showed later, I tend to agree with this last thesis.

But if the meeting at Carbó's house confused and weakened the governmental forces, it also served to deprive its enemies temporarily of their best card—Batista. He was aware that as a participant in the 4th of September coup he was not quite a *persona grata* to the elements who had worked with Céspedes' government (the ABC, the Nationalists, and the American Ambassador) and that they were dealing with him only because of his military position;[23] suddenly he realized how fragile that position was, and how close to disaster he had been, through acting hastily. To strengthen his authority and regain the support of his officers became his essential objective. Consequently, he suspended all meetings with oppositionist groups and devoted all his energies to the army. Sumner Welles, with whom he was always in contact, reported the reason for this strategical retreat: "Batista's own violent animosity to Grau San Martín, which is now growing due to his knowledge of a plot favored by Grau to seize Batista and replace him with another sergeant, makes it inevitable that Batista will move against Grau, *provided he can be reasonably confident of the loyalty of the soldiers in the various Havana barracks.*[24]

Batista's momentary withdrawal from active opposition left

[23] Much later, in a very inaccurate book, Batista still echoed that distrust of the Mediationists. "They consider me unacceptable," he wrote, "because I was a newcomer who had climbed to supreme command of the nation from the humble position of sergeant" (Fulgencio Batista, *The Growth and Decline of the Cuban Republic* [New York: Devin-Adair, 1964], p. 11). In pointing out his "humble" origin, Batista failed to record that he had reached power by "climbing" over a government formed by those very elements who were dealing with him.

[24] *Foreign Relations, 1933,* V, 514 (italics mine). The "plot" evidently refers to the meeting at Carbó's house. This note of the Ambassador shows how wrong Grau was in thinking he had definitely paralyzed Batista's conspiracy.

the ABC and the Nationalists alone to face the revolutionary government. Convinced that the time was not ripe for an open attack and that without Batista's support—or at least his neutrality—an insurrection was suicidal, Martínez Saenz, the principal leader of the ABC, left Cuba for the United States, while the Nationalists softened their criticism of the government. And then, at what seemed the most unfavorable moment, insurrection broke out and the ABC gambled everything on an armed attack against the revolutionary government.

On November 8 part of the small Cuban Air Force and one unit of the army rebelled. Groups of Nationalists, under the leadership of Rafael Iturralde and Colonel Blas Hernández (the anti-Machado guerrilla fighter), were involved, and Carlos Saladrigas, now directing the ABC, ordered his followers to join the rebellion.

At noon of that day the rebels had captured several police stations in Havana, two planes had attacked the Presidential Palace, rumors of a national insurrection were sweeping the city, and one of the ABC's radio stations announced that Grau had escaped to Mexico. Sumner Welles, always predicting the imminent downfall of the government, was once more certain of its impending collapse. After reporting the presence of two thousand fully equipped men fighting against the government, he added: "I anticipate a condition of complete anarchy after nightfall since there is little likelihood that the government soldiers can capture the barracks held by the oppositionists." [25]

But the government did not collapse. Grau remained in the Presidential Palace and announced his decision to stay there "defending Cuba's freedom and sovereignty." [26] Guiteras, the majority of the students, and even members of the ABC

[25] Confidential telegram of Welles, National Archives, Nov. 8, 1933, 837.00/4352.

[26] *Diario de la Marina*, Nov. 8, 1933, front page.

Radical, the Communist party, and the Student Left Wing rallied spontaneously to defend the government and fought the rebels everywhere. Finally, in the afternoon, pressed by his officers and by the inevitability of the situation, Batista ordered the army to fight in favor of the government. By sunset most of the police stations had been recovered and the remnants of the defeated rebels had retreated to Atarés Fortress in the outskirts of Havana, where they were immediately surrounded and attacked by the army.

Although disappointed, the American Ambassador could not give up hope. On November 9, he still gave a bleak picture of the government's situation. It seems that, if exaggeration and wishful thinking could topple a regime, then Grau's government was doomed. "So far as can be ascertained," reported Sumner Welles at 10 A.M., "the total force now defending Atarés amounts to approximately 3,000 men fully armed with ample ammunition. . . . The major part of the province of Santa Clara is reported to have joined the revolution. . . . Reports received early are that the entire province of Matanzas is in arms including the soldiers, all supporting the revolution." One hour later his picture began to deflate: "The total garrison [in Atarés] is slightly over a thousand. . . . Santiago de Cuba and Cienfuegos are reported quiet." [27]

Actually, the rebellion had been utterly defeated, the government was in full control of the situation, and only about four hundred men, poorly equipped, were fighting a hopeless battle in Atarés Fortress. In desperation the ABC sent emissaries to the Ambassador to warn him that they were going to carry out "wholesale destruction of foreign property . . . with the purpose of forcing intervention." The Ambassador took pains to excuse this attitude: "These men have been made

[27] *Foreign Relations, 1933*, V, 517, 518.

desperate by the reports circulated that many ABC members had been summarily executed and by the realization that they can hope for no guarantee of any kind should they be defeated." [28] The phrase "should they be defeated" was a contradiction in itself: if victory hung in the balance, why would the ABC be trying to force intervention?

At 4 P.M. a white flag was hoisted in Atarés. The battle was over. About eighty men had been killed, among them Colonel Blas Hernández, who was shot after he surrendered. At 6 P.M., Grau announced the victory of the revolutionary government, condemned the action of the "false revolutionaries" who had rebelled, and hailed the "magnificent union of the people and the army." [29] On reporting these events, the diehard Ambassador added, "I am advised that the remainder [of those who had fought in Atarés] left the fortress before noon with their arms and proceeded toward the south of the province." Next day he admitted, "Havana has remained fairly quiet on the surface today." [30]

So ended this ill-planned rebellion. The organization that had proclaimed itself "the hope of Cuba" had failed both to retain political power and to regain it by force. The causes for the failure of this second rebellion are difficult to explain—certainly the leadership of the organization gave a weak and confused account of the events [31]—but the consequences of this failure were extremely serious. The futility of the attempt,

[28] *Ibid.* There were so summary executions of Abecedarios, not even a policy of repression after the rebellion.

[29] *Diario de la Marina*, Nov. 8, front page.

[30] *Foreign Relations, 1933,* V, 519, 520.

[31] The retreat to Atarés Fortress, for example, decided at the last moment, was an evident blunder; instead of spreading its forces to prolong the fight and facilitate its escape, the ABC concentrated the fighters in one indefensible position, where the army could defeat and capture them in one single thrust. Three factors can help to explain the poor timing and planning of the insurrection. First, the leaders of the ABC overestimated the internal divisions in the revolu-

the accusation that the ABC had tried to provoke "foreign intervention," the signs of disunion in the top ranks, eroded the revolutionary prestige of the organization. Although it survived for a time as an important political group and later as a party, the ABC never recovered the élan lost in this fiasco and never regained its initial prestige.[32]

After the defeat of the ABC, several revolutionary elements

---

tionary government. Second, they saw in the rebellion of the Air Force the possibility of applying in their favor the same formula which had served to topple them on September 4: a military insurrection backed and expanded by a civilian organization. Finally, and perhaps most decisive, Carlos Saladrigas' ambition to become the real leader of the ABC made him jump at the first opportunity to act without Martínez Saenz. A victorious rebellion, carried out while Martínez Saenz was in the United States, would undoubtedly have made him the hero of the hour.

After the failure, the leaders' justification for their actions was poor. "At the end of October," they argued, "it could be said that the Batista-Grau government had the entire nation against it . . . [the cell formed by the Directors] was in a delicate position; it wanted peaceful solutions, *but the mass demanded energetic action*. . . . The dilemma was solved on the 8th with the rebellion of the Air Force, a rebellion that we joined even if we had not organized it. . . . *The ABC limited itself to offering its cooperation* . . . for the movement had a rectifying purpose which we shared: the intention to reverse [*retroceder*] the revolutionary process and bring it back to the moment when it was halted by a suicidal impatience and a criminal ambition"—referring to the moment when Céspedes' government was toppled ("Manifiesto del ABC," *Diario de la Marina*, Nov. 18, 1933, p. 2; italics mine). A supposedly revolutionary group explained its action by pressure from below, decided to fight not to guide but to cooperate, and was expecting to push the situation back to September. No wonder someone wrote that the explanation did more harm to the prestige of the ABC than the failure itself. For justification of the ABC, see *ibid.* For a harsh criticism of the Manifesto, see "Respuesta," by Luis F. Almagro, *ibid.*, Nov. 21, p. 2.

[32] Only six years after these events, when the election for the Constituent Assembly of 1940 was held, the ABC had already shrunk to a minor political party. After continuous decline, the party dissolved in 1952.

were exultant. Many believed that the worst crisis was over, and could see no reason why Washington could not recognize Grau's government now that it had demonstrated its force and determination. On November 16, the Cuban press reproduced a statement by Horace G. Knowles, former U.S. Ambassador to Bolivia and Nicaragua, accusing Sumner Welles of "openly helping the counterrevolution," and suggesting that the impressive demonstration of the Cuban government deserved diplomatic recognition. The approaching Inter-American Conference at Montevideo revitalized many hopes. So far, only Uruguay and Mexico had recognized the Cuban government, but Montevideo could be a decisive rostrum to turn the diplomatic tide in Cuba's favor. The revolutionary delegation to the Conference included Angel Giraudy, Secretary of Labor; Dr. Herminio Portell Vilá, historian and university professor; and Alfredo Nogueira, Director of Social Legislation. To reinforce its revolutionary image, the government sent two student leaders as secretaries —Carlos Prío Socarrás and Juan Antonio Rubio Padilla. Since the official delegation had already departed, the two young men flew to Miami to catch up with the "S.S. American Legion," the ship that was transporting the American delegation to Montevideo. Also on board were Cordell Hull, Alexander W. Weddell, J. Reuben Clark, and Spruille Braden, along with several other Latin American delegates.

For Antonio Guiteras and other revolutionaries who were less concerned about American recognition, the victory over the ABC cleared the road for more revolutionary reforms; "the opening to the Left" was about to begin. After the defeat of the army officers and the collapse of the ABC, there were no more organized political enemies to challenge the regime. The revolutionary government was consolidated, or, to use an apt and inauspicious expression of Sumner Welles, so it seemed "on the surface."

Under the surface, on the level of basic realities, the defeat of the ABC produced almost no change in the situation. True, the most dangerous opponent of the government had been disabled, and there were now expectations of unifying several political groups around the government, and of obtaining American recognition. But these hopes did not bring political stability (bombs and terrorism continued sporadically in Havana) nor could they give a real respite to the acute economic crisis—a crisis which the approach of the *zafra* transformed into the most urgent and radical concern of almost all sectors of the population. For sugar was king.

Furthermore, the victory over the ABC manifestly increased the importance of the army and, naturally, of Batista. Since Washington and the American Ambassador decided to maintain an anti-Grau policy, it was now almost inevitable for them to regard Batista as the only factor capable of changing the situation and toppling the revolutionary government. All other counterrevolutionary groups with which the American Ambassador had been in contact had collapsed. Only Batista remained, a tenacious and victorious ex-sergeant, obligingly looking toward the Embassy. The Ambassador had no choice, given his firm anti-Grau position, but to accept the situation. Clearly, Batista's moment had come.

Perhaps only one man in the revolutionary government grasped the implications of the new alignments and moved to check Batista. Antonio Guiteras knew that his primary enemy, the American Embassy, was out of reach; he acted then against his natural ally—Batista. But for this move, thanks to Grau's indecision, Batista was also ready. He had learned his lesson. He remained in the barracks, increased his contacts with and promises to the officers, and assumed more and more authority over the army. Guiteras' battle with the ex-sergeant was to be the final act of the revolutionary drama.

15 *The Ambassador, the Army, and the Revolutionary Government*

From the moment of his arrival in Cuba, the attitude and actions of the American Ambassador, Sumner Welles, had been a key factor in nearly every development. Not only that, but from the beginning to the end of the revolutionary government Welles' attitude did not change: he opposed that government in every way possible. He may have been irritated by the crumbling of the political structure he had helped to create in Cuba after Machado and consequently by the shadow cast over his own success as mediator. Maybe he had confidence in the Cuban groups that had been working with him since the mediation and tended to accept at face value their information and reports. Perhaps he was convinced that the groups in power represented a direct and dangerous menace to American interests. In any case, he did not hesitate to use his influence with the American government to prevent recognition of Grau San Martín's government. And to do that, he at times—consciously or unconsciously—distorted the facts, presented a one-sided account, or omitted important points that could have helped to give a better impression of the revolutionary government. He consistently painted a black—and, at times, red—picture of what was happening in Cuba.

The first report Welles sent to Washington mentioned

that the proclamation of September 5, 1933, was signed "by a group of the most extreme radicals of the student organization and three university professors whose theories are frankly communistic."[1] The Ambassador failed to mention, perhaps out of ignorance, that the Communist party and the Student Left Wing had not participated in the movement, and that later—an event Welles never mentioned—they publicly denounced it. Next day the Ambassador cabled another description of the government: "The government of Cuba today is an undisciplined group of individuals of divergent tendencies representing the most irresponsible elements in the city of Havana with practically no support whatsoever outside the capital."[2] If that were the case, one wonders why, in that same report, Welles mentioned that "even so radical a group as the ABC urgently requested me yesterday afternoon to insist that the Department authorize the landing of American Marines both in Havana and in Santiago."

That day the Ambassador also telephoned Secretary Cordell Hull in Washington and asked for the landing of some marines to protect the Embassy. Later he added: "I just had another meeting with the political leaders and they seem to be all of the opinion that the only possible way is for a temporary landing of possibly one thousand men until a new government can be restored [*sic*]." Hull answered that he had talked with the President and they were inclined to land troops only if

[1] *Foreign Relations of the United States, 1933* (Washington, D.C.: U.S. Government Printing Office, 1952), V, 382. Actually there were only two professors among the signers: Grau San Martín and Guillermo Portela. The characteristics of Grau's political position were nationalism, socialism (non-Marxist), and anti-imperialism. Portela never had any definite ideology, but if anything he could be considered a conservative who wanted a quick restoration of order in Cuba. At the University he was famous for a sort of perennial skepticism.

[2] *Ibid.*, p. 392.

the personnel of the Embassy were in "physical danger." No one was in any danger.[3]

In spite of the official unwillingness to send troops, Welles insisted the same day in another telegram that "it was the unanimous opinion" of all political leaders with whom he was in contact that the former government could be restored if the marines landed in Havana, Santiago, "and perhaps one or two other points on the island."[4] Again Hull refused: "If we have to go in there again, we will never be able to come out and we will have on our hands the trouble of thirty years ago. . . . We feel that if conditions would justify your continuing your present and past policy of *absolute neutrality* towards each group, and *especially towards the group in power*, keeping their confidence and good will . . . that would give the Cubans themselves all the more opportunity to do something."[5]

But Welles apparently was not willing to be neutral or to relinquish so easily his desire to restore the Céspedes government. A day after that exchange he endorsed a plan of Colonel Horacio Ferrer to take over one of the fortresses, proclaim Céspedes as the legitimate president of Cuba, and ask for the landing of American marines: "If the legitimate and recognized government of Cuba can make an effective demonstration of its intention to re-establish itself, it would most decidedly appear to me to be in the best interest of the United States Government to afford them immediate support. . . . Such policy on our part would presumably entail the landing

[3] *Ibid.*, pp. 384, 385, 387.

[4] *Ibid.*, p. 388. It is difficult to understand how Cosme de la Torriente could write years later that Welles "always refused to allow or order one single American soldier to put his foot in Cuba." See his "La renuncia de Sumner Welles," *Revista de la Habana*, II (Oct. 1943), 201.

[5] *Foreign Relations, 1933*, V, 389 (italics mine).

of considerable forces at Havana and lesser forces in certain of the other more important ports of the Republic." The Ambassador proposed this plan as the best solution and requested urgent instructions from the President and Secretary Hull. He professed to be "fully prepared to carry out such instructions when the appropriate moment arrives." [6] This request made evident that, in spite of Welles' description of the revolutionary government as feeble and disorganized and opposed by all important Cuban political forces, those forces did not dare to move against the present government unless they could count on American support. They were waiting for Welles' signal, and Welles was pressing his superior for assurance that they could count on his help.

This time Hull's answer was short and rather stern: "We feel strongly that any promise, implied or otherwise, relating to what the United States will do under any circumstances is impossible; that it would be regarded as a breach of neutrality, as favoring one faction out of many, as attempting to set up a government which would be regarded . . . as a creation and creature of the American Government." Cordell Hull seems to have been much more realistic than Welles and thus more willing to recognize the revolutionary government. When Welles suggested, "For the time being we ought not even to consider recognizing any government of this character in my opinion," Hull answered, "until it has shown its ability to preserve law and order." [7]

The Secretary of State, after all, received information about the Cuban government from a variety of sources. As early as September 6, the American Ambassador in Mexico, Josephus Daniels, had informed Hull that the Mexican Minister of Foreign Affairs had told him that "he knows the four men

[6] *Ibid.*, pp. 397–398. [7] *Ibid.*, pp. 402, 390.

composing the junta are educated men with good backgrounds and no taint of Communism." A few days later, Ambassador Daniels gave him an exceptionally clear report on the origin of the rumors of Communist influence in Cuba which he found "very exaggerated." [8]

With the sending of the marines vetoed by Hull, Welles evidently decided to stress the other essential point, the incapacity of the revolutionary government to preserve law and order. In so doing the Ambassador reinforced a vicious circle: as everybody knew, American failure to recognize the revolutionary government encouraged counterrevolutionary forces to oppose the government, and this open opposition justified the view that there was no law and order in Cuba.[9] This tactic is what Grau had called "intervention by inertia"; by simply not doing anything, the American government encouraged other people to do something. That Sumner Welles must have known the consequences of his attitude was shown in his comment after the revolt of the ABC: "I have noted in certain reports from the American press of today that the assertion is made that recognition of the Grau government would have prevented revolutionary outbreaks. . . . Recognition would probably have delayed revolt but it would not have prevented it." [10]

In presenting the Cuban situation as chaotic, the Ambassador seems to have passed along as fact all types of rumors. On September 7 he reported to his government:

[8] *Ibid.*, pp. 394, 414–415.

[9] For example, the first manifesto of the former officers of the army stated that if the American government were to recognize Grau they would decline all responsibilities, but if recognition did not come they would try to reinstate Céspedes. Throughout this period a simple rumor of impending American recognition was enough to weaken the opposition and reinforce the government's position.

[10] *Foreign Relations, 1933,* V, 520.

The situation is breaking fast. Dr. Belt, Secretary of Public Instruction in the Céspedes Cabinet, has informed me that Sergeant Batista has requested an interview with President Céspedes in order to inform him that the army wishes to place itself at his disposal. . . . He further informs me that Carbó, one of the five members of the revolutionary group, has fled and that the others are only waiting in order to seek some solution which will guarantee their safety.[11]

On September 8, he sent this erroneous report: "The army mutiny was originally engineered by a few Communist leaders in Havana under the guidance of Rubén Martínez Villena." [12] And each of these reports, as well as many others that forecast an immediate crisis in Grau's government, was accompanied by the recommendation that the Cuban government should not be recognized.

It is not necessary to burden this book with a multiplicity of quotations to prove the partiality of Sumner Welles. One example is outstanding: the same man who on August 30, when Céspedes' government was still in power, dismissed as almost nonexistent the danger of Communism in Cuba ("I cannot see any indications of the 'red menace' which certain Americans doing business here are fearful of" [13]), just five days later, when his friends were ousted, raised the possibility of an immediate Communist take-over and recommended prompt American action. Apart from his belief in the Communist tendencies of the professors who were in the government, expressed in his first telegram to Washington, he elaborated on September 6: "They [the political leaders, mainly those involved in the Céspedes government, with whom he

[11] *Ibid.*, p. 400.

[12] *Ibid.*, p. 405. As we have already seen, the Communist party opposed the coup. At the time of the coup Martínez Villena was dying of tuberculosis.

[13] *Ibid.*, p. 378.

was in contact] were emphatic in their declaration that the present revolutionary group could not remain in control for more than a few days and would be then in turn forced to give way to an out and out Communist organization."[14]

The same partiality and contradiction are evident in his reports on the Cuban political leaders: these men were considered almost insignificant when they rejected the mediation or criticized Céspedes' government, but they quickly gained in stature and importance in the eyes of the Ambassador when they attacked the revolutionary government of Grau San Martín. The man who, for example, reported on July 7, when ex-President Menocal was opposed to the mediation, that "Menocal has been consistently losing prestige during the last three weeks,"[15] and later dismissed Menocal and his "constantly diminishing group"[16] as lacking importance in Cuba, was eventually using Menocal (who certainly had done nothing to increase his prestige or his followers in the meantime) to prove that all powerful parties were opposing Grau:[17] "I have every reason to believe that it is only a question of a short time before General Menocal will attempt to lead a revolution."[18] (Notice how the Ambassador gave him back the rank of general!) This attempt Menocal, naturally, was wise enough never to try. The Ambassador also always referred to the "exiguous minority" that was supporting Grau,[19] as counterbalanced by his continuous evaluation of the ABC as "in many ways the best organized and most energetic political organization in Cuba."[20] Welles did not mention the growing fragmentation of the ABC—by November there were three different factions in the party—or its internal disputes. It is

[14] *Ibid.*, p. 388. [15] *Ibid.*, p. 318.
[16] *Ibid.*, p. 323. [17] *Ibid.*, p. 479.
[18] *Ibid.*, p. 520. This announcement is still more incredible when one realizes that it was made after the failure of the ABC and when Menocal was on his way into exile.
[19] *Ibid.*, p. 528. [20] *Ibid.*, p. 419.

symptomatic that the first time a failure of a conciliation movement between the government and the opposition was properly attributed "to reported declarations of General Menocal that he would accept no solution involving continuance of Grau as Provisional President *and divergent tendencies in the ranks of the ABC*," it was done when Welles was absent, by Chargé d'Affaires Reed.[21]

Equally revealing is the tendency of the Ambassador to diagnose every minor crisis as disastrous for the revolutionary government. Even before the ex-officers of the army and the ABC created a relatively serious situation, the Ambassador had sent alarming reports to Washington. On September 20 he reported: "In the interior, evidence of armed and concerted opposition to the government is increasing. . . . All evidence I have been able to obtain . . . tends to confirm the fact that the revolutionary government started by Blas Hernández is gaining force and that the number of men now supporting him has increased to over 500. . . . The American Consul at Antilla informs me by telephone that he is advised Major Balan [*sic*] has risen in revolt in Oriente Province with approximately 800 men and apparently sufficient arms; that he took possession of the town of Gibara yesterday and is marching on Holguín today." [22] On November 6, he reported that 11,000 men were ready to revolt in Oriente, "at a moment's notice." [23] As soon as these "powerful" movements dissolved, the Ambassador presented another rumor as the new unsurmountable obstacle for the revolutionary government. He even went so far as to break the established practice of the Embassy and sent to Washington, as pieces of information, anonymous and insulting anti-Grau material received by the Embassy.[24]

[21] *Ibid.*, p. 527 (italics mine). [22] *Ibid.*, p. 450. [23] *Ibid.*, p. 514.

[24] See, for example, his confidential report (National Archives, Nov. 8, 1933, 837.00/4385), accompanying what Welles himself calls "a

When President Grau made an effort to convince the Ambassador of the justice and necessity of recognizing his government and that "everyone in the country would support the government if the United States would accord recognition," [25] Welles lectured him on the firm position of the American government, and pointed out the growing danger of militarism in Cuba. Grau admitted this danger, as well as the unreliability of Batista. "The Department," concluded the Ambassador, "will easily gather from this summary of my conversation how utterly impractical and visionary Grau San Martín is and how little hope of success there can be from a government controlled by him and the students." [26] To this conclusion he stuck to the end of his mission in Cuba.

To these and many more documentary proofs it is worth adding, at least to show how many Cubans regarded Welles' attitude, what is reported to have taken place on board the "S.S. American Legion" en route to the Montevideo Conference. The account is from the testimony of the two student delegates, Juan Antonio Rubio Padilla and Carlos Prío Socarrás, who were on their way to join the official Cuban group already in Uruguay. On November 10 several Latin American delegates invited them to a "celebration," occasioned by the public but unofficial announcement of Cordell Hull that within the next few days the government of the United States would recognize Grau's government, thus eliminating the only obstacle to the harmonious development of the conference. The "celebration" did not take place, and recognition never did materialize. The Cubans were told at Montevideo that on learning the news Sumner Welles rushed to Washington to talk to President Roosevelt and blocked

---

badly written" unsigned piece denouncing almost all members of the revolutionary government as Communists.

[25] *Foreign Relations, 1933,* V, 444. [26] *Ibid.*, p. 445.

Hull's initiative. This story receives some support from statements that appeared in the Cuban and Uruguayan presses, and from the Foreign Documents of the United States.

On November 21, 1933, *Diario de la Marina*, on its last page, published an AP cable which read: "Cordell Hull and President Roosevelt would like to recognize the Cuban government . . . declarations of Cordell Hull on board the SS American Legion." The information was reproduced in several Uruguayan newspapers. On November 27, Hull asked by telegram what were "the controlling facts and conditions to date against recognition of Grau San Martín." At that time Welles was already in the United States. He had asked permission to visit the President on November 13, ending his request with this significant paragraph: "Should the policy we have followed until now be changed, it would be preferable for Caffery to replace me as special representative, as it might be preferable in any event. But the authority of the Embassy would be gravely impaired if any suggestion to that effect were made known now." Obviously, the Ambassador was apprehensive about a change in the policy and, very naturally, preferred not to be present if Grau were to be recognized. Nevertheless, when Hull made the request, Welles had already been talking with Roosevelt for two days. The answer was also illuminating:

> We have maintained that the criteria of Cuban recognition are: (1) popular support, and (2) ability to maintain law and order. . . . The Embassy at Havana insists that these criteria have not been met. With regard to No. 1, Mr. Welles emphatically expressed to me his judgment that Grau does not have the confidence of the mass of the Cuban people but is supported by a minority bent upon remaining in power at all costs. With regard to No. 2, Mr. Welles believes that the Grau government can maintain order only by the most extreme and dictatorial methods

(although it appears to have strengthened itself by the suppression of the November 8th revolt, which has tended to discourage counter-revolutionary movements).

Evidently, the weight of Welles' opinion counterbalanced any trend toward change. After receiving that message, Hull took the trouble to send another telegram denying the press reports which quoted him as being "in favor of recognizing the present government in Cuba." That President Roosevelt had considered recognizing Grau's government can be inferred by this paragraph of a confidential report sent by Acting Secretary Reed to Cordell Hull on November 25: "I cannot but feel that the President would now like to find some excuse to alter his policy if a way can be found to do so without prejudice to his former position." [27]

Naturally, the staunch attitude of Sumner Welles had a tremendous influence in Cuba. From the officers who revolted in October, to the Abecedarios who failed in November and the Menocalistas who were always threatening a revolution, all had always been in close contact with the Ambassador. But their efforts had all failed. Against all expectations the revolutionary government was still in power, still issuing decrees, still attempting to transform the structure of Cuban society.

It is curious to note that the man who would prove decisive in the struggle against Grau San Martín and his government had been trying to reach an agreement with the Ambassador from the very beginning As early as September 5, the very day of the revolt, Sergeant Batista paid an urgent visit to Sumner Welles. He was the only member of the Revolutionary junta who took that step. According to the Ambassador, "the purport of the visit was to ascertain what my attitude

[27] *Foreign Relations, 1933*, V, 521–527, 528; National Archives, Nov. 25, 1933, 837.00/4449.

was toward the so-called revolutionary group."[28] But Mr. Welles did not attach much importance to the visit, probably because he still hoped to restore the government of Céspedes and thus preferred to deal with the former officers of the army, the ABC, and the other political factions who had been involved in the mediation.[29]

Batista was insistent. On several occasions he tried to convince various members of the revolutionary government that "it was necessary to reach an agreement with the American Ambassador,"[30] and he always seemed concerned and worried by what the American thought.

Having more talent and far more ambition than his fellow sergeants, Fulgencio Batista realized immediately that he could not depend on his relations with the students or with Grau. He tried to re-establish contacts with the ABC and with Mendieta, political factions which he knew had the *nihil obstat* of the American Ambassador, but, as we have also seen, he was not totally accepted. These political groups were still counting on a restoration of Céspedes or on a victory over all the forces that had produced the uprising of September. And Batista, willingly or not, was a part of that movement. But then came the first significant failure of the counterrevolution, the battle of the National Hotel. The Sergeants had proved their strength, and Batista immediately paid another visit to the Ambassador. This time he was received with more attention. On apologizing for the accidental death of an American citizen during the battle, Batista assured the Ambassador that he "had personally given orders to sacrifice lives of the

[28] *Foreign Relations, 1933*, V, 383.

[29] The indifference of Sumner Welles is more striking when one remembers that, from Washington, Cordell Hull insisted on September 6 that "everything now revolves around the army" (*ibid.*, p. 389).

[30] Julio César Fernández, *Yo acuso a Batista* (Havana: Construyendo a Cuba, 1940), p. 90.

soldiers themselves rather than endanger foreign lives." [31] When Batista asked for Welles' opinion and advice, the Ambassador obliged. It is easy to imagine the impact that the polished and meticulous arguments of the elegant Ambassador, dispenser of recognition and power, had on the tough and unsophisticated ex-sergeant who was avidly listening.

To begin, Batista was told that in the Ambassador's judgment his anti-Communist and anti-radical stand had made him the sole representative of authority in Cuba. But, Welles added, it should also be evident to Batista that the government of Cuba did not fill any of the conditions required by the U.S. government for diplomatic recognition, and that it had actually lost most of the small popular support it had once had. Furthermore, the affair of the National Hotel had very definitely removed any probability of recognition by the Latin American republics. The Ambassador added that all that stood in the way of a national and equitable solution was "the unpatriotic and futile obstinacy of a small group of young men who should be studying in the University instead of playing politics, and of a few individuals who had joined them from selfish motives." "In the interest of the Republic of Cuba," the Ambassador suggested, "Batista should act as intermediary between the opposing groups and through the force of authority insist on a fair and national solution."

Evidently, the ex-sergeant was dazzled by the possibilities opened for him if he knew how to use his "authority." "Batista," reported the Ambassador, "most emphatically agreed. . . . He declared that while in his opinion the ABC was unquestionably conspiring against the army (something that the Ambassador knew better than Batista did), he felt the leaders of the ABC were both patriotic and able men with

[31] The quotations in this and the following paragraph are from *Foreign Relations, 1933*, V, 469–472.

whom he could work." Before leaving, Batista asked whether the Ambassador would let him come back frequently to talk over the Cuban situation. Welles assured him that he would be "very happy to see him at any time." In reporting that meeting the Ambassador concluded: "The situation as regards my relations with Batista is, of course, anomalous. . . . In the event of further disturbances which may endanger the lives and properties of Americans or foreigners in the Republic it seems to be essential that this relationship be maintained."

It was after that interview that Batista initiated conversations with Mendieta and the ABC, trying to form a united front against the revolutionary government. Counting on its own elements and its own plan, the leaders of the ABC were not enthusiastic about dealing with him. Nevertheless, on October 7, Batista told the Ambassador that he was now completely convinced "that the present regime was a complete failure," and proclaimed his willingness to support Mendieta as provisional president. But, as we have already seen, by the beginning of November the Student Directory was fully aware of Batista's maneuvers and had forced him to recant his counterrevolutionary sins. In his retirement in Columbia military barracks,[32] concentrating on reinforcing his authority in the army, Batista had to face the unexpected insurrection of the ABC. Since no political agreement had been reached with that organization, and his own officers were very distrustful of any change in the situation, the ex-sergeant was forced to fight on the side of the revolutionary government. Immediately after victory, however, he sent his aide, Captain Hernández, to visit the Ambassador. Havana was full of rumors

[32] After the meeting at Carbó's house Batista seldom ventured out of the military barracks, and when he did he was accompanied by a rather numerous bodyguard, something that was widely criticized in the press.

about the "coming American recognition," and Batista wanted to know if there was any truth in those speculations. Busy with preparations for his trip to the United States and full of misgivings himself, Welles was quite laconic and limited himself to reiterating the basic points of the American position. "It was plain," wrote Welles, "that Batista is very much exercised as to my own views concerning the present situation." [33]

The sudden departure of Sumner Welles a few days after the defeat of the ABC, the widespread belief in the forthcoming American recognition, the beginning of conversations between the government and different sectors of the opposition under the initiative of the Uruguayan Ambassador, and the expectation of results from the Inter-American Conference in Montevideo produced the highest degree of optimism in Cuba. In a new effort to consolidate the situation, Grau addressed an urgent letter to President Roosevelt stating that his government had quelled every rebellion against it, that its goal was only to enact a constitution which would be submitted to a plebiscite of the nation at the earliest possible time, thereby ensuring freedom of suffrage and fulfillment of international obligations, and that as soon as the program of renovating Cuba was accomplished Grau would retire to the peace of his home. In his name, and in the name of his government, Grau also requested that President Roosevelt put an end "to the perturbing actions of Sumner Welles," who repeatedly disclosed his partiality by communicating and dealing with the enemies of the government.[34]

The letter was personally delivered by Alfredo Betancourt at the White House. As Roosevelt was at Warm Springs, his secretary Stephen Early wired the Acting Secretary of State

[33] *Foreign Relations, 1933*, V, 523. [34] *Ibid.*, p. 524.

Phillips asking if it were proper "for the President to receive this communication." Phillips answered negatively: "I believe the President should not receive the communication, as method suggested for transmitting it is not the proper one to be used in the circumstances." [35] Consequently, it appears that Roosevelt did not read Grau's dramatic appeal, at least not at that time.

The optimism declined, but did not die out, when the press announced that Roosevelt had confirmed "his confidence in Sumner Welles" and that "the American attitude toward Cuba had not been changed." [36] Four days later, on November 24, when it was officially announced that Sumner Welles had been replaced by Jefferson Caffery as special representative in Cuba, many Cuban circles interpreted it as proof that the American government planned to recognize Cuba, but first had to save Welles' prestige and reputation. On December 1, the Committee for the Defense of the Zafra (sugar crop), formed by many important *hacendados* and *colonos*, announced their support of the revolutionary government.[37] One day later the man who would become the most famous of Cuban *hacendados*, Julio Lobo, expressed the necessity of uniting all national economic factions to fight against the Chadbourne Plan [38] and to promote the reconstruction of Cuba. Touching on a note of radical nationalism, Lobo proclaimed that "it is better to be ruined but free, than to be ruined and subjected to the will of a few foreigners."

Increasing his energies in the meantime, Guiteras, who re-

[35] *Ibid.* [36] *Diario de la Marina*, Dec. 1, 1933, front page.

[37] *Ibid.*, Dec. 2, p. 4.

[38] The Chadbourne Plan was the scheme implemented by Machado to reduce the Cuban sugar crop and avoid the decline of the sugar price (*ibid.*, p. 3).

garded Batista as the next enemy to be defeated, tried to improve relations with labor groups,[39] appealed to all revolutionaries to close ranks with the government and, above all, began to forge an armed instrument which could counterbalance or paralyze Batista's. Realizing that, after what they considered Grau's betrayal (at Carbó's house), most of the officers were now reluctant to act against Batista, Guiteras, without decreasing his propaganda in the army, organized a corps of *Infanteria de Marina* (marines), sought the support of top navy officers, and proposed the necessity of creating "student militias."

Batista was naturally alarmed by all these maneuvers. Cautious by nature and still uncertain about the real meaning of Welles' replacement, Batista adopted a conciliatory tone toward every sector,[40] and re-established his contacts with the ABC, Mendietistas, and Menocalistas. He also publicly backed the formula of the Uruguayan Ambassador, while trying to convince Mendieta to accept the provisional presidency if Grau were forced out. He did not visit Welles again, but the Ambassador, who had returned to Cuba at the end of November, was "au courant" of his strategy, and of his silent and critical battle against Guiteras. "Dissension among the leaders of the army is sharply on the increase," reported Welles on December 4. "I was reliably informed yesterday by an authoritative source that the Secretary of Interior Guiteras, in connivance with the leaders of the Cuban navy and of two of the Havana barracks, intends to create a new mutiny directed against Batista and Grau should any compromise agreement

[39] Among other activities to that effect, on November 22 the press published the account of how Guiteras had personally freed 15 workers who were in prison in Matanzas (*ibid.*, front page).

[40] See, for example, Fulgencio Batista, "Al pueblo de Cuba," *ibid.*, Nov. 18, 1933, p. 3.

for a concentration government be entered into, their objective being the creation of an extreme Left dictatorship." [41] Quite concerned about the march of events, Welles decided to remain in Cuba at least until the conversation between the revolutionary government and the oppositionist groups reached some crisis or decision.

Probably fearing that the continuation of the "conciliation" between Grau and his opponents would only result in weakening the government or in strengthening Batista's position (all the groups represented in the conversations were also in contact with the ex-sergeant), Guiteras and the most radical elements of the government decided on December 9 to force the issue. The result was the Cabinet crisis already mentioned, the suspension of the meetings with the opposition, and the opening to the Left. This defiant attitude, which closed the way to any political compromise, was for Welles the signal for departure. He knew, as Guiteras also knew, that Batista was still in Cuba and still commanding the army. He also knew that Guiteras' gauntlet would force the opposition to seek a united front against the government and that there was no longer a Student Directory to stand behind Grau.[42] He knew something else: he knew well the man who was going to succeed him and the policy that man would apply. He let the Cubans speculate about the implications of his departure; he did not have to speculate. Nothing was going to change. In a farewell speech at the American Club, he pointed out the failure of the efforts for conciliation and commented softly: "As you may see by the latest events, it has been impossible to

[41] *Foreign Relations, 1933,* V, 531.

[42] As a matter of fact, by this time many of the members of the Student Directory were in the opposition or had abandoned the struggle.

carry out the plans that the United States had to help Cuba." [43] And with that parting arrow he abandoned Cuba.

[43] *Diario de la Marina*, Dec. 14, 1933, front page. Some time later, Welles insisted that "the Government of the United States did not believe it had the moral right to recognize a government which unquestionably met with the whole-hearted opposition of all important elements in Cuban life"; see Sumner Welles, *Relations between the United States and Cuba* (Washington, D.C.: Government Printing Office, 1934), p. 6.

16 *The Downfall of the Revolutionary Government*

While these events were taking place in Cuba, the Cuban delegation to the Inter-American Conference in Montevideo was fighting a gallant battle for the revolution. At the opening of the debates only two Latin American countries, Uruguay and Mexico, had recognized Grau's government. It was the mission and the hope of the Cuban delegation to turn the tide of Latin solidarity in their favor and to obtain American recognition.

In his first speech before the general assembly, to a tense and silent audience, Cuban delegate Angel Alberto Giraudy made a passionate and eloquent presentation of the Cuban case:

> Among my first words permit me also to refer to Cuba, a country to which great suffering has fallen. I believe it absolutely essential to express the attitude of the Cuban government under the present circumstances. . . .
>
> We represent a government formed by the free will of the people of Cuba, and through the initial efforts of the students, professors and workers who waged a cruel and tragic strife against tyranny, and who aspire . . . to reconstruct the national life upon the basis of its most complete sovereignty. . . .
>
> Our government is ready, therefore, freely to consult the opinion of its people in the certainty that popular will will con-

stitute the backbone of the program of national regeneration which Cuba enacts.[1]

He then appealed to "the people of this indigenous and ragged America" to form "a confederation of free countries," invoked the memory of Martí, expressed his faith in the future of America, and saluted Cordell Hull who was "one of those brave Americans who fought with our *mambises* in San Juan and El Caney in 1898." Later Mrs. Dania Padilla spoke for Cuban women:

> I have the enormous satisfaction of making known before this American Assembly, and through it to the whole world, that the Cuban woman, who side by side with man fought to secure her rights, has seen her emancipation realized with the triumph of the revolution.
>
> Today in our country we share with men the right to live as civilized human beings, and the duty to work to make our country great, prosperous, happy and definitely sovereign.[2]

But their efforts were of no avail. In vain, in and out of the meetings, did the Cuban delegates reiterate the popular support that their government was accorded, the accomplishments and the democratic structure of a regime that had already announced its intention to hold free and honest elections in the next ten months. In vain did Giraudy repeat that nonrecognition was a form of intervention. The Latin American governments did not change their attitude. The Cubans were, as an observer put it, "quixotic and heroic," [3] but their

[1] *Seventh International Conference of American States* (Montevideo, 1933), Plenary Sessions, pp. 27–30.

[2] *Ibid.*, p. 53. *Mambises* were the Cuban soldiers in the war for independence.

[3] Jonathan Mitchell, "Pan American Prelude," *New Republic*, LXXVII (Dec. 27, 1933), 192; Hubert Herring, "Pan Americanism, New Style?" *Harper's Monthly Magazine*, May 1934, pp. 683–694;

efforts could not break the powerful influence of United States policy.

Some of the events taking place in Montevideo were reported by the Cuban press as Cuban revolutionary victories.[4] The situation in Cuba since the departure of Welles continued to be a confused mixture of optimism and despair, of chaos and radical action. The oppositionist groups, in spite of their evident disorganization, persisted in declaring their intention to combat the government in every possible way. The revolutionary government, where Guiteras was now both force and symbol, pushed forward its program and confirmed its radicalism. On December 8, Guiteras announced that any person caught stealing or damaging government property would be shot on the spot. Three days later a national labor congress was convened, and Grau announced general elections for a constituent assembly in April. On December 22 there was a huge popular demonstration in front of the Presidential Palace to thank the government for its nationalistic stand and its laws in favor of the people.[5] On December 24, *Alma Mater's* front page announced that the government was "practically recognized by the United States."

But the economic crisis continued, and the basic weakness of the revolutionary government was by then becoming more and more apparent: deprived of any political organization or party to mold the masses into a permanent, effective supporting instrument, the government looked like an isolated and gesticulating minority, occasionally applauded, usually criti-

---

and Herminio Portell Vilá, *Cuba y la conferencia de Montevideo* (Havana: Imprenta Heraldo Cristiano, 1934).

[4] "Anti-imperialist Victory in Montevideo," announced *Alma Mater* (front page) on Dec. 16, 1933, commenting on the acceptance by the conference of the principle of nonintervention.

[5] See *Alma Mater* and *Diario de la Marina* of that date.

cized, seldom understood, always incapable of creating the impression of real control. Recognizing this dangerous gap growing between the government and the masses, Enrique C. Hernández criticized the numerous students who by then were either in the opposition or had abandoned the struggle, pointed out that "the government does not know how to explain its programs and accomplishments," and urged the immediate formation of a revolutionary political party. In the same tone, Sergio Carbó, who had vainly struggled to form a national revolutionary party, exhorted President Grau: "An isolated government is a doomed government. . . . To survive the government needs to expand in the national atmosphere, needs to create one or two political parties and promote a vigorous propaganda. . . . We cannot rely indefinitely on the support of the bayonets." [6] But the confusion of the revolutionary groups was by then too serious. The revolutionary party was never formed.

That the frail government was not yet facing a major crisis was due largely to the lack of unity and leadership among the opposition—who were again begging Mendieta to become their rallying figure—and to Batista's caution. Still holding his control over the army in spite of Guiteras' maneuvers, Batista was unwilling to take any action against the government until he could be certain of the American attitude. While resuming his conversations with oppositionist groups, especially with Mendieta, Batista also displayed his support for the revolutionary government. He went so far as to accompany several student leaders (Rubén de León, Segundo

[6] For Hernandez' words see *Alma Mater*, Dec. 26, 1933, front page. Sergio Carbó, "Que cosa quiere y adonde vá el Partido Nacional Revolucionario," *La Semana*, Oct. 14, 1933, p. 3; and "Como y por culpa de quien cayó Grau San Martín," *Bohemia*, Mar. 25, 1934, pp. 28–29, 40–42.

Curti), who immediately after Welles' departure went to the Embassy to defend the policies of the revolution. While León made a fiery speech to Chargé d'Affaires Matthews expressing the students' determination to fight "for the aims of the revolution, which means not only a change of leaders but a change of system," Batista calmly expressed his anti-Communist convictions and backed León's contention that every opposition to the government "would rapidly subside once the regime were recognized by the American government."[7] Matthews merely replied that the new special representative of the United States would arrive soon and that he would surely be glad to hear those arguments.

On December 18 the new personal representative of the American government, Jefferson Caffery, arrived in Havana. Caffery belonged to the same school of suave diplomats as Sumner Welles. Without any previous personal involvement in the Cuban imbroglio, he had a chance to be impartial and to judge the situation from an objective standpoint. He had, nevertheless, similar and possibly even stronger convictions than Welles about whom the American government should or should not support. A political conservative of elegant manners, Caffery was once described as a "somewhat frostbitten diplomat of the old school, who holds to the Hamilton belief that those who have should rule." "Diplomacy, as I interpret it," he declared in Havana, "nowadays consists largely in cooperation with American business."[8] It was natural, then, that the shouting revolutionaries should be greeted with something like contempt by Caffery. Apparently he even had a personal dislike for the man whom he knew to be his best

[7] *Foreign Relations of the United States, 1933* (Washington, D.C.: U.S. Government Printing Office, 1952), V, 541–542.

[8] E. Wilder Spaulding, *Ambassadors Ordinary and Extraordinary* (Washington, D.C.: Public Affairs Press, 1961), p. 262.

potential ally: rough, ill-mannered Batista. But in this case he sacrificed his personal distaste to the interests of American diplomacy as he interpreted them.

Although he was more reserved and less prone to action than Sumner Welles, Caffery let his attitude toward the Cuban regime be known as soon as he arrived in Havana; he remarked to an expectant press: "My country's policy toward Cuba will remain the same." [9] It was his first blow to the hopes of many Cubans who had interpreted his arrival as proof of a change in American policy. A few days later, when Secretary of Agriculture Carlos Hevia visited him to ascertain his position and to assure him once more that the revolutionary government intended to hold free elections, Caffery stated: "As the situation appears today, we cannot recognize your government." He went on to indicate the American concern about "certain seemingly Communistic tendencies in the present regime," and added, "I do not feel that you offer adequate assurances for guaranteeing free elections." [10] Caffery expressed these opinions even before he had tried, as he reported on December 26, "to explore the situation thoroughly." [11] Thus, his conclusions after that careful exploration were predictable. On January 10, 1934, Caffery voiced his opinion of the revolutionary government: "I agree with former Ambassador Welles as to the inefficiency, ineptitude and unpopularity with all the better classes in the country of the de facto government. It is supported only by the army and the ignorant masses who have been misled by utopian promises." [12]

In spite of that opinion—and unlike Welles—Caffery did

[9] *Diario de la Marina*, Dec. 19, 1933, front page.
[10] *Foreign Relations, 1933*, V, 544. [11] *Ibid.*, p. 545.
[12] *Foreign Relations of the United States, 1934* (Washington, D.C.: U.S. Government Printing Office, 1952), v, 95.

not praise the ABC or any other opposition group, nor did he make an effort to talk to them. He apparently was skeptical about their capacity for action and believed that the Cuban political situation was deteriorating so rapidly that a firm and open anti-recognition policy was enough to bring about the crisis of the regime. He was probably correct.

At the beginning of 1934 the economic conditions in Cuba were so bad and the uncertainty about the coming *zafra* so widespread that large segments of the population—from *hacendados* and *colonos* to labor groups, to the urban middle class—were clamoring for a political solution that could restore normality and assure some degree of economic security. Furthermore, another break had occurred in the high ranks of the government. Tired of the struggle, or perhaps resenting the growing prestige of Guiteras, President Grau San Martín was now willing to accept a compromise with the opposition.[13] Finally, Caffery's unmistakable position had dispelled Batista's doubts about American policy and the possibilities of diplomatic recognition. During the first days of January, Batista was organizing a united political front against Grau and putting pressure on Mendieta to accept the position of provisional president. On January 10 he bluntly asked what had to be done to obtain American recognition. Caffery's answer was a gem of diplomatic savoir faire: "I will lay down no specific terms; the matter of your government is a Cuban matter and it is for you to decide what you will do about it."[14]

Two things hindered Batista's plan to replace Grau: the

[13] On Jan. 11, 1934, Grau told Caffery, in Batista's presence, that he was willing to give place to a nonpolitical successor to guarantee fair elections, or to change his cabinet in order to admit representatives of the opposition (*Foreign Relations, 1934*, V, p. 97).

[14] *Ibid.*

possibility of armed opposition from pro-Guiteras revolutionary groups (including the navy, which had been courted by Guiteras), and the hesitancy of Mendieta, who wanted to reach power without bloodshed or violent opposition. Concerning this second aspect Batista at times appeared so desperate that even cautious Caffery moved to give him a hand. When Mendieta reiterated to Caffery that he would be willing to accept the provisional presidency "only if he knows in advance that the United States will recognize him," Caffery requested authority to do so immediately, for "if this is not done, Batista will probably turn definitely to the left with definite disaster for all our interests here (or declare himself military dictator)." [15]

On January 14, Batista convened a civilian-military junta at Columbia's military barracks, with representatives of the most important political groups, to decide on a plan of action. He still insisted on Mendieta's candidacy, but to avoid a possible clash with revolutionaries and friction with the navy, the junta decided to ask for Grau's resignation and to support Carlos Hevia, Secretary of Agriculture in the revolutionary government, as provisional president. On January 15, faced with a united political front and an ultimatum from the army, Ramón Grau San Martín decided to resign.[16] Guiteras was asked to make known his position, since he had been mentioned as a possible substitute. His answer was typical of the man: "If the junta designates me, I will accept. If the army opposes, we'll fight the army." [17]

[15] *Ibid.*, p. 98. The State Department refused to authorize any "previous" declaration.

[16] Later, Grau wrote that he was forced to resign because of military pressure, the perturbing influence of illegitimate interests, and the handiwork of Caffery. See his "The Cuban Terror," *The Nation*, April 3, 1935, p. 381.

[17] *Diario de la Marina*, Jan. 15, 1934, front page.

On January 15, before a vast crowd, Grau made his short farewell address: "I have dictated some laws which are beneficial for the entire country. . . . I have never submitted to any foreign embassy. . . . I have tried to benefit the people, and I have used a firm hand against big companies." A week later he departed for Mexico. He assured the large multitude who had crowded the Malecon to see his ship pass: "In saying *hasta luego* [a Spanish goodby which implies "I'll see you again"] to the Cuban people, I repeat that I shall continue with unshakable faith to work for the liberty, the dignity, and the progress of our country." It has been said that when Carlos Prío, who had just returned from Montevideo, embraced him with deep emotion, Grau assured him softly: "Don't worry, Carlos, we'll return to power soon." And indeed they did.[18]

Grau's resignation and the designation of Carlos Hevia as provisional president triggered Guiteras into a final desperate action. Immediately he attempted to rally all dispersed revolutionary groups; he appealed to his friends in the navy, and made an all-out effort to organize a general strike. But he was struggling against a general desire for peace and security. The revolutionary groups were now dispersed and weak; all Communists and many extreme radicals considered him an enemy; and labor lacked the necessary organization—and probably the will—to paralyze the nation. Not only did Guiteras fail in his attempt, but ironically his efforts strengthened Batista's position. Alarmed by the rumors of a general strike and of possible disturbances in the interior, the junta at Columbia decided that only a truly national figure, backed

[18] *Ibid.*, Jan. 16 and 22, front pages; interview with Carlos Prío. Ten years after these events Ramón Grau San Martín was elected President of Cuba for the term 1944–1948. He was succeeded by Carlos Prío Socarrás, 1948–1952.

by Batista, could calm the tensions and avoid another crisis. Mendieta's partisans had disavowed his promise to support Hevia and were demanding Hevia's resignation. On January 17, after hasty consultation with the leaders of the navy and with Mendieta himself, the Junta accepted Hevia's resignation—which Hevia had sent addressed to Batista—and proclaimed Carlos Mendieta as the provisional president of Cuba.[19]

Once again cheering multitudes marched in Havana to celebrate the restoration of peace and order. After months of tension and turmoil, there was among many Cubans a sensation of relief. That very day Rubén Martínez Villena died in Havana, a relatively unnoticed event. On the following day Grau San Martín went into exile.[20] His government had lasted more than four months and had not received American diplomatic recognition. Five days after Mendieta was sworn in as President, Caffery received a momentous telegram: "Under authorization of the President you will please extend immediately to the Government of Cuba on behalf of the United States a formal and cordial recognition." [21] Bitterly, Julio César Fernández commented:

> The guns of the "Wyoming," the same guns which threatened to exterminate our revolution when it began, joyfully saluted yesterday the new reactionary government. And the salvos of the "Wyoming," noisy and powerful as the Empire they represent, were echoed by thousands of shots fired—to proclaim their presence—by the masochists of the "diplomatic recognition." . . . American diplomacy has many resources; when the steel

[19] M. Márquez Sterling, *Proceso histórico de la Enmienda Platt* (Havana: Imprenta El Siglo, 1941), pp. 402, 404.

[20] The Mexican Socialist Youth asked the Mexican government not to give asylum to Grau becuse he was "a servant of imperialism and of Wall Street" (*Diario de la Marina*, Jan. 23, 1934, front page).

[21] *Foreign Relations, 1934*, p. 349.

of her warships is not convenient, she uses the docile backbone of her native lackeys.[22]

These were the bitter words of a student leader who could not realize, at the time, that many of the forces and aspirations unleashed by the revolutionary episode of 1933 were to continue influencing and changing Cuba, but the words were quite fitted to express the situation in January 1934. For the thunderous salvo of the "Wyoming" did represent the turning of a page in the history of the island. The turbulent, radical, forging revolutionary period had come to an end. A new and different era began in Cuba.

[22] *En defensa de la revolución* (Havana: n.p., 1936), p. 149.

17

Reflections on the Cuban Revolutionary Process

For those who have "discovered" Cuba and Cuban history only after, and under, the impact of Castro's revolution, it is easy to dismiss as unimportant the revolutionary episode of 1933—and, for that matter, all Cuban history before Castro. On the other hand, the similarities between the earlier episode and the later revolution are so obvious that they suggest a point-by-point historical comparison which could be as dangerous as ignoring the 1930's altogether. After all, the same Fulgencio Batista whom Guiteras failed to defeat in 1934 was defeated by Castro in 1958; a student leader of 1933, Eduardo Chibás, sponsored Fidel Castro at the beginning of his political career in 1951;[1] the same Blas Roca who justified the "opportunistic" mistake of the Communist party in 1933 is now a full-fledged, though not very influential, member of the Executive Committee of the Cuban Communist party, which, at least theoretically, rules the island. As in 1961, so also in 1933, Cuba was diplomatically isolated, surrounded by American warships, and fighting at Montevideo's Pan-American Conference for her right

[1] Castro ran as candidate for the House of Representatives in Chibás' Party of the Cuban People. On March 10, 1952, a military coup put Batista in power, and the elections were never held.

to develop her revolutionary programs. And was not Raúl Roa, for a time the most important spokesman of Castro's government, one of the members of the Student Left Wing of 1933?

Yes, the links are obvious. They could be further dramatized by remembering the chilling prediction of Rubén Martínez Villena in 1933, when Fidel Castro was only six years old: "The red flags hoisted in the silence of dark night upon the factory chimneys of the Armour Company sugar mills herald the raising of those other red banners which will float in the glare of the sunlight over all the factories of the whole sugar industry. . . . *Eyes that are young today will not yet have grown old when they look upon this marvel.*" [2] Or one could ponder the conclusion of Ezequiel Ramírez Novoa: "If the United States in 1933 had respected the decision of the Cuban people, the process of independence would have been freely carried out, and there would have been no need for the sacrifices which the present generation of Cubans have had to make." [3] Perhaps, perhaps if what we have called "the Right" had not frustrated the revolution of 1933—and killed the attendant reforms—then the Left in 1959 would not have needed extreme radical measures, or perhaps there would have been no need for revolution. But let us avoid the game of conjecture to dwell upon the actual reasons and results that make 1933–1934 a crucial time in Cuban history. One fact at least appears certain: the Cuban society that Castro found in 1959 was basically forged by the forces that emerged and grew out of the revolutionary episode of 1933.

[2] Rubén Martínez Villena, "The Rise of the Revolutionary Movement in Cuba," *The Communist*, XII (1933), 569 (italics mine).

[3] Ezequiel Ramírez Novoa, *Historia de una gran epopeya: Cuba y el imperialismo yanky* (Lima: Ediciones 28 de Julio, 1960), p. 108.

The long struggle against Machado and the turbulent period following his downfall have characteristics usually attributed to true revolutionary phenomena: violence, participation of the masses, radical programs, and some basic changes in the social and political structure of the nation. By profoundly shaking the political order in Cuba, by defying with a measure of success the hitherto unchallenged position of the United States, and by partially applying some of the radical ideas and programs that had been gaining ground since the 1920's, revolutionary groups of 1933 effected a profound change in Cuba. The revitalization of nationalism, the opening of new economic opportunities for several national sectors, and the weakening of foreign dominance in Cuba were some of the consequences of their actions. The vanguard of the 1933 revolutionary forces—the students, Grau, Guiteras—did fail to remain in power for long and, as a consequence, were able only to "offer" the nation their ideas and projects. But the mere realization of the necessity and possibilities for change created a new national conscience and initiated a trend that was afterward almost impossible to reverse. As early as August 1933, when the real revolutionary period was about to begin, an alert Spanish writer had already noticed the new dimension of events in Cuba: "In comparison with the usual Latin American revolution —which seldom is anything more than a *pronunciamiento* [4] —the fall of Machado offers a new aspect: the weapon with which he was defeated. That weapon was a general strike, that is, the none-too-frequent intervention of the masses in the fight for their claims." [5] The awakening and politization

[4] *Pronunciamiento* is a word used mainly in Spain to indicate an act of rebellion of an individual, or some small group, usually of the armed forces, who generally represent no interest other than their own.

[5] Quoted in Ramón Vasconcelos, *Dos años bajo el terror* (Havana: Cultural, 1935), p. 20.

of the Cuban masses was indeed one important result of the conflict but, as we have already seen, there were many others.

Of the three political parties of the prerevolutionary era, Liberal, Conservative, and Popular, only the Liberals reappeared later to play a role, a minor one, in Cuban politics. New parties, more or less imbued with the ideas of 1933, dominated the scene after the revolution.[6] The Congress, the courts, the bureaucracy, and the University were purged of corrupt elements. The feeble labor unions of the 1920's evolved into the powerful CTC (Confederation of Cuban Workers), the only central labor organization of Cuba, bringing together all organized workers. In 1942, four years after its founding, the CTC had a membership of more than 400,000 workers.[7] Under the growing power and pressure of the CTC, which was dominated by Communists from 1939 to 1946, labor legislation was augmented steadily before and after the promulgation of the Constitution of 1940. Simultaneously the *colonos*, who were almost defenseless before the revolution, joined forces in the Cane Growers Association of Cuba (created by the revolutionary government in January 1934) and fought successfully for their economic security and for a more just distribution of sugar profits between them and the *hacendados*. The Law of Sugar Coordination, issued on September 2, 1937, which gave them the right of permanent occupancy of the land they were occupying under any title, was a radical advance for the Association, which soon became one of the most important

[6] "It is axiomatic among Cubans," wrote William S. Stokes some years later, "that the only parties capable of winning a national campaign are those which opposed the dictator Machado in the 30s." See his penetrating article, "The Cuban Revolution and the Presidential Elections of 1948," *Hispanic-American Historical Review*, Feb. 1951, p. 38.

[7] José R. Alvarez Díaz *et al.*, *A Study on Cuba* (Miami: University of Miami Press, 1963), p. 584.

socioeconomic forces on the island. The economic nationalism that Machado timidly began was expanded by these and many other measures adopted by the Cuban governments after 1933, and the recovery of Cuban resources by Cuban native capital was impressive and continuous. In 1939, sugar produced in Cuban-owned mills still was only 22.42 per cent of the total production; in 1958, Cuban-owned mills were producing 62.13 percent of the total. The commercial banks under Cuban management, which had completely collapsed in the 1920's, held 60 per cent of total deposits in 1958.[8]

The revolution of 1933, while opening the way for remarkable economic and social progress and increasing the role of the state in economic affairs, also gave the Cubans a taste of nationalism and a new sense of sovereignty. The Platt Amendment was officially abrogated in 1934, and Cuban politics gained a visible measure of independence. No one doubted the still enormous weight and importance of American influence in Cuba, but in comparison with a very recent past—with the era of Crowder, Welles, and Caffery, when almost all eyes were fixed on the American Ambassador as the supreme political arbiter—the new period brought a refreshing sensation of liberation and the feeling that Cuba was beginning to be the master of her own destiny.[9] Protected by an expanding web of nationalistic legislation, the Cubans ceased to be pariahs in their own land, squeezed by the double pressure of American companies and Spanish commercial interests.

[8] *Ibid.*, pp. 521 and 467.

[9] While interpreting it according to Marxist ideas, Castro's historians and economists do recognize this decline of American influence in Cuba during this period. One of them, Oscar Pino Santos, described this as the moment when American imperialism "sort of silenced itself" ("Historiografía y Revolución," *Casa de las Américas* [special issue of the 10th anniversary of the Cuban Revolution], IX, Nos. 51–52 [Nov. 1968–Feb. 1969], pp. 105).

Cuban literary expression, influenced by international currents but also reflecting these new national conditions, moved from a tone of social protest and political involvement to a more purely artistic concern. If the most important literary magazine of the twenties was *Avance*, whose name had been symbolically linked by the editors to a ship penetrating new horizons, the most significant magazine of the postrevolutionary movement was *Origenes* (which lasted from 1944 to 1956), whose editors were more concerned with creating a pure, transcendent poetical form. Under the influence of José Lezama Lima (b. 1909), a new generation of Cuban poets adopted an almost metaphysical, extremely elaborated form of poetry.[10]

The emphasis on education in the revolutionary government of 1933—a new educational program, autonomy for the University, reduction of tuition, and free education for poor students—did not diminish during the following years. In 1936, Cuba inaugurated her first national plan for rural education; in 1953 she had six universities, had expanded the scope of higher studies, and could boast of having one of the lowest illiteracy rates in Latin America (22.1 per cent).

Politically, the period 1933–1952 represents a general progress toward democracy. Batista's ten years in power (1934–1944) after the collapse of Grau's government should not be viewed simply as a period of counterrevolution and military oppression. Batista was too smart and too realistic not to try to use in his favor the popular energies liberated by the revolutionary government of 1933. He never hesitated to use force when necessary—the ruthless methods employed to prevent a general strike in 1935 were proof

[10] There were, of course, other groups and other tendencies including those who, like Nicolas Guillén in his poetry and Paco Alfonso in his dramas, kept an accent of social protest in some of their works.

enough[11]—but force and brutality were not his natural tendencies. In power, as when he was struggling to reach it, he relied more on his political skill, maneuverability, and cunning. In 1936, when president-elect Miguel Mariano Gómez refused to act like a puppet and tried to oppose Batista's dominance, the former sergeant did not resort to the usual method of deposing the president and establishing a military dictatorship; instead he used all his political influence to force the Congress to depose the president and call for new elections. Shortly afterward a general amnesty was proclaimed and all political prisoners were freed. If the validity of Batista's self-proclaimed title of "revolutionary"[12] is debatable, it is not easy to overlook his sociopolitical record during those ten years. He took charge of a nation convulsed and divided by long years of turmoil and terrorism, and he restored order. He allowed political parties to act freely, convened a constitutional assembly where many of his political opponents sat as delegates (including Ramón Grau San Martín) and which proclaimed the Constitution of 1940 (one of the most socially advanced constitutions in Latin America), and finally crowned his period in office by presiding over free national elections and by stepping down when Grau San Martín was elected president in 1944. As Fulgencio Batista was about to leave the presidency, a group of well-known Cubans who had never been

[11] In March 1935 almost all revolutionary groups—the Auténticos, Guiteras' Joven Cuba, the ABC, and the Communists—joined forces to topple Batista through a general strike. The loyalty of the army, severe methods of repression, and the usual division among revolutionary groups saved the government. After that failure, the majority of the groups decided to abandon violent tactics and organized themselves as political parties. Antonio Guiteras was killed while trying to escape into exile to continue the fight against Batista.

[12] See Fulgencio Batista, *Revolución social o política reformista* (Havana: Prensa Indoamericana, 1944), p. 51.

suspected of pro-Americanism or reactionary tendencies, saluted him in a public letter:

Honored President and Esteemed Friend:

The National Assembly of the Socialist Party [Communist] . . . wants to take advantage of its meeting today to address a letter to you . . . At this time, as you relinquish the presidency, our party wants to declare that it is satisfied with the collaboration we have maintained and the support we have given you in your task of governing. . . . The free and sovereign constituent assembly, the political amnesty that wiped out all of the tumultuous proceedings of 1934–37, the solution of the critical phase of the university problem and the pacific spirit with which, despite all this, it was possible to reintegrate all parties into the legal civil battle and to restore normalcy, were the first fruits achieved by your actions. . . . Since 1940, our party has been the most loyal and unswerving supporter of your governmental measures, the most energetic promoter of your inspiring platform of democracy, social justice and defense of national prosperity. . . . In the record of your acts as president, the public works, the progressive measures, the democratic declarations shine with such luster that they obscure and reduce any stains that have tarnished your administration as a legacy of the past. . . .

Juan Marinello
Blas Roca [13]

Thus the Communists spoke of Fulgencio Batista in 1944.

In 1944, Cuba offered the refreshing, and in Latin America, infrequent, spectacle of a strong man abandoning the presidency to a democratically elected rival. From 1944 to 1952, the Cuban Revolutionary party (the "Auténticos"), a political organization created by the principal revolutionary leaders of 1933, ruled Cuba, first under Ramón Grau San

[13] From "Los socialistas y la realidad cubana" (pamphlet of the Cuban Communist party, 1944), quoted in Luis E. Aguilar, *Marxism in Latin American* (New York: Knopf, 1968), pp. 133–138.

Martín (1944–1948), and then under Carlos Prío Socarrás (1948–1952). Under the Auténticos, Cuba enjoyed the prosperity brought about by the high price of sugar after the Second World War, and a remarkable period of political freedom and democracy. Social and economic legislation continued to expand, the army lost its pre-eminence, the Communists were forced out of the leadership of the CTC, and freedom of expression reached a very high level.

How can we explain, then, that after such remarkable progress brought about by a revolutionary process, a nation considered prosperous by Latin American standards—where the middle class was expanding, labor legislation was advanced, and the most dramatic aspect of the usual Latin American spectacle, a miserable and defenseless mass and a handful of rich people, was absent—was to enter after a few years into the terrible throes of a socialist revolution?

There is no easy answer. Even after considering all the factors involved—including the most decisive and elusive, the character and personality of Fidel Castro—there is still wide margin for uncertainty and doubt. That is why, when reflecting upon this entire period, one must consider inadequate the usual leftist simplification of gathering some figures about the imperialist exploitation of Cuba, and about the famous and favorite "corruption" of Havana, to conclude that in 1959 Cuba was ripe for a socialist revolution. That ripeness as late as 1958 no Marxist in or out of Cuba had foreseen or predicted. The easy anti-Marxist explanation (so dear to many Cuban exiles) which presents a paradisaical Cuba falling through deceit and betrayal into the grip of a group of international Communist conspirators also misses the mark.

Where then is the answer? Who knows it? Historical causes are always difficult to discover, and sometimes it appears that, as in Plotinus' theory of beauty, they exist primarily in the eyes of the observer. After revolutions, theories multiply. Impressed by the spectacular explosion, investigators scrutinize the past, searching for clues and portents of the impending revolution, and in their eagerness they transform any suitable episode, no matter how trivial, into a significant event. This entire prerevolutionary period, then, acquires a new, and largely artificial, dimension: its events were only the prelude to the revolution. What seems evident is that in the period following the revolution of 1933 a series of events occurred in Cuba that created a national crisis and produced a situation for favorable exploitation by anyone capable of confronting the crisis. Surely those events do not explain the emergence of Fidel Castro or the decisions he made (or was forced to make) radically to alter the course of Cuban history, but they do help us to understand the historical moment in which Castro appeared and some of the actions and reactions of the Cuban people when he became the new champion of a national cause.

But before we consider those significant developments of the postrevolutionary period, it is essential to emphasize the obvious: the revolutionary episode of 1933 was for Cuba a step forward, but only one step, and a step fraught with frustration and disillusion. The relative progress that Cuba enjoyed from 1933 to 1952 did not solve many of her problems, nor did it change many unjust conditions. The existence of *latifundia*, the periodical unemployment of thousands of cane-cutters, the basic dependence on one product (sugar) and one market (the U.S.A.) were still dramatic and at times agonizing problems for thousands of Cubans.[14]

[14] After reading some of the most recent studies of Cuba's economic problems (for example, René Dumont, *Cuba: Est'il Socialist* [Paris: Gallimard, 1970]), and after witnessing the tremendous and not quite

And there were many others: public corruption, an absurd concentration of political power in the city of Havana (a Cuban Minister of Education once said "Havana is Cuba, all the rest is landscape"), some vestiges of racial discrimination, and the poor conditions of Cuban rural population were some of the most evident.[15] But these were old problems that Cuba shared in a greater or lesser degree with the rest of Latin America and should be considered only as the background for some important specific developments that give the period we are dealing with its special characteristics. These developments are keys to understanding the Cuban situation in 1959.

First, there was the bitter, general disillusion brought about by Ramón Grau San Martín's second administration. In June 1944, when it was officially announced that the famous and respected leader of 1933 had won the presidency, a wave of joy and confidence swept the island. At last the revolutionary president of 1933, the first Cuban leader who had openly defied American dominance and favored the lower classes, the champion of nationalism and social legislation, was back in power. And now he and his *muchachos*, the student leaders of 1933, were the representa-

---

successful effort to produce 10 million tons of sugar—pushing Cuba back to the state of a sugar factory—plus the undeniable economic dependence on Soviet aid, which is always accompanied by growing political pressure, one feels compelled to ask a somber but realistic question: To what extent is it possible for a small, nonindustrialized nation really to free herself from foreign influence?

[15] "How can we fail to tremble for the future of our political institutions," I wrote in 1954, "and of our nation, if a large section of our rural population is illiterate, reduced to support 'rights' they do not understand and 'liberties' that have no meaning, . . . an easy prey for the demagogue or the Marxist of the future, capable always of using for his own benefit this kind of tragic situation" (Luis E. Aguilar, "La Verdadera Tragedia," *Bohemia*, Nov. 15, 1954, p. 76).

tives of a legitimate government, recognized by all nations, free to consolidate and expand the ideals of the revolution and to stop public corruption once and for all. Everybody hailed the "glorious journey of June"—Chibás' phrase for the electoral triumph of the Auténticos—as the dawn of public honesty and civilian democracy in Cuba. The Auténticos were in power from 1944 to 1952 and, although they advanced several beneficial laws, restored civilian authority in the government, and kept a religious respect for freedom of expression, they displayed an almost legendary capacity to steal public funds. What had happened to the gallant leaders of 1933? Again one can only guess.[16] Perhaps ten years of exile, struggle, and petty politics had effaced their idealism. Perhaps the absence of the best of them—such men as Antonio Guiteras and Enrique Fernández—had opened their ranks to opportunists and cynics. Maybe the continuous repetition of the same ideas and programs in the name of the "revolution," in a nation where revolutionary programs had become a standard political procedure, had deprived the words of their true meaning and transformed the leaders into something close to "professional" revolutionaries.[17] We do

[16] During an interview with former president Carlos Prío, I asked him, rather bluntly, for the causes of the Auténticos' public dishonesty. "It was basically a matter of generation training," he answered. "As Machado was despotic and pro-American, we learned to fight for democratic freedom and nationalism. But as Machado was honest, we failed to incorporate honesty as one of the objectives of our program; we didn't learn to associate dishonesty with a basic evil."

[17] A glance at the programs of the twelve Cuban political parties in existence in 1940 shows how common revolutionary terminology and rhetoric had become (*Los partidos cubanos y la asamblea constituyente* [Havana: Editorial Atenas, 1940]). Ortega y Gasset loved to say that when a human activity becomes "professionalized" it gains in efficiency what it loses in spontaneity. One of the most unfortunate results of the episode of 1933 was the proliferation of revolutionary groups which, like the UIR (Unión Insuruccional Revolucionaria),

not know the causes for that transformation (or revelation), but we do know quite well the full extent of its results. The failure of the Auténticos to live up to the popular expectations and the bitterness, resentment and loss of faith among the Cuban masses, after the initial shock of disbelief, were to have profound and tragic consequences for the island. If the initial damage was not total, if some measure of optimism and faith survived to be rekindled into a national cause, it was owing principally to two factors: economic prosperity, and the emergence of a new leader who raised the fallen banner of revolutionary decency and became rapidly the champion of many popular aspirations. This man was Eduardo Chibás.

The son of a wealthy engineer, Chibás was involved in the fight against Machado since his early youth. In 1946, partially disillusioned with Grau's public corruption, and partially frustrated at not being able to obtain his party's nomination for the next presidential elections, Chibás broke with the Auténticos and initiated a crusade against governmental corruption. Adopting the broom as his emblem and proclaiming a catching slogan, "Verguenza contra dinero" (dignity versus money), he appealed to the Cuban people to join him in his effort to clean Cuban politics and rescue the revolution. His success was impressive and significant. With improvised political machinery, resting his cause more on his unblemished record and recognized honesty than on any radical program,[18] Chibás ran as presidential candidate

---

used terroristic methods to obtain political positions or bureaucratic spoils. They became a plague during the Auténticos' regime.

[18] It is significant, and expressive of the condition and aspirations of the Cuban people, that throughout this period the essential political issue was not radical reforms or revolutionary objectives, but public honesty.

in 1948—only two years after founding his Party of the Cuban People, known as the Ortodoxo party—and pulled almost 20 per cent of the votes. The candidate of the Auténticos, Carlos Prío Socarrás, won a majority of the votes, but he had relied more on the money the government spent freely (to buy votes) and on the mistakes of his adversaries [19] than on the prestige of his party, which was declining.

After those elections Chibás continued to gain political force. His Sunday programs on CMQ radio station in which he incessantly, and at times immoderately, attacked anyone remotely associated with any dubious affair, became a landmark on the Cuban national scene. As the elections of 1952 approached, the growing popularity of Chibás and the impact of his public accusations were so great, the clamor for honest politicians was so general, that to keep alive a hope of winning the elections the Auténticos were forced to look for an honest man to be their candidate. It took some searching, but they found one: Carlos Hevia, former Minister of Agriculture of the revolutionary government of 1933, President of the Republic for forty-eight hours (the brief moment between the resignation of Grau San Martín and the proclamation of Mendieta in January 1934), a quiet, diligent man, lacking charisma, but honest.

A third man announced his candidacy for those elections, a man who had lived in a sort of self-imposed exile since 1944 and who, reassured by the democratic atmosphere that Cuba was enjoying, had recently returned to the island—Fulgencio Batista.

As the electoral campaign began to unfold in 1951, every

[19] Instead of taking the offensive against governmental corruption, the third candidate, Dr. Ricardo Núñez Portuondo, a well-known physician who was backed by an impressive political coalition, spent the entire campaign defending himself from the charge of Machadista hurled at him by the Auténticos.

national poll showed that the real contenders were going to be the Auténticos' candidate, Hevia, supported by the political machinery of the government, and Chibás, backed by the enthusiasm of thousands of Cubans. Observers of the Cuban situation gave Batista only a remote chance of winning. Then, in August 1951, at the end of one of his radio programs, after a dramatic appeal to the Cuban people to continue the fight for an honest government, Chibás shot himself. Four days later he died.[20]

After the disillusion caused by the debased political practices of the Auténticos' government, the death of Chibás was a staggering blow for the popular forces in Cuba. The most important champion of honesty and decency, the only man whose voice could rally masses of Cubans and infuse real fervor, had abandoned the struggle. His funeral was a massive demonstration of grief and consternation. The absence of his familiar voice left a somber silence in Cuba, and events were soon to demonstrate how essential his presence had been in the struggle for democratic and social gains.

After Chibás' death the electoral campaign was less dramatic. Trying to avoid internal dissension and to assure unity, the leaders of the Ortodoxo party chose as Chibás' substitute a candidate amenable to everybody: a rather unprepossessing professor of the University, Dr. Roberto Agramónte. While the Auténticos redoubled their efforts to restore their de-

[20] Chibás was a nervous and mercurial man, obsessed by his popularity. He was deeply disturbed by the fact that, having accused President Prío and one of his ministers, Aureliano Sánchez Arango, of illegally acquiring vast lands in Guatemala, he was unable to produce any proof when challenged. This failure resulted in loss of prestige and popularity, and was reflected immediately in the electoral polls, which Chibás avidly followed. He was depressed by the situation and was certainly overreacting; there are sources who maintain that he wanted only to wound himself, perhaps in an effort to regain the confidence of his people.

teriorated public image, the Ortodoxos appealed to the Cuban people to save "the legacy of Eduardo Chibás." At the beginning of 1952, Fulgencio Batista realized that his chance for an electoral victory was worse than hopeless.

Then, on March 10, 1952, three months before the elections, Fulgencio Batista climbed to power, through a military coup: he suspended the elections and proclaimed himself as provisional ruler. It was a bloodless coup; in another demonstration of decay the Auténticos offered no resistance. In a matter of hours the elected President of Cuba was in exile, and all his ministers had vanished (former president Ramón Grau San Martín stayed in Cuba and opposed Batista publicly and privately). As in January 1934, Batista had managed to defeat and disperse the students of 1933, only this time the reasons for his victory and their defeat were sordid on both sides. Almost twenty years of political progress were interrupted; with criminal ease the republic had been pushed back into a dangerous path of military dictatorship. Using the undeniable corruption of the Auténticos as a pretext, Batista imposed his own brand of corruption: "March 10th illegalized order and legalized violence in Cuba." [21]

I remember the incredulity and the sadness of many Cubans when news of the coup broke. But I also remember the prevailing sensation of detachment and the stolid reaction of the majority, as if the political drama did not affect them. There were no true and recognized leaders who could guide the masses in a moment of national crisis. Batista was still ruling Cuba when I published my impressions of those fateful moments: "Those who were deposed lacked prestige enough to rally the people to fight for a system they had degraded; those who came to power were too well known to

[21] Luis E. Aguilar, "Fidel entró por la Posta 6," *Diario de las Américas*, March 10, 1962.

arouse any enthusiasm. . . . March 10th brought to Cuba many old things that are not good, and some new things that are very bad." [22] Among the old things were corruption and militarism; some of the new evils were Batista's proclaimed will to remain in power, his lack of any valid national program, and the destruction of a political structure that he himself had helped to build two decades before.

After Batista's military coup the horizon clouded in Cuba. The basic unresolved questions were no longer honesty and decency in public life, but much more essential ones—a return to legality, to a true democratic process, to the principles of the Constitution of 1940. And then, on July 26, 1953, amid confusion and disarray, while the political groups and civic institutions of the nation were beginning to define their positions and their line of action in the crisis provoked by the military coup, a people who had neither faith in any leader nor a leader with any faith, learned that a group of young men had tried to overthrow Batista's government by attacking the military barracks of Moncada in Santiago de Cuba. Neither the name of the leader, Fidel Castro, nor the news of the attack provoked any general reaction. Faith is something that is regained slowly, if at all. But the atmosphere was open and propitious for a new voice to remake the broken dream, for a young figure to replace the worn-out leaders of the 1930s and give fresh meaning to unfulfilled aspirations.

From the very beginning the new champion interpreted correctly the signs of the times: he spoke the language that the people wanted to hear. He mentioned Chibás, Guiteras, and Martínez Villena; he spoke against Batista and militarism; he promised to restore the Constitution of 1940, to

[22] Luis E. Aguilar, "Tres generaciones en la crisis cubana," *Cartéles*, Feb. 2, 1957, p. 46.

call for elections, and to move the republic forward with an honest government and a true social democracy. Who this new champion was, how he succeeded in embodying the general aspirations of the Cuban people, and how he drastically changed his course and the course of Cuban history toward an unexpected, formidable, tragic, and still unreached objective is quite another story. But this story cannot be understood if one ignores the historical current that emerged from the violent episode of 1933—the accomplishments and failures, the hopes and despairs, that preceded Castro and, to a certain extent, formed the essential prologue for the new situation.

Index

BOOKS ON LATIN AMERICA IN THE NORTON LIBRARY

Cuba 1933: Prologue to Revolution
by Luis E. Aguilar

The Latin American Policy of the United States
by Samuel Flagg Bemis

Empire in Brazil: A New World Experiment with Monarchy
by C. H. Haring

Journeys Toward Progress: Studies of Economic Policy-Making in Latin America by Albert O. Hirschman

An Affair of Honor: Woodrow Wilson and the Occupation of Veracruz by Robert E. Quirk

The Mexican Revolution, 1914–1915 by Robert E. Quirk

Cuba: The Making of a Revolution by Ramón Eduardo Ruiz

The Making of the Good Neighbor Policy by Bryce Wood

The United States and the Independence of Latin America, 1800–1830 by Arthur P. Whitaker